MAZEPPA

THE LIVES, LOVES AND LEGENDS OF ADAH ISAACS MENKEN

A BIOGRAPHICAL QUEST BY
WOLF MANKOWITZ

STEIN AND DAY/Publishers/New York

First published in the United States of America in 1982

Copyright © 1982 by Imeartas Ltd, Dublin
All rights reserved

Printed in the United States of America

STEIN AND DAY/Publishers
Scarborough House
Briarcliff Manor, N.Y. 10510

Library of Congress Cataloging in Publication Data

Mankowitz, Wolf.
   Mazeppa, the lives, loves, and legends of Adah Isaacs Menken.

   Bibliography: p.
   Includes index.
   1. Menken, Adah Isaacs, 1835-1868. 2. Actors — United States — Biography. 3. Poets, American — 19th century — Biography. I. Title.
PN2287.M6M3   792'.028'0924 [B] 81-48534
ISBN 0-8128-2868-2   AACR2

Contents

	Preface	1
1	Enter Mazeppa – on a fiery steed	5
2	Enter Ada Theodore – as Adah Menken, the Creole in Texas	29
3	Enter Adah Isaacs Menken – as actress	49
4	Enter Menken – as Cleopatra	61
5	Enter the Menken – as Poetess to a Puritan	79
6	Enter Adah I. Menken – the Southern Star of the West Coast	89
7	Enter the Menken – into the *Golden Era*	101
8	Enter Menken – as the Belle of London	123
9	Enter La Belle Menken – the delicious corruption from America	135
10	Enter Mrs. Newell – with a Prince of Gamblers	151
11	Enter La Menken – as Dada, the Queen of Paris	163
12	Enter Infelix Menken – in tales of old Vienna	181
13	Enter MENKEN ("no *A* and no *I*") – luxuriously printed, artistically designed, and dedicated to Dickens	195

14	Enter Dolores Menken – as Dolorida with a whip	209
15	Exit Menken, Adèle Isaac Barkley – and a curtain call with a bouquet of artificial gardenias	231
	Postscript	245
	Appendix – A Selection of the Poems of A. I. Menken	247
	Bibliography	259
	Acknowledgements	263
	Index	265

Preface

ABOUT A CENTURY or so ago, when gentlemen believed themselves to be free, and knew that ladies had no inclination in that direction, a few bright female souls sought total liberty for themselves by applying their talents and beauties to the art of manipulating men. And some of them seemed to succeed at it – for a time. Lola Montez, bored little wife of an Anglo-Indian officer, danced herself from regimental charades into the ball-rooms of Bavaria and ruled a kingdom. Cora Pearl, very ordinary *horizontale* if you like, but truly *grande*, became richer than many actual queens. Other such iron butterflies were smothered with honours and diamonds, until their beauty rusted away and men pillaged their spoils. I have always felt a sincere admiration, compassion, and fellow-feeling for them, these great female free-lances of that artistic Bohemia, the republic of free creative souls, which struggled to survive the two great wars of this century and finally failed when television, paperbacks, and *Playboy* centre-pages made all our *horizontales* huge but essentially *petites*.

For me the greatest of the last century's iron butterflies is the long-forgotten Adah Isaacs Menken, an artist whose only true work of art was herself, a Galatea who insisted on being her own Pygmalion. Her talents, her beauty, her fantasies, her impertinence, her courage, and her will (together with the new American skill for marketing), were all the strength, power, and capital she possessed; and for a brief decade she used them with superb intelligence and folly to make herself into a queen in Bohemia. In 1856 she was first heard of; by the end of the theatrical season of 1868 she was dead and almost forgotten. But I believe that the Menken deserves to be sought out and rediscovered, not only because she played, unintentionally, a key role in the evolution of the American theatre's great achievement, the modern musical, in which her contribution is remembered in *Gypsy*:

> Once I was a *schlepper*,
> Now I'm Miss Mazeppa
> With my new revolutions in dance
> Oh, you've gotta
> Have a gimmick
> If you wanna get ahead ...

Menken's life and career should also be remembered because they epitomise the courage of those, today, even rarer butterflies, the free-souled, free-lance, free-thinking, free-lovers, who take the inane fragments endowed to them by God and their genes, and make, out of the chaos, works of art. I consider the entire process quite meaningless, but, like Mazeppa herself, absurdly magnificent; and to the memory of her creator, Adah Isaacs Menken, this search for all her selves is dedicated.

The earliest picture of Adah Isaacs Menken, aged about 18. Extremely beautiful, highly appealing, insanely confident, yet deliciously vulnerable.

One

Enter Mazeppa – on a fiery steed

THE GREAT AMERICAN TRAGEDIAN, James E. Murdoch, describes the nightmare experience of playing *Macbeth* with Adah Isaacs Menken. It was in Nashville in February 1858 and Menken had assured the theatre manager that she was more than up to Murdoch and the part. But just before the performance was to begin Adah came to Murdoch, timid, charming, her lovely eyes full of entreaty, and confessed that, except for impressions gained from seeing another actress once play the role, she knew nothing whatsoever of Lady Macbeth. She made her confession with touching shame, terrified of the ordeal before her; but she was enormously impressed (if a little frightened) by Murdoch's high status in the tragic arts, and was certain that he would carry her through. "I must act it! I must!", she simultaneously entreated and demanded, a tone of command she was already adept in assuming both with horses and with men.

Murdoch, great actor he might or might not be, man he certainly was. Menken was beautiful and available, and so she persuaded him. "I found her to be a mere novice", he wrote (of her acting), "and not at all qualified for the important position to which she aspired. But she was anxious to improve and willing to be taught. A woman of great personal attractions, she made herself a great favourite. She dashed at everything in tragedy and comedy with a reckless disregard of consequences until, at length, with some degree of trepidation, she paused before the character of Lady Macbeth."

But the pause was only momentary. Murdoch playing her Pygmalion, agreed to teach her the part there and then, mere hours before the performance. Adah pointed out encouragingly that there were not really very many lines to it. "But dear lady," Murdoch explained, "it takes years of study and experience to play a great Shakespearean role. And now there is barely time for you to learn the lines – much less for you to become familiar with my business."

"Don't worry, dear master," Menken assured him huskily. "I can commit the lines in a few hours, if you will run over them and mark the emphases for me."

Such eyes with such a figure and such self-confidence were irresistible to the good-natured Murdoch with his well-known weakness for lovely women; and Adah was, indeed, extremely beautiful, highly appealing, insanely confident, yet deliciously vulnerable. So he tutored the "timid tragedienne", as he dubbed her, enjoying the experience but, an old hand at the game, he also prepared for the worst. Inevitably it came. Murdoch describes the first act on the night with, "Miss Menken arrayed to personate the would-be queen. She grasped the letter and read it in the approved style, holding it at arm's length and gaspingly devouring the words with all the intensity of ferocious desire; then, throwing her arms wildly over her head, she poured out such an apostrophe to guilt, demons, and her own dark purposes that it would have puzzled anyone acquainted with the text to guess from what unlimited *variorum* she could have studied the part." Yet, amazingly, the audience, as ignorant of Shakespeare as was Menken, greeted her lovely violent display with more applause than they awarded the great actor himself.

In the next scene Menken worked her way crab-wise over to Murdoch. Surprised he glanced questioningly at her, and was appalled to hear her loudly whisper that she had completely forgotten the part's few lines. "From that point Macbeth ceased to be the guilty thane and became a mere prompter in Scotch kilts and tartans", recorded Murdoch. "For the rest of the scene I gave the lady the words. Clinging to my side in a manner very different from her former scornful bearing, she took them line by line before she uttered them, still, however, receiving vociferous applause, and particularly when she spoke of dashing out the brains of her child; until, at length, poor Macbeth, who was but playing second fiddle to his imperious consort, was glad to make his exit from a scene where the honours certainly were not even."

The audience's enthusiasm helped Menken to recover from her unaccustomed stage-fright. For the remainder of the performance Murdoch assisted her in "winging it", the actors' term for leaving the book in the wings when going on stage to study again when off. A nerve-racking experience, yet afterwards, Menken could honestly claim that she had played Lady Macbeth to a principal leading-man. Her ambition to become the Rachel of America was nurtured by the credit, even though Murdoch's final advice to her was that she should search out for herself some "sensational spectacle" in which "your fine figure and pretty face will show to the same advantage as the prosperous curves of, say, Madame Celeste", a French gymnastic dancer currently enjoying popularity in daring tights. It wasn't quite the future that Menken had in mind for herself but, as always, she would consider seriously the advice of respected professional friends. At least she never played Lady Macbeth again.

Every actress needs the right appreciative impresario to achieve the fullest exploitation of her special personality and talents. Theatrically Menken may be said to have been discovered by Captain John B. Smith, who had the Green Street Theatre in Albany. There he was currently reviving an old three-act drama

The arrogant and victorious Mazeppa on Broadway.

based upon Byron's romantic poem, *Mazeppa*. It was a stand-by piece which had never enjoyed any great success, its sole attraction being that it culminated in a desperate ride around the stage upon the back of a "fiery untamed steed of Tartary". The actor at this point, was usually substituted by a dummy strapped to the horse's back, and though in Albany the part was played by R. E. J. Miles, a second-rate actor who, being a first-rate horseman, rode the untamed steed himself, the production was still hardly paying its way. But Smith had no wish to write off the expensive costumes, props and scenery for *Mazeppa*. Pondering salvationary alternatives, he came up with a brilliant and thoroughly show-business notion. Why not have a girl play the part? Girls dressed in tight men's costumes were always appealing and, in the present case, the chosen lady would be wearing precious few of them in the final scene. Indeed, what a sensation it would make if the very final scene itself, the desperate ride on the back of the stallion, were to be played by an apparently naked lady! At once Smith knew he had conceived the greatest idea of his career. His only problem now was to find a lady capable of riding the horse and willing to look naked while doing so.

Captain Smith was familiar with the shows and talents available on the various circuits. In the previous two years Menken, advertising herself as "The Star of the West" - "The Female Soldier" - "The Accomplished Actress" - "The Sterling Tragedienne" - "The Enchanting Songstress" - "The Bewitching Danseuse", had been playing Jack Sheppard and (her chosen *alter ego*), Lola Montez, in which parts she duelled, rattled sabres, and wielded a pretty horsewhip; she had often announced herself to be a fearless horsewoman. True, she had also played Lady Macbeth and was said to have inclinations towards tragedy; but perhaps a good offer might overcome her classical inclinations.

Smith approached Menken with his proposition. Initially she dismissed it as absurd, outrageous, and not very original, having been attempted, with no great success, by Mrs. Rampton. But Smith was a first-rate salesman. He described eloquently the fame, furore, and high fees waiting for the first successful female Mazeppa. Suddenly Menken saw it all before her with total clarity; without another word of argument she agreed to Smith's proposition. That "other self", the impulsive and instinctive *geist* by whom she was directed throughout her life, suddenly told her that the fiery steed would bear her into theatrical history.

Rehearsing his star Smith wrote: "I found her nervous and anxious. Full of trepidation she dressed, or rather undressed. I assured her that there was no danger, and that she had only to hold on like grim death and the mare, Belle Beauty, would do the rest."

The actor Miles, excellent horseman that he was, had trained the mare for the act, riding her bound with a single strap. Menken would simply follow the routine Miles had set. The strap ran through a loop on the band around the horse, supporting the performer's body. It was devised so that the closer he drew the ends held in his hands, the closer he was grappled to the animal. He could free himself by letting go of the straps at any time. Smith demonstrated the technique himself. Strapped to the mare he easily rode up and down the eighteen-inch run of the painted mountain scenery. Menken agreed to give it a try, but stubbornly insisted on introducing a variation into the horse's routine. Instead of starting from the footlights she would commence on the run itself. Smith and Miles both advised against it, but Menken assured them that it would look better. At her first try, she was thrown. The change in its routine confused the mare, and the nervous beast crashed off the runway on to the supporting timbers below; a scene of more than theatrical terror which horrified Smith on two counts. "My heart was in my mouth, for not only was there danger that the woman was killed, but also that my two-thousand dollar mare was ruined forever." Yet in spite of concern for the horse, "we lifted up the Menken, pale as a ghost, nearly lifeless and the blood streaming from a wound in her beautiful shoulder. Then, with the help of tackle, we got up Belle Beauty."

Would Menken continue with the experiment, Smith wondered? "Nobody ever saw the Menken wear a white feather", replied Adah, gritting her teeth with pain. The first public performance of *Mazeppa* with Adah Isaacs Menken in the great Protean role would take place, as announced, at Smith's Green Street Theatre, Albany, on 7 June 1861, three months after another historic and theatrical event, the inauguration of Abraham Lincoln as President. A week after that, in Montgomery, Alabama, the Congress of the Confederate States of America had adopted a Constitution by unanimous vote, proclaiming its sovereignty. From that moment a civil war was known to be inevitable; indeed, shots had already been fired at Fort Sumter, Charleston, South Carolina on 12 April. And yet the press conference announcing the forthcoming début of an unknown actress prone to nakedness and riding accidents, was still able to draw representatives of six important daily newspapers, three weeklies, and two monthlies. Recruiting sergeants with drummers were parading the streets of New York; the ports of the Confederacy were blockaded; Tennessee was about to become the eleventh state to secede from the Union; Congress was planning the introduction of an outrageous tax on income to pay for a war; ladies were arranging genteel tea parties at which to roll bandages. And still, for the American public, an actress in negligée on a trained horse was adjudged a lead story.

Actually, in spite of (or perhaps because of) the crisis, theatre business was better than ever; Dion Boucicault's play *Colleen Bawn*, which had opened a year ago, was still drawing full houses. New York, always a gutsy city, didn't permit political catastrophes to spoil its pleasures, provided always that they were unusual. The aggressive penny newspaper, the *Sun*, put it fairly and squarely: "Boston and Philadelphia are conscious of their cultural heritage. In those dusty cities people attend the theater, read books and listen to music out of a sense of duty. That duty impels these worthies to suffer through many a dull evening. We of New York are not fettered by such conventional restrictions. We seek pleasure in literature, the arts and drama for the sake of that pleasure itself..." The leader-writer added, almost as an afterthought: "... ever mindful, to be sure, that the bounds of propriety and good taste are observed."

The gentlemen of the press who travelled to Albany to meet Menken were, however, reasonably confident that those bounds would be deliciously exceeded by Captain Smith's new star, for whose show the poster was having a more sensational impact on the public than the distant pistol-shots in South Carolina. The poster presented a huge black stallion, its teeth bared, rearing high, front legs pawing the air. Lashed to the brute's back was what seemed, at first sight, to be the nude figure of a woman. On closer examination (and the poster received a lot of it), only arms, neck and legs were certainly bare. The torso may or may

THEATRE

Managers, — Newark — S. H. France & B. McAuley

Doors open at 6 1-2. Performance to commence at 7 1-2 o'clock.

ADMISSION: Dress Circle, Lady and Gent. 50 cts.; Single Tickets, 38 cts.; Parquette, 25 cts.

ST. PATRICK'S NIGHT

Thursday Ev'ng, March 17, 1859

ERIN GO BRAGH.

THE GREATEST BILL OF THE SEASON

SINGING AND DANCING.

On which occasion will be played, — THREE PIECES

Fourth Night of Miss

ADAH ISAACS

MENKEN

☞ THE STAR OF THE WEST, ☜

The Female Soldier,   The Accomplished Actress
The Sterling Tragedienne,
The Popular Comedienne,   The Enchanting Songstress
The Bewitching Danseuse,

THE GREAT ACTRESS,

The evening's performance will commence with the

UNPROTECTED FEMALE!

POLLY CRISP,   -   MISS A. I. MENKEN

With the the Songs of "The Captain with the Whisker," and "Billy Grimes, the Drover."

Nicodemus Crisp, - - - - - - - - H. Russell
Tom, (an apocryphal gentlemen), - - - - - B. McAuley

Menken, star of the West; heralded in an 1859 playbill.

not have had some close covering, but it was enough to suggest to New Yorkers, satiated by the unusual, that even they would find Menken's *Mazeppa* worth fifty cents unreserved, seventy-five cents reserved, an orchestra chair for a dollar, or a box for six for ten dollars. The free list, incidentally, would be suspended during Miss Menken's engagement.

The famous journalist Horace Greeley, obsessed with the future tragedy and horror of the civil war, nevertheless found space to comment in an editorial: "We cannot believe that the actress scheduled to appear before our citizenry in *Mazeppa* would so shock and revolt decent people by exposing her body in the nude." Here, at the conference in Albany, the press were hopeful of being able to confirm or deny such anxieties. That significant occasion has been variously and colourfully reported; it has a curiously contemporary tone. First Ed James, Menken's press-agent and well-known as a contributing editor to *The Clipper*, explained over drinks at the hotel bar, that discussion of the details of her actual forthcoming performance might be unnerving to Miss Menken. Its quality they would have to wait to appreciate; he had no doubt they would find it unique even in their extensive experience. For the present they were free to ask the actress anything else within the realms of reason and decency, but they would please remember that they were talking to a lady who had played the Scottish queen with the great Murdoch. "Now gentlemen", he concluded, "if you will follow me to Madame's suite, I will have the honour of presenting you to one who, I sincerely believe, will soon be heralded as one of the greatest and most courageous artistes of our theater. This way please." And they were ushered by a liveried attendant into the Menken's suite, the most expensive in Albany. There, in careful light, waited Menken, reclining on a tiger-skin, sipping champagne, feeding bonbons to a French poodle, and smoking a cigarette!

After assimilating the shocking impact of the tableau, one journalist reported Miss Menken as a "true beauty"; another described her as "bewitching" in her daringly short skirt. One observed a total absence of petticoats. All dazedly noted that her hair was outrageously short-cropped, and that she wore a white blouse, the collar open at the neck, in the Byronic style of Lola Montez, the greatest of courtesan-actresses.

Exploiting the advantage of her initial impact, Menken at once took over the interview. She dismissed and deplored her successes to date (such unserious pieces!), but she hoped her lack of early judgment would be generously attributed to her tender years. Although, she hastened to remind the gentlemen of the press, that in the theatres of the South and West she was generally recognised for her Shakespearean roles, being specially acclaimed for her Lady Macbeth, in which role she had been supported by the great Murdoch. Occasionally she had undertaken non-Shakespearean roles. Which? Oh, Lady Teazle in *School for Scandal*, for example, was one of her favourite lesser classical roles.

A courageous reporter interrupted to ask why, then, was Miss Menken now

A coquettish Menken in London for the first time.

appearing in *Mazeppa*, which was a pretty poor sort of melodrama, far away from Shakespeare and Goldsmith?

"Sheridan", Menken corrected him and then burst into a paean of praise for her present author, the great and noble poet Lord Byron, with whom she had always felt so close an affinity. Lord Byron? The reporters looked at one another, and James. They had no idea that Lord Byron was writing for Miss Menken. James shrugged, smiled and nodded smugly as Menken continued, pointing out that both she and the aristocrat poet were rebels and lovers of liberty. Like him, she adored danger, and longed always to attempt what had not been done before. She would be the first serious actress ever to play his lordship's male character-creation in what was an enormously improved version of Byron's *Mazeppa*. She regarded it as a personal mission to retrieve that great subject from neglect.

A less than sober gentleman asked her now, whether she didn't also feel something of a personal mission to find theatrical fame any way she could. Menken turned the blinding searchlights of her eyes upon him and sincerely admitted to a determined passion for theatrical fame, both nationally and internationally. She regarded herself as kindred to Lola Montez, she told them, the lovely eyes flashing, though spiritually and poetically she was more closely related to Goethe, whom she had studied much in her childhood.

The journalists were impressed but a little confused. Why, one asked, if she was so famous and respected as Menken, had she appeared in the somewhat less than first-class Old Bowery Theatre in New York under the name of Mrs. Heenan? Oh that, said Menken, that was at the insistence of a manager who hoped to exploit her marriage to the champion heavyweight pugilist. But, she added proudly, the name of Menken would soon be better known than that of John C. Heenan. She didn't want to discuss her marriages and anyhow, "what's in a name?" she quoted, from her familiar Shakespeare; *apropos* of which she would now reveal to the Press of the World a fact never before published. Her real name was neither Heenan nor Menken. They were merely the gleanings of past and present husbands. No – her true identity was Dolores de Ricardo Los Fiertes; she was the daughter of a Spanish Jew, and an aristocratic French Creole lady of New Orleans. She had left Madrid at the age of twelve and made her dancing début in Havana, where she enjoyed instant fame as the "Queen of the Plaza". Ed James would confirm her statement, she concluded, staring at him. James quickly pointed out that the Menken spoke French and Spanish which, he suggested, was pretty conclusive evidence of her assertions. Under further questioning, Menken modestly admitted that she also had "a smattering of all Slavic tongues". Of course she spoke Italian and Portuguese fluently. Not to mention a reasonable familiarity with the sacred language of her people, Hebrew; but only a schoolish relationship with Latin, she regretted.

At once an eager reporter asked her a long question in Portuguese. She cut him short, saying she would be delighted to converse with him in what was one of her favourite languages, on some other occasion, but that it was discourteous to use a tongue before people who did not understand it. Next question?

A journalist produced a clipping from the New York *Sunday Mercury*. He quoted its revelation that Menken's true name was Marie Rachel Adelaide de Vere Spencer, and that she was the daughter of a fabulously wealthy Englishman, the second son of a duke. She had been educated in a convent in Rome, escaping from it, at twenty, by scaling its walls. "Isn't there some kind of a confusion there?" he modestly suggested.

Yes, replied Menken, she did often seem to confuse gentlemen of the press who were not of the first calibre as were her present guests. "And now", she concluded, "I must regretfully leave you. The wild steed must be tamed daily."

"Had Miss Menken recovered yet from the accident and was the horse still giving her trouble?", asked a reporter quickly. "No stallion gives the Menken much trouble for long", Adah answered with the smile of a confident centauress. "And now gentlemen", added James hastily, "rehearsal time is upon us." Then thanking the press grandly for their attentive interest, the Menken left on Mr. James' arm. The gentlemen of the press breathed out and agreed that the lady was enchanting, beautiful, powerful and quick-minded. "But was she completely candid?" asked the unanswered genealogical questioner. "Well, at any rate", replied one lighting a cigar, "she is rather Jewish I would say." But, as we shall discover later, he may have been wrong.

Menken's *Mazeppa* rehearsals had been, for those days, unusually extended. Normally a leading artiste moved into a theatre with a complete repertoire to hand, ready-learned. The reach-me-down supporting parts might stumble here and there, but the star gave a fully prepared (and frequently over-prepared) performance. Not so the Menken. Repeating her approach to the Bard and Murdoch, she confessed to Captain Smith, once their contract was signed, that, in fact, "she knew nothing about the play – business, lines, nor anything else". Thus she, by temperament, initiated the normal practice of the modern theatre where artists study the piece in concert under a director. It was not to be the last of Menken's modern touches. She also found, and perfected in Ed James, one of the first truly great and inventive press managers.

James had arrived in America as Edwin James and his story, naturally, is almost as incredible as some of those which he invented in the course of his career as Menken's mythographer. He had, he said, been an actor himself but had given up the stage to devote his talents to the study of civil and criminal law. In 1858, at the peak of his career, he defended Dr. Simon Bernard, who was one of those accused of attempting to assassinate Napoleon III. The following year James was elected a Member of Parliament. It seemed that his career would have no bounds, but extravagance and a strong inclination towards powerful and beautiful women involved him in a series of scandals, lost him his money, and, eventually, in 1861, at the age of forty-nine, resulted in his being disbarred. An English critic described him as "a fat florid man with a large hard face was Edwin James, with chambers in the Temple and rooms in Pall Mall: his practice was extensive, his fees enormous. I had many consultations with him, but found it difficult to keep him to the subject of my case: he liked talking, but he always diverted the conversation into other channels." James also maintained that he was the original for Stryver the Barrister who defends Darney in Charles Dickens' *The Tale of Two Cities*. If so, Dickens' description of him sounds very much like that of a successful publicity man: "A man of little more than thirty, but looking twenty years older than he was, stout, loud, red, bluff, and free from any drawback of delicacy, had a pushing way of shouldering himself (morally and physically) into companies and conversations, that argued well for his shouldering his way up in life." James first met Menken following a letter she wrote him, thanking him for arranging publicity for her in the New York *Clipper* to which he had become a contributing editor. Apparently he did, at some point in their association, present himself to her as a possible lover, but she neatly turned aside his approaches by calling him her "dear brother" and herself his "dear sister". Certainly they shared a kind of family taste for the bravura, for James genuinely enjoyed and appreciated

An example of one of Menken's letters to Ed James. The letter from Liverpool reads: Dearest Ed, You have often been kind enough to write and send me lots of nice papers, and I thank you for all very, very much. You must never think (I) neglect you through forgetfulness. I think of you all the time, but I have to work very hard, and see so many people, answer so many letters, that I let my loved ones wait. But ...

Menken and remained a gifted servitor of her career until her death, and even beyond. He protected her secrets, projected her legends, supported her reputation, and adored her at all times. His handling of Menken's first open press conference set a pattern for many future personality presentations, and committed him to her interests forever.

After the conference James escorted Adah to the theatre for rehearsals, having invited the reporters back to the bar for continuing free drinks. They both felt the meeting had gone very well, although James had been somewhat surprised at Menken's daring revelation of her true Jewish identity and name, since he, too, had previously been favoured with the Spenser account. "Ed dear", cautioned Menken. "From this moment on I am only Mazeppa." Respecting the painful and dark secrets of her origin James never did argue with her on the matter.

Mazeppa or *The Wild Horse of Tartary*, was adapted in 1830 by Henry M. Milner from Byron's poem, itself inspired by a confused but Romantic incident in Polish history. In the theatrical version, Ivan Mazeppa, a handsome young Polish nobleman, loves Olinska, a beautiful aristocratic lady, betrothed against her inclinations to a terrifying count. Mazeppa challenges the count to a duel, in which the cowardly villain consistently breaks the rules of noble combat but is eventually brought down by the gallant Ivan. Mazeppa spares his adversary in return for a safe conduct from the count's castle. Not entirely unexpectedly, the count breaks his word and orders his men to take Mazeppa alive. In the following scene, in the courtyard of the castle, the count and his barbarous moujiks attack Mazeppa, stripping him of all his clothing, and then leading him off to Stage Left where flaring torches now reveal a winding ramp supported by scaffolding. From the footlights it runs, at an upward angle to the backdrop, then veers to the right across the stage, rising ever more steeply until it disappears into the right wing. At the drama's high point which was, wrote a reviewer, "enough to unnerve the strongest of men", Mazeppa is dragged to his feet. The count cries out, "bring forth the untamed steed!", and to a long roll of the drums and a musical crescendo, the fiery animal is led on, in Byron's words:

> A noble steed,
> A Tartar of the Ukraine breed,
> Who looked as though the speed of thought
> Were in his limbs; but he was wild,
> Wild as the wild deer, and untaught,
> With spur and bridle undefiled ...

Described in the playbills as a coal-black stallion, "a wild horse" that "pawed the dust", the animal had in past productions been a gentle mare, a well-broken hack or sometimes even a child's pony. So long as it was sure-footed, and hungry for a feed after its trip, it had been taken, by willing suspension of disbelief, to fill

The Broadway Theatre programme announcing Mazeppa *in 1866.*

Byron's noble description. Bearing Mazeppa such a beast would be led up scaffolding while the count declaimed: "Let scorching suns and piercing blasts, devouring hunger and parching thirst, with frequent bruises and ceaseless motion, rend the vile Tartar piecemeal!"

The difference now was that Belle Beauty, Miles' trained mare, had style, breeding and dash, and had promptly propelled Menken into the Pit on their first dramatic encounter. But Menken now had mastered Belle, making her as flashing a performer as herself. Her magic on horseback was assisted by all the effects that the Green Street Theatre could produce. Music. Thunder off. Lightning. Snow falling. A moving panorama of mighty mountains and abysses in the background; the Dnieper River; wolves beside, and vultures overhead; a formidable array of theatrical illusions. But the two most sensational illusions of all were, the voluptuous figure of Adah Isaacs Menken as Ivan Mazeppa, a sexual transformation requiring an extremely willing suspension of disbelief; and, more sensational still, the nakedness of the star. For Menken had given much thought and experiment to improving the style of tights used by the notorious Madame Celeste, the French entertainer whose fame and example Murdoch had recommended to her. She had developed Celeste's basic dress nearer to the modern close-fitting body-stocking in which, flesh-coloured and carefully-shaped, assisted by sound, movement and

1866 Sarony carte of Menken in a pose much favoured by herself and the public at the height of her career.

light, Menken seemed, to the eager imagination of the audience, to be actually naked beneath her short, flimsy tunic.

Yet Captain Smith must be credited for much of Menken's initial impact as Mazeppa. He had built up public interest by heavily publicising the danger of the ride, and the fact that Menken had already suffered a serious accident, and would be nightly confronting the same dangers. He had paraded through the streets of Albany thirteen trained horses with placards describing them as "The Menken Stud", suggesting that, in spite of the dangers, the stallions would be worn out well ahead of Miss Menken. Smith knew his town very well. He recognised that the moral fury of its top families, all of Puritan Dutch or Scottish descent, would add to the sensational impact of his protégée. And, without the support of modern psycho-analytical studies, Smith also understood, with a showman-of-the-world's experience, that a voluptuous naked lady strapped with leather thongs to the back of a wild horse must play a powerfully erotic role in the fantasy life of his audience. Puritanism, he recognised, produced even more extraordinary unconscious erotic tableaux than that which he had devised at the Green Street Theatre. In being the first impresario daring to produce the erotic dreams of his audience, Green was convinced that he would make box-office history.

We may, with our permissive pretensions today, think that the highly

A semi-nude pose by Menken.

inflammable receptivity of the Albany audience in 1861 was a little laughable. But what did our own times' long-running theatrical stimulant, *Oh Calcutta!* do, much beyond devising full frontal exposure of theatrical performers in *Playboy* jokes, simulating a high degree of excitement which anyone could easily see was not actually realised there on the stage? The naked human body, absurdly enough, seems to keep its ability to shock and excite in public display, even in a deteriorating urban desert littered with hard and soft porn garbage, stretching to infinity. Thus "a naked hussy on horseback" in Green Street in 1861 was a not inconsiderable theatrical coup, well confirmed by houses quickly sold out, with hundreds of standees producing the largest audiences ever recorded in an Albany theatre.

On the first night Menken's duel, in tights and a black cloak, received great applause. The villainous count was hissed, and the cat-calls were so loud that the unusually well-rehearsed lines could not be heard; the performance was halted until the excitement subsided. But when, partially shielded by actors, Menken performed the first public striptease act ever witnessed in a theatre, the audience was almost religiously silent. Then, in her invisible tights and flimsy tunic, she was revealed by the light of the flickering torches, and the great shocked and excited gasp assured Smith that he had, indeed, secured his place in the history of the American Theatre. An American audience had seen, for the first time, a naked lady on the stage, for as one reviewer was to put it, "the Menken is without a rival in her special line – but it is *not* a clothes line!" Reported a pale and amazed first-nighter: "It had to be seen to be believed! Parts of the body of this actress were exposed that God never intended to be seen by any eye other than her mother's!" And when they saw them, that audience, after its momentary stillness, and its great gasp of shock, rose to its feet and hailed Mazeppa with a great roar of applause and protest. That deliciously thrilling and purely animal sound was to echo through the remainder of Adah Isaacs Menken's sadly short but always sensational life.

The transfer of *Mazeppa* to the Broadway Theatre was arranged by Captain Smith with very little argument after the Albany reception, although the brutal *Sun* was already sniping: "We recall Miss Menken on our stages in one or another roles that were mercifully brief. She is a dreadful actress." But George Wood, the owner of the Broadway, was hardly less shrewd in his judgement of the taste of the New York audience than was the gallant captain. Wood advertised the forthcoming attraction just as aggressively, and by opening night on 13 June, Mr. Collins, his theatre manager, was able to put up on the box office that notice which is the ultimate ambition of all in the theatre: "All seats for this performance have been sold." The notice added that "tickets may be purchased for the next four weeks at the prevailing rates. Evening performances at 8.00 p.m., matinees at 1.30 p.m." Already the ticket-touts were queuing to buy blocks of seats which their business experience told them would show high profits.

Walt Whitman, the poet and philosopher whom Menken thought poetically centuries ahead of their contemporaries, in his respectable old age.

When Menken arrived for her début on Broadway, she was escorted by James, already well-known in café society for his colourful English background and his present power as an editor of the New York *Clipper*, a popular sports, racing and show-business paper. Menken's other companion was another notorious eccentric, a former newspaper editor and present poet. His name was Walt Whitman, and he was ignored by a crowd whose attention was focused entirely upon Adah. Her large startling eyes, her full crimson mouth, her figure in the simple dark velvet close-fitting Byronic dress, and her shockingly short hair, were all great talking points. But with one simple prop she amazed them all. She was smoking a cigarette in public. The ticket-touts increased their demands for even larger blocks of tickets for the next four weeks.

That night Menken eclipsed her victory in Albany, and she knew it. And yet she was relaxed and calm before the curtain went up. Gerson, Menken's most imaginative biographer, quotes James recalling that evening:

> Adah's calm on the night that would either make her a great star or send her back to a life of squalor was monumental. Wood, Whitman and I dined with her at Pfaff's, than which no finer restaurant catering to the theatrical trade has ever existed.
>
> There she accepted the good wishes of Edwin Booth and Ada Clare, the reigning King and Queen of our theater, as though she were monarch and

A sad Menken, over made-up in Vienna.

> they her subjects. Fitz-James O'Brien, who would have become the greatest American poet of our century had he not suffered a tragically premature death, offered her a toast in champagne. She accepted with great dignity, but replied by sipping water, explaining that she preferred not to drink alcoholic spirits until later in the evening. She showed her wisdom, for the calamitous power of those spirits had marred her soul.*

---

* A reference to the alcoholic dependencies of both of Adah's husbands (to date). She herself was generally abstemious with drink.

Her appetite was exceptional, and neither then nor on any other occasion in the many years I knew her did she eat with anything but the gusto of a working man. She consumed a dish of raw clams, a thick soup of chicken, a hearty steak and a deep-dish pie containing, if memory does not err, a compote of fruits. Charlie Pfaff also prepared for her a roast turkey sandwich at her request, so she could eat it during one of the play's intermissions as a means of maintaining her strength.

Adah had known such great poverty that, in my belief, her hunger of past years had given her an insatiable appetite. She could eat more than anyone I ever knew, man or woman. Yet some strange quality in her nature held down her weight. When I first met her, she was hungry to the point of near-starvation, and weighed less than the one hundred and twenty-five pounds that was her normal weight. I never knew her to weigh more, even when she enjoyed a huge income and was so much in demand that wealthy citizens vied with each other in the attempt to present her with rare and delectable treats from the world over.

But I digress. At Pfaff's on the fateful night, Whitman and I had no zest for food, and found it difficult to converse. Wood, always a silent man, looked down at his plate and replied in a few words when one of us spoke to him. Adah, bless her, was the life of the party, chatting happily about a thousand and one things, yet never once mentioning the test that awaited her at the theater.

Perhaps she betrayed a trace of apprehension while smoking a cigarette in the coach whilst driving to the theater. She betrayed neither fear nor other nervousness when bidding us farewell at the stage door, and I later learned from Minnie, her wardrobe woman, that she sang to herself in the dressing room as she prepared for her great assault on New York.

In that audience there were nine Union generals in full uniform, one rear-admiral and seventeen colonels. Adah's friends, Edwin Booth and Ada Clare (with her current millionaire), were also present, as were members of the Astor and Schuyler families; and a heavy contingent of fashionable ladies as curious as their men to know how far the notorious Menken would go in her finale. It had been speculated that a Lady Godiva-like trick would be used; the tresses of a long wig would protect what was left of Adah's virtue. On the other hand, it was rumoured that the nakedness in Albany would be even more complete on Broadway. It certainly took one's mind off the endless talk about income tax and war; and the stylish audience buzzed with anticipation.

The sophisticated and sceptical New York critics, however, were not as easily impressed as the reporters who had visited Albany. Robert Henry Newell of the *Herald*, who made Lincoln laugh with his satirical writings under the somewhat heavily comic pseudonym of Orpheus C. Kerr ("Office Seeker"), had the direst expectations:

My colleagues and I knew that Adah had been riotously received in Albany, of course. All of us had heard that she appeared on stage nude, lashed to a horse, and we expected some such spectacle as the climax of her performance.

That expectation did not relieve our knowledge that we faced a dreary evening. *Mazeppa* was one of the worst plays ever written, and its history had been dismal. It had failed miserably at Niblo's Gardens, and at Mike Herman's National Theater. In London it had been hissed from the stage.

We were not comforted by the fact that the play had been revised, for none of us had heard of the playwright. I, myself, having learned something of Adah's own literary pretensions and earnest attempts to publish some of her poems, was inclined to suspect that she had rewritten *Mazeppa*.

George Wood had called on me, as well as on my colleagues, to assure us that Adah would ride the horse herself in the final, fifth act of the play. It had been customary for a horseman to take the part for those few moments when a great beast, no doubt prodded by hirelings backstage, crossed from the wings on one side to those on the other. I wondered, privately, whether tedium would propel me from my seat into the velvet air of a June night before the fifth act came.

Newell little knew that destiny was planning to propel him much further than that, for he was, in the fullness of time, to become a Menken husband. But there were important scenes to be played yet, and all of them surprises. The first came before the curtain went up. Ushers entered and respectfully distributed leaflets to the members of the audience, as if administering sacred wafers. On one side of the single sheet they read:

The Management of the Broadway Theater wishes to announce that attacks on the patriotism of Miss Adah Isaacs Menken are without warrant. Miss Menken makes no secret of her birth in Louisiana, but proclaims no fealty to that misguided state. She is a loyal and trustworthy Citizen of the United States of North America, and joins with other patriots in the devout wish that those states which have seceded will return to the fold of the Union.

No one in New York had actually heard, at this point, that Miss Menken was anything but "loyal and trustworthy", though now, of course, there would be speculation about her position in the dispute. To put a stop to such calumnies in advance she offered, on the reverse side of the printed sheet, verses entitled *Pro Patria – America, 1861*. They were signed with a block of her already bold and distinctive signature and would make, their patriotic evidential value apart, a wonderful souvenir of her Broadway début. Ed James assured members of the press in his immediate vicinity as they studied the verses, that Walt, in spite of rumours to the contrary, had given Menken no help whatsoever. It was all, he

The New Broadway Theatre, from a photograph by Howe.

insisted, the Menken's own work. Ten minutes later the brilliant gas jets dimmed and a fife and drum band, playing *Yankee Doodle*, came on to the stage. The combination of Menken's patriotism and the popular anthem of the North had the audience cheering before the curtain had yet risen on the first scene of Mazeppa's fiery ride on to Broadway and into theatrical history.

Menken in Children of the Sun.

Two

Enter Ada Theodore – as Adah Menken, the Creole in Texas

WHO WAS ADAH before she became Mrs. Alexander Menken, wife of a pit musician and conductor, a touring actress *en route* to becoming the Broadway star of *Mazeppa*? The journey seems to have begun in Louisiana, in the exotic capital of the South West, the City of Sin, New Orleans. Most biographical entries on Menken accept her statement (through Ed James) that she was born in "Chatrain" or "Chartrain". But since there is no such village or township in the vicinity of New Orleans, the assumption must be that the alleged birthplace was the terminus of the Pont-Chartrain Railroad on the lake of that name. This station developed into an area called Milneburg, "a favorite suburban place of amusement which offered hotels, bars, restaurants, bathing facilities, and shooting galleries". No doubt it also offered all the less reputable amusements which citizens of New Orleans expected to find when taking a vacation by the sea. Locally mispronounced "Millenburg", this inconsequential seaside suburb disappeared in the first quarter of this century; it is remembered now only by esoteric jazz-lovers familiar with a number called *Millenburg Joys*. But though the lost Milneburg has a hundred years or so of history, there is no mention existing in the records of the New Orleans Board of Health or in the archives of the French cathedral of that city, of the birth of the woman who became Adah Menken, under any of the names which she used from time to time in the course of her career.

The confusion about Menken's place of birth is more confounded by the extraordinary range and variety of origins and birthnames which she claimed as situation or fancy demanded. The Louisiana historian John S. Kendall studied the mystery with great application, and in 1938 published the results of his researches in the *Louisiana Historical Quarterly*. "Who were her parents? Where was she born? What was her name?", he asks:

> Sometimes her father was James McCord, and sometimes Richard Irving Spencer, Ricardo La Fiertes (or Fuertes), or James Campbell. Once she

described him as "Sir" Campbell. Her mother was alternately a Creole or a Jewess of Franco-Spanish descent. Adah was as vague about her mother's name as about her father's. There were moments when it was Dolores Adios Fuertes, although at other times Adah claimed this appellation for herself. According to the daughter, the lady was left a widow in 1837, and thereupon married Dr. J. C. Campbell, of the United States Army; but this identification has been denied, and the honor of being Adah's step-father has been transferred to a man named Israels.

Allen Lesser, the distinguished Jewish historian, thought it might be a Josephs, of New Orleans, since Adah's sister was called "Annie Josephs". But that may only have been her married name, and the obscurity remains.

Kendall went on to examine the McCord attribution of paternity, one frequently found in Menken's biographical entries. Apparently there was a James McCord in Milneburg, an Irish-born Londoner, operating as a "general merchant". Some have described him (apparently influenced by Menken's later insistence that she was born a Jewess) as an "old clo'" man – an unusual trade for an Irishman. But according to Kendall, Milneburg in 1835 had no dealers in second-hand clothing. There was a McCord in New Orleans, but he was not a James; he lived in Triton Walk, and, according to the Directory, was not in the "old clo'" line.

Lesser, always deeply committed to proving Menken's Jewish origins, further discredited the McCord paternity, concluding that:

> Most important of all is the evidence against the Adelaide McCord story. The absence of such a name in any of the church or parish records of Louisiana is not too conclusive in itself, for apart from the lack of any registration laws, fire and other natural catastrophes have been responsible for many gaps in American vital statistics of the period. Fortunately, proof of the Menken's source of inspiration for the name and adventures of Adelaide McCord is available. It is contained in the New York newspaper *Wilkes' Spirit* of March 3, 1860, which published Adah Menken's reply to the charges of Alexander Menken on that day (*regarding her bigamous marriage to Heenan*). In the same column as her letter, and only a few paragraphs above it the following "item" appears:

> "The *Cincinnati Independent* gives a romantic sketch of an actress named Miss Ada McCord, a ballet girl at the Varieties, New Orleans, under Placide's management, some years since, who has since been Mrs. Bouxary, Mrs. Ned Buntline, etc., etc., etc."

Lesser, believing that the McCord name was adopted from this source, concludes, "the inference is clear".

It is an interesting and feasible theory, and whether the inference is as clear as Lesser believes it to be or not, it is certainly strongly supportive of Kendall's evidence.

Kendall then proceeded to demolish the "Dr. J. C. Campbell" (also known as the "Sir" Campbell) possibility. He discovered that:

> No such person figures in the Army list. If he (*Campbell*) took his stepdaughter with him to the Army post in Baton Rouge, where, according to Adah, the family lived for several years subsequent to 1838, no record of the fact remains. There was, however, in New Orleans in that epoch a very distinguished physician, Dr. George W. Campbell, a relative of the Duke of Argyle; and Adah's ascription to her supposititious parent of a title suggests that she was assimilating that gentleman into her pedigree with the sublime indifference to the truth which was characteristic of all her utterances on the subject.

Lesser confirms Kendall's dismissal of the Campbell connection. He checked the United States War Department records for 1844-1855 and found no Joseph or Josiah Campbell listed there among army surgeons. He also believed that there was no "doctor by that name in the New Orleans directories for the period", presumably having failed to locate the medical relative of the Duke of Argyle.

Adah occasionally claimed that she had married, while in the course of a brilliantly successful theatrical career in Havana, Cuba (of which there are no local records), a Spanish nobleman named Juan Clemente Zenea. Zenea did, indeed, exist. He was a noted Cuban revolutionary poet who lived in exile in New York from 1852 to 1855, the very years during which Menken claimed she married him in Cuba. So farewell Zenea.

The Ricardo La or Los Fiertes or Fuertes (*fuerte* is Spanish for *strong*), seems to have convinced no one; no attempts have been made to prove or disprove it since Menken first revealed this paternity in 1865. At the time it was a solemn revelation, a flat denial of all previous statements. She was, she then insisted, the daughter of a Spanish Jewish aristocrat who had married an equally aristocratic French woman in New Orleans. Her real name, she declared, was Dolores Adios Los Fiertes; she also deducted six years from her hitherto official date of birth, stating that she was born in 1841.

With his profound understanding and experience of Creole history in Louisiana, it is to Kendall we must now return for more interesting biographical research into the deliberately obscured origins of the woman we know as Menken. On one key point he was wrong. He believed that Adah married Alexander Isaac Menken in Galveston, Texas. The marriage, in fact, took place in Livingston, and is recorded thus:

> STATE OF TEXAS,   To any Regularly Ordained Minister of
> COUNTY OF POLK.   the Gospel, Judge of the District Court,
> Chief Justice of the County Court, or Justice of the Peace.—GREETING:

You are hereby authorized to celebrate the Rites of Matrimony between ALEXANDER I. MENKEN and ADA B. THEODORE; and make due return of this License to me within 60 days thereafter.

Given under my hand and Seal of the said County Court at my office in Livingston this 3rd day of April, A.D. 1856.

L. S. McMickin,
Deputy Clerk County Court P.C.

I celebrated the Rites of Matrimony between the above named persons on the 3 April 1856 in Polk County, Texas.

D. D. Moor,
J.P.P.C.

Returned & filed April 4th, A.D. 1856.

L. S. McMickin,
Depy. Clk.

STATE OF TEXAS,
COUNTY OF POLK. I certify that the foregoing License and Certificate thereto were this day recorded in my office in Record Book B of Marriages on page 77 at 5 1/2 o'clock P.M.

Witness my hand & seal of office April 4/56.

L. S. McMickin, Depy, Clk. C.C.P.C.

Rumours of an even earlier marriage in Galveston, Texas, are, however, well supported by a record (see p. 33) of a union between a W. H. Kneass, said to have been a composer of sorts and Miss Adda Theodore. If Adda is Adah (which seems not unlikely) then our heroine was already married when she eloped with Alexander Menken in the spring of 1856. Kneass, and others, later claimed to be former husbands; but neither Menken nor anyone else gave their claims very much attention. At least it begins to seem certain that Adah's true born name was Ada Berthe Theodore.

Bearing her Creole reference in mind, it occurred to Kendall that "Theodore" was likely originally to have been "Théodore". He investigated the Théodores of New Orleans in great detail, and uncovered the following fascinating material.

In 1838 there were in New Orleans two families named Théodore. One was that of a widow, who had a little millinery business at No. 41, Condé Street. This Mme. Théodore was apparently white. The other family was that of a "free man of color". He was Auguste Théodore, and he was a wheelwright by trade. In that year he resided at 35, Bagatelle Street - or Chartres Street, as we say to-day - probably in the vicinity of Elysian Fields. One year later he moved to a house on Love Street (now Rampart), between Elysian Fields and Marigny.

It is an interesting fact that between the years 1819 and 1848 there is no

THE STATE OF TEXAS:
COUNTY OF GALVESTON.

To any Regular Ordained Minister of the Gospel, Judge of the District Court, Judge of the County Court, or Justice of the Peace:

I hereby Authorize any one of you to Celebrate the Rite of Matrimony between *W. H. Kneass* and *Miss Adda Theodore* and due Return of your Proceedings to me, at my Office, make within Sixty Days, as the Law directs.

In Witness Whereof, I, OSCAR FARISH, Clerk of the County Court of Galveston County, hereto subscribe my name, and affix the Seal of said Court, this 6th day of February A.D. 1855.

Oscar Farish CLERK, C. C. G. C.

RETURN.

The above named Parties were duly United in the Bonds of Matrimony, on the Sixth day of February A.D. 1855 by the Undersigned, a Justice of the Peace.

Galveston, Feby. 6th, 1855.

Marriage certificate of Kneass and Theodore, 6 February 1855.

record of any child being born in New Orleans to parents named Théodore except to this "free man of color". That eliminates the shopkeeping Mme. Théodore. In the case of the wheelwright, however, there were two girls, one who came into the world in 1839 and the other in 1848. "Free man of color", be it observed, did not mean necessarily a person of black complexion; rather, it referred to one of those of indeterminate tint, who were the shame and romance of New Orleans in the first half of the nineteenth century – one of those individuals, then, in whose veins coursed a more or less considerable infusion of white blood.

Was Adah Isaacs Menken one of these girls? There is not a scintilla of evidence to that effect. Yet if we accept the "free man of color" as her progenitor, we can account for much that is otherwise difficult to reconcile with the probabilities. For at midnight on 3 May, 1839, Auguste Théodore became the father of a child to whom was given the name of Philomène Croi. She is described in the Board of Health record as the "legitimate offspring" of him and his wife, Magdaleine Jean Louis Janneaux, a native of Pensacola. Eight years later, to the same parents was born another child, a girl named Bénigne. Are we to suppose that Auguste Théodore had no other children, and was one of those persons rare among the colored population of New Orleans who were meticulously careful about registering the arrival of his offspring? Or was there something special about these two girls which made him desirous to place their births on record with the legally constituted authorities, while neglecting to do so with other little additions to his family circle? For after all, eight years was a long time between children among Creoles, and especially among free people of color. And Adah claimed to have a sister, and one only.

If Philomène Croi Théodore was really the girl who subsequently became known throughout Europe and America as Adah Isaacs Menken, then we have an explanation of a circumstance which has always puzzled the present writer. Why did she go to Texas to be married? If she were white, and her mother (according to Adah, the only surviving parent) consented, there could have been no objection to celebrating the happy event in New Orleans. But if she were a quadroon or octoroon, there was a law in Louisiana which forbade her union with a white man. In Texas, however, who was there to question her racial status? So to Texas the two young people hied themselves, and there the nuptial knot was tied.

The theory that Adah was of mixed blood also explains why she did not live in New Orleans after her marriage. Only once did she revisit her native city and that was in 1858, when for six days she played at the Varieties Theatre. She ran no danger of being molested by the bailiffs on that occasion, for her husband was not with her, and her offense, if any, had been committed beyond the jurisdiction of the local tribunals. Moreover, if our suppositions be justified, there were abundant motives why Adah should thereafter avoid telling the truth about her origins, and why she should devise one fantastic tale after the other about her family. Perhaps, too, that explains her beauty as well as her stormy temperament, indomitable ambition, and sketchy morals; for the octoroon women of New Orleans were reputed to be almost uniformly lovely.

It may be argued that there was no need for her to falsify her paternity in the Northern part of the United States or in Europe, but that is to ignore the deep impression which would have been made upon a spirit such as Adah Isaacs Menken's, in her childhood, in a community like New Orleans, where white blood had an almost celestial prestige. Adah would have imbibed that prejudice with her mother's milk; she would have craved nothing so much as to be included in that sacrosanct social caste, even when a touch of the tar-brush might elsewhere have invested her with a special and picturesque attraction for the public.

Menken poses as the "French Spy".

Now although Kendall himself agreed that it was "easy to pick flaws in this argument", the case he makes for Ada Theodore having such a background is convincing. He observes that "among the negroes and half-breeds" there was a pronounced laxity in the keeping of records; whilst acknowledging that "in the case of a child born on the outskirts of the city, whether white or colored, chances of it being registered were highly dubious". But, continues the assiduous Kendall:

> ... it is precisely these facts which make Auguste Théodore's certification of his daughter's birth so significant. And there is no mention in the Cathedral archives of any baby named Fiertes, Fuertes, Campbell, or Theodore born in the years required to fit into the erratic chronology of Adah Isaacs Menken's life.

Kendall, however, is unable to account satisfactorily for the assumption of the names *Ada* and *Berthe*. But Menken also, at other times, called herself *Adèle*, *Adelaide*, and *Dolores*, so perhaps we need not expect the systematic and thorough Louisiana historian to find archival evidence for feminine whims as well-understood and familiar as age-lopping and name-fixing.

Kendall then considers the problem of Menken's birth year, given at the time of her marriage as 1835:

> That made her a bride of twenty-one, lacking about five weeks. How, then, can she be identified with Philomène Croi Théodore, born in 1839? Of all persons Adah was least likely to add four years to her age unnecessarily. But if we suppose that she was really only 16 or 17 years old, would it not have been imperative for her to pretend to be of full legal age, in order to contract a valid marriage under the Texas law? Even the officials of a frontier town would have hesitated to marry an eloping couple unless assured that the bride had attained her majority.

The Livingston marriage certificate is not the only evidence of Ada Theodore in Texas. In the *Liberty Gazette* on 8 October 1855, the following advertisement appears:

> SHAKESPEARIAN READINGS
> Miss Ada Theodore
> Will Give Four Readings
> From Shakespeare in This
> Place Shortly
> Due Notices Will be Given of
> First Reading

During the months of November and December of the same year, three poems were published in the *Liberty Gazette* signed "Ada Bertha T——e". One of them, called *The Bright and Beautiful*, is dedicated to her sister "Josephine" (Annie Josephs?) and is datelined Washington, Texas. Another dedicated to "R.M.T****" is headlined *New Advertisement!!!* It is, indeed, an extraordinarily open declaration of availability, and with its dateline of Austin City, 23 November 1855, clearly indicates that Ada was seriously on the look-out for a Texan husband. It also denies later descriptions of her eyes as being violet, blue or sea-grey, for girls may be relied upon for accuracy in such details. Ada versifies lightly:

> I'm young and free, the pride of girls,
> With hazel eyes and 'nut brown curls';
> They say I am not void of beauty –
> I love my friends, respect my duty –
> I've had full many a BEAU IDEAL,
> Yet never – never – found one *real* –
> There must be one I know somewhere,
> In all this circumambient air;
> And I should dearly love to see him!
> Now what if *you* should chance to be him?

"R.M.T****" never came through, but perhaps Alexander Menken, touring Texas as a pit musician and conductor followed up the tantalising invitation. Certainly it was very soon after the *New Advertisement!!!* appeared that Ada and Menken met and fired one another with passion and ambition.

In his deductions regarding Ada's age and his conclusion that she was, unlike the majority of actresses, actually younger than she gave out, Kendall is perhaps supported by the *Notice Biographique sur Miss Adah Isaacs Menken* published during her season in Paris in 1867, in which it is startlingly revealed that she "was born in 1841, in New Orleans, of Franco-American parentage, of the Jewish religion". Now while it would seem extremely unlikely that this date is accurate, certainly Adah looked and was acceptable to her Parisian admirers as being still on the right side of 30, regardless of her extraordinarily long and variegated career. Her age, like the colour of her eyes, are matters concerning which she seems to have been able to confuse even her most ardent and intimate admirers. Charles Reade, the famous author of *The Cricket on the Hearth* and an escort of hers in London, commented on the devilish things she did to her eyes, and her use of a heavy white-base make-up. Even so, in her photographs, up to the last year of her life when she suddenly put on weight and seemed to be ageing rapidly (which is to say, looked thirty-five), she appeared both on and off-stage to be still in her late and extremely vigorous twenties.

We should also bear in mind the extraordinary youth of many South Western wives and mothers in the mid-nineteenth century. With or without the benefit of civil law approval, marriages were commonly contracted with girls still in their early adolescence. They were mothers in their teens, and not unusually (if they

Menken was one of the first actresses to recognise the value of photography for both publicity and posterity, and was a frequent visitor to the Sarony Photographic Studios in New York.

survived annual pregnancies), grandmothers in their early thirties. As to the deliberate gullibility (or purchaseability) of the officials who celebrated marriages, one should recollect the extraordinary case of Poe's marriage to his cousin Virginia Clemm. It was witnessed on oath in Richmond in 1836, that Poe's bride "is of the full age of 21 years". In fact, "Sis", as Poe called his cousin and wife, was 13 years, 9 months, and 1 day old at the time of their marriage. Twenty years later, Livingston, Texas, was much nearer the frontier and far behind the relatively sophisticated Richmond, Virginia, of twenty years earlier. It would not have been difficult in Polk County, Texas, where men were men and there was a chronic shortage of women, for all parties concerned to be fairly free and easy about the precise age of a determined young bride-to-be, with a gentleman able to pay the requisite fees and buy drinks all round.

It was not altogether surprising that the Liberty poetess should be misinterpreted. Ada, it seems, was already experiencing the dark side of even the smallest local fame, that shadowing notoriety which a travelling, pretty, talkative, and conscientiously liberated young lady in her teens would attract inevitably. She reacted with outrage and vigorous counter-attack, the style which characterised her behaviour in such situations throughout her life, writing emotionally in the *Liberty Gazette*:

> There are many young men, alas! too many! who imagine it adds to their dignity to play off mean jests, to bandy unclean doubts of woman's honor;

and this even passes as a wretched substitute for wit. Let those remember, who dare to whisper vulgar suspicions of any woman's purity (even though it is darkened) if compared to their own would appear as the immaculate white of angels! And they should also remember, that for her blasted character *they alone* are answerable.

Ada insisted that women, even teenage girls with no apparent means of support, apart from their ability to write articles and give Shakespeare readings, were not to be the helpless objects of even the macho men of Texas. In her column in the *Liberty Gazette* the teenage female liberationist addressed herself to a womanhood committed to lives of domestic slavery. "Oh! mothers!", she wrote, "believe me, there are other missions in the world for women, other than that of wife and mother." In other *Gazette* "Fugitive Pencilings", Ada quoted sharply:

A *man* discovered America, but a *woman* equipped the voyage. So everywhere; man executes the performance, but woman trains the man. Every effectual person, leaving an impress on the world is but another Columbus, whose mind was trained and furnished by some Isabella, in the form of his Mother, Wife or Sister. Will men never learn to be grateful?

Exposed as she was to the inevitable notoriety that followed such unconventional opinions, she sadly observed:

Public opinion is a terrible tyrant – cruel are the sacrifices it demands – many the hearts it has broken.

Alone in Liberty she fantasised about the loving mother she had left behind in Louisiana. We know from a letter to her sister Annie Josephs, that in fact, her mother was not very fond of Adah. But here she poeticised clumsily, "*My mother!* around thee blessings doth move", and she dreamt of a home she never had:

My Home! oh, what a scene of bliss is there,
A paradise of innocence and love;
It seems a spot of Heaven's peculiar,
A haven for the peace-alighting dove.

Meanwhile she still insisted that it was wrong that the daughters of such mothers and such homes should be:

... trained that the ultimate end of every accomplishment is to please the opposite sex. To win for herself a wealthy husband, is the lesson. She is taught all the feminine arts that woman is capable of teaching and learning, and every thought is concentrated in this all-important event. It matters not how the poor fellow is secured, so he is safely bound with the hymenial halter.

So Liberty saw the two faces of Ada Theodore – the female liberationist, who also wrote the coquettish "New Advertisement!!!" for a husband, and the contradiction puzzled its citizens as Menken has puzzled her followers ever since.

From the material published in the *Liberty Gazette* we have conclusive evidence that Adah was giving public readings, writing articles and poems, and searching for a husband in Texas, visiting Livingston, Liberty, Austin, Washington, and, probably, Galveston. There is also a considerable body of folklore in Texas concerning her early schooling in the small pueblo of Nacogdoches. But although Colonel Ochiltree and other eminent gentlemen of that township, reminisced freely about their early school-day associations with Adah, there is no

Dreams of Beauty.

(Inscribed to Emma Hardinge)

"And full the truths eternal
Oer the yearning spirits steal:
That the Real is the Ideal,
And the Ideal is the Real!"

Visions of Beauty, of Light, and of Love,
Born in the soul of a Dream;
Lost, like the phantom-bird under the dove,
When She flies over a stream.

Facsimile of the first two verses of Dreams of Beauty.

definite evidence of her presence or of that of her father (again described as an "old clo'" man) in that town.

One later piece of documentary evidence of Menken's presence in Texas relates to Livingston. The diary of a local lady records that the Menkens were "stopping at the Minter Hotel and that he was trying to get up a class to teach dancing (the Highland fling, polka, and mazurka)". This would seem to have been the first show-business enterprise of Ada Theodore as Mrs. Menken. It gives Livingston, Texas, the honour of being the first town in which Adah Isaacs Menken appeared. We may, then, conclude with some reason, that Menken, the artiste-performer, was, theatrically-speaking, born in Livingston, Texas, wherever she may have originated as Ada Theodore.

The tallest of Adah Menken's Texas-style tales was her often recounted Ned Buntline-style dime Western version of her capture by Indians. George Lippard Barclay, "comedian", published in Philadelphia a pamphlet called *The Life and Remarkable Career of Adah Isaacs Menken* soon after her death in 1868. In it he briefly and inaccurately summarises Menken's life, making the substance of his pamphlet the Indian story as told by Menken to his friend "Mr. Wm. Wallis of the Arch Street Theatre, while he was on a visit to Paris". It has been largely ignored by Menken's biographers because of its typically Western obviously mendacious quality; but it does, in fact, hit a significant bell-note in Menken's extravagant personality. Here, for the first time since Barclay "the comedian" related it in 1868, is the tale in full:

> I rode a splendid horse belonging to Captain Gonzalez, who kindly loaned it to me. Both the horse and myself were in excellent spirits, as indeed was the whole party, with one exception, a man named Gus Varney. A more inveterate coward I have never seen! We had scarcely gone fifteen miles when he commenced hinting as to the probability of Indians being in the vicinity. Several ladies became alarmed at his suggestion. The men, however, attempted to make sport of Varney's fears, but his cowardice was predominant over his sense of shame. A practical joker proposed to raise a cry of "Indians are coming", to frighten Varney, and then ridicule him. Having communicated the plan to us, we consented to act our parts by screaming and pretending to be greatly alarmed. At a given signal, our joker cried: "Run for your lives, Indians are coming." I was about to do as directed when a sight I never shall forget presented itself to me. Far over the hill were plainly visible a number of Indians, not mere spectres but solid matter-of-fact bodies. The thought of those savages sent a chill through me! I lost my balance, my consciousness left me, and I remembered no more until I awoke within a wigwam, with a dusky "son of the feather" gazing intently upon me!
>
> "Pretty squaw – you mine now – me big chief!" murmured the Indian, in broken English.
>
> "Were any of my friends captured?" I asked.
>
> "One – little mole – big coward – no fight."

I understood from this that Varney had been caught as well as myself.

"You see little mole?" asked my captor.

At first I was disgusted at the idea, but having thought that Varney might possess a knowledge which would assist in escape I consented. The Indian gave a peculiar signal, which was immediately answered in person by a young Indian girl. In appearance she did not possess any refined beauty, but there was something about her which drew me towards her; there was something grand about her, as with stately step she answered the summons.

"Why am I called?" she enquired.

"Laulerack is more proud than ever!" said the Indian in Spanish. "Bring the white man!"

She glanced toward me with a look of pity, and then, as if the act was a condescension on her part, obeyed the command.

"Is the maiden your wife?" I asked in Spanish. The Indian started as if some immortal power had addressed him, as hitherto I had spoken English.

"No," he answered; "as each moon passes she grows more proud, and although I am determined that she shall be mine she is determined not to be."

"If you would marry her, why do you wish that I, too, shall be your wife?"

He replied: "The white beauty in summer, the red beauty in winter!"

I saw that it was useless to try to direct his mind from having two wives at once! As the Indian did not seem inclined to converse further, I commenced to think of the future, when Varney entered.

"Oh, Miss Theodore," he said, in piteous accents. "Do contrive some means whereby I can escape, and then I'll send out armed men to rescue you!"

Varney, finding me in no mood to talk with him, retired. I then expressed a desire to speak with Laulerack, which my dusky captor consented to comply with. She entered, and at the same time the Indian stationed himself outside the wigwam.

"What does my pale sister want?" asked Laulerack, in a more pleasant voice than she had used in addressing her Indian admirer.

"Thy sister is named Bertha Theodore", I said in Spanish, "and although I have seen you but once I already love you!"

"My white sister has my pity."

"And pity in a woman amounts to love", I quickly added.

"My sister is right", Laulerack answered, "and my pity has thus soon become a love!"

"Thanks, thanks", I muttered.

"No thanks to me but to the Great Spirit who has willed it. The Great Spirit has given thee the power of speaking in winning speech."

I perceived the advantage gained, and immediately followed it up.

"Then will you help me escape? My friends perhaps think I am dead!"

"We can but try", she said. "With the darkness to-night we will start towards your home, and before the moon rises we shall be far on the path."

Bidding me prepare, she quitted the wigwam, having first placed her finger upon her lips as a warning to act silently. Night came at last, but how long seemed the time! My heart beat as a footstep sounded nearer the tent. I was sure it must be her, and I sprang up to greet her. A chill, however, came over me as I beheld not Laulerack but my captor, Eagle Eye!

"The pale face maiden seems anxious to meet me", he said.

"I thought it was Laulerack come to talk with me as I am so lonely."

"Eagle Eye would gladly stay with you", he answered. "Does the pale face maiden wish for anything?"

"Nothing!"

With a smile, which he intended for a loving one, but which in my eyes appeared hideous, the Indian left the wigwam.

A long time elapsed before Laulerack made her appearance. "I have kept my word. Follow me quietly", was all she said.

We had proceeded quite a distance when sounds of pursuit followed us.

"Keep behind me and run", said Laulerack.

I did as directed, but found myself unequal to keep up with the Indian maiden, who ran more like a deer than a human being. I consequently was far behind, when she stumbled over a stone. As I came up, I was about to assist her to her feet, but she said; "Do not stop for me, but run for your life." She was not so badly hurt as I had supposed, and presently came within hailing distance. "On, on", she cried, and I endeavoured to quicken my pace, but found it impossible to run at all!

By this time we could hear guns, and I, expecting to be shot, expressed my fear to Laulerack, who laughed as she said, "They fire up in the air, not at us!"

Suddenly we came in view of an encampment, and a voice shouted "Indians!"

I knew these were white men, and I shouted, "A white maiden seeks protection".

But a volley was fired in our path, and Laulerack was shot! In a faint voice she called out to me to drop, which I did. The Rangers (for such they proved to be) finding all quiet, advanced cautiously. In a loud scream I said, "There are no enemies, but a white woman and an Indian maiden, whom you have shot."

"Well, I would have sworn there were Indians in ambush", said a rough voice, and presently he was joined by others, who came towards us, and lifting Laulerack carefully from the ground carried her to the encampment.

"We'll pursue these darned redskins", said the man.

"Their village is but a short distance from here, and they hold a white man prisoner", I added, forgetting that Varney did not deserve the blood that might be spilled by these brave fellows.

"My white sister", said Laulerack, "I am dying."

"You will get well", I muttered, "and then we will never leave one another. Had I not asked you to assist me to escape all would have been well."

"No, fair maiden, it was no fault of yours. I will soon be with my father and mother in the Happy Hunting Ground far, far away. May the Great Spirit watch over you."

The three men, who had been left to protect us from danger, now came near, and bending down raised their hats, for within the circle lay the inanimate Laulerack!

On the return of the other men I listened to the plan of the attack, their capture of some Indians, and the rescue of Varney, whom I saw conversing with the Rangers.

Among the captives was Eagle Eye, who was deeply affected at the death of Laulerack. In Spanish he said to me: "White man gave alarm when you escaped, in hope of gaining his liberty!" I did not translate this to the Rangers! As I knew their tempers were of a violent nature, I felt sure that Varney would swing if they learned the truth.

After a march of many miles, we arrived at Austin, where for three months I was kindly taken care of by General Harney, who was stationed there.

Now although it is quite impossible not to regard Menken's Indian experience as being a highly embroidered patch-work of Western tale-telling, the Texas author and historian J. Frank Dobie, has truly observed that "the facts of Texas history dwarf in comparison the products of the most imaginative minds". In the mid-fifties, Texas, the former fierce republic, had been a State of the Union for less than a decade. One of the principal reasons for joining the Union had been the inadequacy of the local Texan military resources to deal with the opposition offered by fierce Comanche and other Indian nations in their resistance to the ruthless drive to the West of the white-eyes. Not so very far from Austin, the capital of the State, skirmishes with Indians were still occurring in the mid-fifties. A valiant Indian fighter and Texan commander was the General Harney Menken mentioned in her story, who had a ranch in Travis County near Austin. In her *Notice Biographique* Menken enlarged upon her relationship with Harney. There she says that after her deliverance she was "taken to the Federal General Harney's quarters, then based in Austin. Welcomed with open arms by her compatriots, she spent three months in the barracks in an apartment arranged for her. The Harney family received her, and she translated Spanish documents into English for the General. Miss Adah went out riding with him on review days, could give orders in the military fashion, and commanded a company like a true soldier."

Certainly Adah learned her excellent horsemanship, and her style with gun, dagger and pistol from someone military somewhere in Texas.

As for the extraordinary relationship with her "sister", the Indian girl

"Laulerack, the dark-eyed one", Adah wrote a poem celebrating her beauty, her sacrifice and their love:

> I see her yet, that dark-eyed one,
>   Whose bounding heart God folded up
> In His – as shuts, when day is gone,
>   Upon the elf the blossom's cup.
> On many hours like this we met,
>   And, as my lips did fondly greet her,
> I blessed her as Love's amulet;
>   Earth hath no treasure dearer, sweeter.
>
> The stars that look upon the hill,
>   And beckon from their homes at night,
> Are soft and beautiful, yet still
>   Not equal to her eyes of light.
> They have the liquid glow of earth,
>   The sweetness of a summer even,
> As if some angel at their birth
>   Had dipped them in the hues of Heaven!
>
> They may not seem to others sweet
>   Or radiant with the beams above,
> When first their soft sad glances meet
>   The eyes of those not born for love;
> Yet when on me their tender beams
>   Are turned, beneath love's wild control,
> Each soft sad orb of beauty seems
>   To look through mine into my soul.
>
> I see her now, that dark-eyed one,
>   Whose bounding heart God folded up
> In His – as shuts, when day is done,
>   Upon the elf the blossom's cup.
> Too late we met. The burning brain
>   And aching heart alone can tell!
> How filled our souls of death and pain
>   When came the last sad word, Farewell!

In her collected poems, these verses retitled *A Memory*, seem to reveal a need for a sacrificial sister-figure. The poem has also been said to contain strongly homosexual elements. But in the complex erotic history of Adah Menken, there is not a single close relationship with a woman recorded. One senses in the poem more a profound need in Menken for "sisterhood", and for a real and positive mother. She may have found some fulfilment of that need in her relationship, years later, with Georges Sand in Paris. But in 1856 in Texas, untrained but worldly eyes observed only an extraordinarily talented and complicated girl of dubious origins about to provide an unforgettable experience for the BEAU IDEALS who might succeed in catching her but would never be able to hold her for long.

Menken with Georges Sand.

The Orleans Theatre, founded in 1819 in New Orleans by a group of French actors.

Three

Enter Adah Isaacs Menken – as actress

WHEN ADAH BECAME Mazeppa she had been Menken and an actress for only six years. Her theatrical career moved on from the Liberty Shakespeare readings to performing with the amateur Crescent Dramatic Association of New Orleans in 1856, her first recorded appearance on any stage. She was still in her late teens, lovely, but already rather dashing, and giving herself out to be twenty-one in order to justify both extensive claims to theatrical experience and her marriage. Her career had begun, she said, when she was a mere child. Then, with her sister Josephine, she had performed in the French Opera House in New Orleans as "The Sisters Theodore", a dancing act. Research has not produced evidence of this childhood booking, and the truth may be that, like so many other little girls, she was exaggerating the importance of a school production. It would have been elementary for Menken to elevate such a childhood experience into a professional booking. Later she would add more and more to her early background as a dancer but, at the moment, the Crescent did not ask for much in the way of qualifications other than vivacity, determination, and a sense of the theatrical. Adah showed enough of these qualities to draw the attention of James S. Charles, a former New Orleans comedian and now the manager of the first regular stock company to exploit the greater hunger for entertainment in the Red River towns of Louisiana and East Texas. It was Charles who discovered in a converted hall in Opelousas, Louisiana, that there was money to be mined in those cultural deserts.

By 1856 the Charles Company had developed a profitable circuit, including Shreveport, Alexandria and Texas towns as remote as Nacogdoches. For the 1857 season Charles wanted to introduce some new talent into his company, and the energetic and beautiful amateur "debutante", with her remarkable eyes and more than ordinary figure (which she was already skilled and confident in presenting), seemed a good bet. Furthermore, Adah, young as she was, had another useful qualification for a professional theatre in which the ladies were too often bravura *demi-mondaines* and, consequently, a doubtful attraction in the more respectable dates. She had been married for a year to the dark, handsome and distinguished-looking Alexander Isaac Menken, a member of a prominent and wealthy Cincinnati Jewish family in the dry goods business. The family founder Solomon, born in Prussia, arrived in the United States from Holland in 1820, as a packman. He had prospered as Cincinnati grew into the "Queen City of the West". Alexander was the son of his first marriage and something of a black sheep who may well have been disowned by the Menkens (for there is no record of his name in the family Bible), perhaps for becoming a theatrical and a musician. But if being stage-struck made Alexander unsuited to the dry goods business, it certainly qualified him to become Adah's husband. Together the attractive young couple dreamed of double booking their way up the provincial ladder to the highest dates. The Charles Company would be the first step on that ladder; and so at Shreveport in March 1857, "Mrs. A. I. Menken" was booked to appear in a local favourite, Bulwer-Lytton's *The Lady of Lyons or Love and Pride*, a five-act drama in blank verse set during the French Revolution. The local reviewer commented on Mrs. Menken's performance: "The debutante was self-possessed, graceful, pretty, and capable of reading with correctness and force" in the leading role of Pauline. With such a success behind her Adah (for from marriage onwards her name was to be spelt with an "h", Hebrew-style), was cast by Charles in leading roles throughout the season.

But 1857 was to be a bad year for the American economy. The great railroads' bubble suddenly exploded, banks called in their money, and finance-houses closed down, having lost the savings of their stockholders and depositers. Credit was non-existent, business died, factories closed, unemployment increased. The Menken fortunes were inevitably affected. Alexander, who had, up to now, been in receipt of some kind of income (perhaps from a family grateful to pay him to keep away from Cincinnati), was suddenly short of cash. Theatre bookings were poor and the companies touring were hungry, but not for the talents of Adah. Nevertheless she had added something to her fame and name. She was not only Ada*h*, but Isaac*s* Menken, a slight but distinct differentiation from her husband's name.

The summer produced no work for the Menkens and so Adah, with calculating impulsiveness, volunteered her services to the good old Crescent for a benefit performance, in a leading role, of course. The benefit was to take place in New Orleans and would provide her with a first-class showcase for, following practice, she, as star, had the privilege of choosing the play. She carefully settled for Henry Hart Milman's *Fazio or The Italian Wife's Revenge*. Milman was an English clergyman who wrote extremely rotund fustian, and his style fitted Menken's idea of her scale. The play is the tale of Bianca and her philandering husband, Fazio. She is a lovely passionate girl, innocent and wholly trusting, but transformed by the inner violence of her character when she discovers her husband's infidelity. She warns him, thus: "Take heed; we are passionate; our milk of love doth turn to wormwood, and that's bitter drinking. If that ye cast us to the winds, the winds will give us their unruly, restless nature; we whirl and whirl; and where we settle, Fazio, but He that ruleth the winds can know!" Not surprisingly, Fazio ran off with another lady, financing his escape from Bianca quite simply by murdering a rich miser. The Italian wife now seeks her revenge. She betrays her dishonourable husband to the police and enjoys her greatest moment after the blackguard has been executed, with the curtain finally descending after a powerful and stirring blank verse homily on the wages of sin. It was a perfect part for flashing eyes, but a bad night, the last Saturday of an unbearably hot August. It did not prevent New Orleans theatre-lovers from attending the Gaiety but the more influential citizens were cooling off in the country. Still, as it was a charity show, the Menkens were more concerned with exciting the press than the groundlings. Adah was now to establish that close rapport with journalists which characterised her entire career; they were kept informed of every up and down in this really not very significant amateur production. Rehearsals, they were told, had not gone easily. The amateurs had thought of postponing; but Adah had lifted their spirits and, drilling them night and day, had welded them into a true company of Thespians, perfect in delivery and movement. She, it was, who had insisted, trouper-like, that the show must go on. Naturally, lovers of true Theatre would want to see the beautiful and wonderfully talented girl who could command such theatrical discipline and who had such a superb figure to boot.

And so they did. The *New Orleans Daily Picayune* gave Adah a perfect puff. "The accomplished and talented Menken", it said, "received constant applause throughout her performance and an enthusiastic call at the termination." The benefit, then, turned out to be highly profitable to all, perhaps even its nominal beneficiary, a poor old actress forgotten in the excitement. A second performance was arranged for the following week, but this time it would be totally in aid of Mrs. Menken, who would show how varied and extensive her talents were by playing two pieces: *The Soldier's Daughter*, for drama and tears; and for laughter and comedy, *A Lesson for Husbands*. Again the theatre played to an enthusiastic audience, and the young star was "profusely bouqueted, wreathed and coroneted in flowers" after the final curtain. Certainly one husband present received a serious lesson. While Adah quoted the *Picayune* reviewer's conclusion that she "has decided talent, joined with a good person, a beautiful face, a musical voice, graceful action and perfect self-possession and ease on the stage and would be a valuable accession to one of our stock companies, and with the practice she would have in that capacity might soon attain a high popularity and celebrity", Mr. Menken was thinking of the cost of all the drinks and flowers, the clothes, and the hotel. He seemed quite depressed when Adah quoted the great critic, John W. Overall of the *Sunday Delta*, who had compared her with famous actress-beauties of the American theatre and concluded that she was, "beyond all question …

more graceful and elegant than Mrs. Hayne, and more vivacious than Agnes Robertson".

"What do you think of that, Alexander?" cried the almost-famous, almost-actress.

Mr. Menken sighed. "It has all been very, very expensive", he said. Not surprisingly, there followed the first of their really serious marital disagreements, after which Adah went to see Mr. Overall. His praise and admiration soothed her disappointment with the unappreciative and cruel Alexander who, she could see quite clearly, was destroyed by jealousy at her success while he had been ignored in the pit. During supper Mr. Overall wisely pointed out to Adah the dangers of theatrical marriages and of the personal problems which accompany success. Moved by the lovely girl's great-eyed concentration on his words, he advised her on her career, offering her his influence and protection. It is not known what Menken offered in return, but it is certain that her recognition of the possibilities of writers and journalists of all qualities blossomed at this time.

Overall daringly suggested two more performances in New Orleans under Mrs. Menken's own producership. He recommended the part of Parthenia in Mrs. Lovell's play, *Ingomar or The Barbarian* as being particularly suited to her talents and Adah's sister might present a group of dances in the course of the evening. But in spite of Overall's wise advice, influence and tutelage, and the combined talent of The Theodore Sisters, that show was a total fiasco. Mrs. Menken's thrown-together company missed cues, dropped lines and props, and only by the most flagrant projection of her powerful figure and personality was Adah able to prevent the normally patient and sympathetic New Orleans audience from walking out. Yet a month later she dared to produce a second show, but now she chose her company carefully. She played her great success Bianca again, drilling the actors about her like a guards captain. Again the piece went down well and there was praise from the critics. The *Picayune* stated categorically that Mrs. Menken "would be a good card for one of our managers in want of a useful and attractive 'leading lady' ". Mrs. Menken made sure *that* review was placed on the desk of Mr. William H. Crisp, the manager of the Gaiety Theatre, and the most important of Southern theatrical producers. She made her intentions clear in a letter to a friend.

"My mind", she wrote on 2 November, "has been in a constant state of suspense regarding my theatrical business lately. You must know that I for some time negotiated with Crisp for the leading business in Memphis. When Crisp arrived he was waited upon by some of my friends, and consented to make me an offer to play at both his houses ... I accepted, but there being no articles, and his business being very bad at both places he wilfully broke the engagement – as related – but offered me leading business at Vicksburg where he plays a season of *6 weeks*! I declined of course. He has made a great many enemies by treating me so badly ... You know it is very difficult for an actress to get an opening in any theater when she has no position as a star actress in that profession – no matter what talent she may possess. My circumstances are anything but flattering; I mean privately. You see I have not been playing for some time – waiting for engagements till my means have run out ... Do not think me ungrateful – I am not indeed; but fortune has not been kind to me lately."

But Mr. Crisp was soon brought to heel. Adah now added to her sales presentation a thoroughly convincing account of her intimacy with Shakespearean parts, knowing Crisp was already committed to Murdoch and the Bard. With such invaluable additional repertoire she suddenly seemed to Crisp too good to miss. A satisfactory contract was completed and Crisp proceeded to arrange the *Macbeth* production in Nashville where Menken played the unforgettable Lady to James E. Murdoch's Thane, thus bringing to a not unsatisfactory conclusion Mrs. Menken's first year in the professional theatre. It would have been encouraging to most beginners but Adah could never rest upon her laurels. She gave another one-night stand in New Orleans, then played a month on tour – after which there really wasn't much more she could do on the local circuit. After the Crescent, and Charles and Crisp, to what heights could one climb? There was no alternative but to move up the Mississippi Valley, towards Cincinnati. And wasn't that the home town of Alexander? And didn't she, the most famous of the Menkens, have in his family, a wealthy and influential caucus who could do her career no harm at all? How dreadfully sad it was that Alexander had fallen out with his family! So unsuitable amongst Jewish people like the Menkens and the Theodores. It was, perhaps, the first time that any noticeable mention was made of Adah's "Jewish" forebears, starring the distinguished sephardic aristocrats, the Los, Les or Las Fiertes.

Alexander Menken was amazed. He had no idea that he had married a Jewess. As he considered the revelation, Adah flashed her eyes at him. Her hair fell in long ringlets, dark and gleaming and she looked more Jewish all the time.* She pointed out with the sad patience and subtlety of her people, that old Solomon Menken, the patriarch of Alexander's tribe, would be thrilled to know that his oldest son had married within the Faith. Was it not time, she appealed, for all of us Menkens to become one big, happy, extremely wealthy Cincinnati family?

Eventually Alexander succumbed to Adah's reason, persuasive flattery, and other caresses. She convinced him that he had inherent talent as an impresario and was wasted in the pit. Why should he fiddle away his talent when he could drive star vehicles which would bear them both to the heights of fame and fortune? And where better to start the journey than Cincinnati, where the influence of his family would certainly not prevent them getting a booking at Wood's Theatre, not at all a bad date. Alexander followed her reasoning, but he was reticent to face his family again after all the hard words. Impatiently Adah reminded him

---
* Falk, Menken's biographer in his *The naked Lady* (1934) was convinced that Menken was born Jewish by her Jewish appearance and hair style at this time (see illustration p. 4).

that his own brother Jacob had published a poem in her honour in the Cincinnati *Israelite*, the local Anglo-Jewish paper. They were proud of her, for had she not brought honour to their name? And was not a little of the credit his? Members of his family had written warm Jewish letters to her full of invitations to come home and eat wholesome meals and so on.

"But", interposed Alexander, knowing his family well, "all that's if we go back into the dry goods business. They won't feel quite the same if we're booked at Wood's and the whole town can see your – well." He hesitated.

"My talent and success are exactly what the Menken family want to see in Cincinnati!" declared Adah. "No one, my dear", she added with all the worldly wisdom of her nineteen, twenty-one or twenty-two years, "no one", she insisted, "and that includes the wealthy Menkens, turns away from success."

Adah's better notices were now sent with a carefully phrased letter, neither too eager nor too haughty, offering the Menken for a season on, for the sake of family associations with Cincinnati, an exceptionally reasonable basis. Adah drafted the letter and Alexander signed it. When Wood's replied that they were eager and available for his wife, Alexander began to feel that Adah had discovered his true vocation.

Adah viewed the long trip up the Mississippi River as a parallel to the forty-year journey of her Chosen People through the desert to the Promised Land. As the steam-boat got nearer to Cincinnati she grew increasingly Jewish, utilising her time studying back-numbers of the Cincinnati *Israelite*, and questioning Alexander endlessly about his family, their history, his Jewish experience, and the general state of the theatre and the press in Cincinnati. She was effectively putting together her new role, that of a nationally famous Jewish actress. And, for the first time, she was studying a part in depth.

Adah had continued publishing poems and spirited literary pieces ever since *Liberty Gazette* days. *The New Orleans Sunday Delta* had run an essay shimmering with the indignation of a Jewish Portia, on Shylock, and poems were appearing here and there. The Cincinnati *Israelite* had reprinted her verses in October 1857. Encouraged, she sent the editor others, piously dated in Hebrew. Her *Dum Spiro, Spero* was dated Tishri 11/5618. She also gave some of her poems Hebrew subtitles. By April 1858 the *Israelite* was full of pride at having discovered an American Jewish poetess, naming Adah (sight unseen), as "a first class star on the stage all over the southwest". Its editor, Rabbi Isaac M. Wise, a leading exponent of Judaism in America, was a pillar of the new American Jewish establishment, and his opinions carried weight. Rabbi Wise had responded to Adah not only by publishing the poems; he also reprinted her articles, and featured the better reviews of her productions. With the Rabbi's assistance, Adah was becoming a star in Cincinnati even before arriving there.

When the Menkens did arrive in early June, Rabbi Wise and The *Israelite* were proud to greet Adah as, "our favourite and ingenious poetess ... who comes to us from the south, crowned with the brilliant success, genius and talent always meet". So far as the local Jewish communities were concerned, Rabbi Wise's enthusiastic acceptance made Adah undeniably *kosher*. However Jewish she may or may not have been up to this point, she would be, from now on, effectively a convert to the Cincinnati Jewish Community. Through Rabbi Wise she now began actually studying Hebrew; and even the most respectable of the Cincinnati Jews when they heard that were able to overcome their prejudices against theatricals, and feel proud of, and support, the Menken season at Wood's.

The Menken season in Cincinnati was a huge success. The audience adored her in *The Soldier's Daughter*, *The Jewess*, and cried over her sufferings in *The Hunchback*, a touching new piece she had found. The literary set around Rabbi Wise and the *Israelite* were delighted to have a national celebrity as a focal point for their otherwise ordinary provincial cultural activities. Adah read her poems to them, and gave addresses on subjects of social, religious and artistic significance, including the famous civil rights issue of the admission of Jews into the British Parliament. She also spoke on the position and status of women, pointing out that the wives of the Jewish patriarchs had power and respect, and that a woman could, among the Jews, be elected a judge and a leader. The spirit of the great matriarchs, the passion of Judith about to behead Holofernes, descended upon Adah when she spoke on these themes. A certainty for popularity among the Jewish gentlemen of Cincinnati, she also became the heroine and idol of the ladies. Parties and dinners were given in her honour and Adah grew in spiritual stature in the heat of the Jewish warmth to become a queen among the local princesses in Israel. The physician and novelist Dr. Nathan Mayer, composed quatrains in her honour, and she replied in print with a poem describing him as the "young Genius of our ancient race". With this steady and powerful cultural input, the new *persona* she was creating for herself blossomed. She developed a studious style in conversation using Latin phrases she had learnt by heart. French she knew from her New Orleans background and spoke with the charming erratic accent of the Creoles; but then who, in Cincinnati, spoke perfect French anyway? Her eccentricities were regarded as natural and necessary to an intellectual and a poetess; furthermore, was she not a courageous exponent of the new liberated attitudes towards themselves being adopted by some of Europe's bravest and most intellectual women?

Then Alexander booked Adah for Dayton, Ohio, to play *Sixteen-String Jack*, her own version of the life of the notorious English highwayman Jack Sheppard (affording her great gymnastic possibilities in boy's dress). She was greeted by the Dayton press as if she were already the equal of Rachel and Lola Montez. In the intermission, a little drunk with success, she continued to hold the stage, singing "Comin' thro' the Rye", and performing a Spanish dance which the *Dayton Empire* described as, "done with that grace and abandon that ranks her as a finished and fascinating danseuse". It is the only record of her, up to this time, dancing in public, and however good or bad she was, she had a personal *claque* of seventy-five young men who applauded her every turn, convincing the audience of her greatness, and building up enthusiastic applause to a rapturous final curtain. After the show all of them marched backstage, where they introduced themselves as the Dayton Light Guards, a volunteer corps of militia. Their captain invited Adah to dine with them as their guest of honour. As Alexander was back in Cincinnati, and she was hungry and all alone, it was hard for her to turn down seventy-five stalwart young men.

That night many toasts were drunk to Adah, with the guards finally bestowing upon her the honorary commission of Captain. By the time Adah returned to Cincinnati the news had already reached her husband of her long night with her admirers. He suggested coldly that the dinner was scandalous, that her commission was a crude joke, and that if she had drunk a toast with each of the seventy-five guards, she must have been carried back to her room, and who knows what else. The Menken name, insisted Alexander (who knew how such things happened), had been trampled in the sweat and grease-paint of the footlights. As Adah turned her great eyes upon him, brimful with tears, appalled at his coldness, Alexander Menken suddenly looked like a prematurely middle-aged Cincinnati businessman in dry goods. Her "inner self" knew that their great love affair was in crisis.

No doubt what Alexander had heard concerning the Dayton affair was much exaggerated; but in no circumstances would Adah agree to forego her new title. She would use it in her publicity, she insisted. "Captain Adah Isaacs Menken of the Dayton Light Guards", suited her specialisation in male parts perfectly, and where was there another artiste in the American theatre who held a comparable military honour? Alexander seemed, infuriatingly, to have become increasingly conventional and middle-class since their return to Cincinnati. While she had grown in spirit and achievements, he was dwindling before her very eyes to tradesman-like proportions, making him more boring than the most ordinary of storekeepers. But what could she do? There she was, entirely alone, except for the Menkens. If they deserted her, she knew her reign over the local intellectuals would be rapidly terminated. She would have to try and make her marriage work. Somehow she must bring Alexander back, for he had, after the Dayton controversy, actually walked out on her. He stayed away till the end of August when, overlooking the gross creative discrepancy between them, she sought him out and, at her most excitingly vulnerable, begged a forgiveness which, after long nights of absence from her, he was inclined to award her fairly easily. There was a passionate reconciliation.

Adah now returned to more straight-laced cultural activities than those of which Dayton still whispered. She studied German, the mother-tongue of many of the Cincinnati Jews, and increased her activities in religious and social matters. She became fascinated by all the current speculations regarding the Millennium which fear of the impending civil war encouraged, and studied the Books of the Prophets, discussing calculations with Rabbi Wise about how long the world was likely to last. With relief she concluded that there was still time for her career to be accommodated. As was her wont, Adah threw herself totally into her pseudo-cabalistic studies, and they acted as a powerful stimulant upon her poetic inclinations. In full spate, under her new daemon's influence, she could now enter totally into another character, that of a Biblical prophetess heralding the imminent arrival of the Messiah. As such she called in free verse upon her people to defend themselves against injustices, and to prepare for the return to Zion.

Adah had already revealed an inclination towards the political aspects of the Jewish Question. Her Shylock essay was being quoted by lecturers on Shakespeare. Her essay on the *Jew in Parliament* (*Israelite*, 3 September 1858), a powerful plea for the right of Baron Lionel de Rothschild to sit in the British Houses of Parliament as an elected member, was responded to nobly and gratefully by the Baron who had called her (she said) "the inspired Deborah of our People". Each week during the last three months of that year she contributed an article or poem to the *Israelite*. Her protest against the papal kidnapping of an Italian Jewish boy, Edgar Mortara, was one of the first pieces on the subject to appear. Some of

Menken, "truly brilliant Reader and Poetess".

her protests were picked up by Jewish and other newspapers in America and England.

Apart from lectures, Adah also gave dramatic readings, a more serious form of public display, less likely to provoke scandal; she even ventured as near to Dayton as Piqua, twenty-five miles away, to lecture and recite. There "this truly brilliant Reader and Poetess", read from *Richard III*, and *Romeo and Juliet*, and delivered a poem for which her style was perfect, Edgar Allan Poe's *The Raven*. The reading was to a small audience but was accounted a great success. A fortnight later she ventured back into Dayton and there repeated her victory over the hearts and applause of a loyal public, although the militia members found it a touch tame after tight knickerbockers and champagne. But Alexander and all the Menkens were now very anxious whenever Adah appeared in public, and after Dayton further readings were not encouraged. They preferred her other *persona*, the literary, even the political, for though the prophetess was a little embarrassing to the rational Reform Jewish citizens of the United States, even a Deborah was more acceptable than a cavorting theatrical gymnast.

Adah's serious cultural efforts were certainly gaining attention. In December a poetic tribute to her appeared in a national weekly newspaper, the *Sunday Mercury* of New York. Other papers ran the story of her captaincy in the Dayton Light Guards, and she pointed out to Alexander, delightedly, that they had, all of them, taken it perfectly seriously. Her victory over the squeamish Menkens was complete when she was able to show them a published quotation from a popular Shakespearean actor, Stuart Robson. On hearing of the Menken's entry into the civic and political field, he was said to have exclaimed: "By the living jingo, what next? In the case of female suffrage, Adah Isaacs Menken will be nominated for the Presidency – yes, and be elected too!" With such support from her professional peers and the media, offers materialised and, doubtful as he still was about the moral character of Adah's theatrical *geist*, Alexander booked her for the spring. The first two weeks would be in Louisville supporting a young member of a famous acting family named Edwin Booth, whom people thought had some kind of a future.* Even though Booth had, as yet, no fame comparable with her own, Adah was delighted to get back on to the stage with anyone. Overwhelmed by gratitude and love for her loyal if still resentful husband, she composed her *Wife's Prayer* for him, and published it in the *Israelite*:

> Oh, Thou great God of Israel! Bless and preserve that dear person, whom Thou hast chosen to be my husband; let his life be long and blessed, comfortable and holy; and let me also become a great blessing and comfort unto him, a sharer in all his joys, a refreshment in all his sorrows, and a meet-helper for him in all the accidents and changes of the world; make me amiable forever in his eyes, and very dear to him. Unite his heart to me in the

---

* He was never to achieve the historic notoriety of his younger brother, the assassin of Lincoln.

dearest union of love and holiness, and mine to him in all sweetness, charity and compliance. Keep me from all ungentleness and ill-humor, and make me humble and obedient, useful and observant, that we may delight in each other, according to Thy blessed word and ordinance, and both of us may rejoice in Thee, having our portion in the love and service of our God of Israel, forever, for Thou art the King, the Help and Savior: Thou mighty shield of Abraham, and all Israel – Thy dear people!

But apparently the Lord God was a little preoccupied at the moment, trying to save the marriage of the Northern and Southern states from total catastrophe, and the Menken match was not much improved by Adah's prayers. Christmas came and, with it, a lead for Adah in Sir Walter Scott's *Ivanhoe* at the new National Theatre in Cincinnati. Because of the season an additional attraction was booked for one night only. John Carmel Heenan, the American heavyweight title-holder, would box a round with a sparring partner. Alexander thought it somewhat *infra dig*, but at least it offered the advantage and convenience that Adah could leave the theatre immediately after her performance, and get home early. But the Benecia Boy, a six-foot-two Irish Galahad, called at her dressing-room to present his compliments, and Adah's return to the Menkens was dangerously, if deliciously, delayed.

John Carmel Heenan sketched at the time of his famous battle with Tom Sayers for the World Championship.

Four

Enter Menken – as Cleopatra

ACCORDING TO experts on pugilism, J. C. Heenan had all the attributes of a great boxer, other than first-class fighting ability. He was tall, handsome, muscular and flashy and, provided he wasn't confronted by a real killer, could look after himself well enough. One quality he shared with Adah Menken; that of immodesty. He had declared himself heavyweight champion of America, afterwards matching himself carefully, to ensure that he retained his self-awarded crown. Heenan's history till then was typical enough of the emigrant son. He was born in West Troy, New York on 2 March 1835, his father Timothy being a foreman in the Federal arsenal there. On leaving school John Carmel was apprenticed to a machinist; at seventeen, like many another adventurous youth, he left for California and gold. And like many others found himself stranded there without a cent. But there was work for a trained machinist in the factory of the Pacific Mail Steamship Company in Benicia, and there it was that fame first touched Heenan's shoulder. He won a local contest by keeping going with a thirty-two pound sledge-hammer for twelve consecutive hours. After that, dubbed the Benicia Boy, and regardless of his ignorance of the noble art, he won himself numerous exhibition bouts as a pugilist.

As the Menken was found by Captain Smith, so Heenan was discovered by Jim Cusick, a sports promoter who observed that, even without too much skill, the Boy had star-quality in his looks and theatrical style. Cusick took Heenan to New York and there introduced him to Irish friends at Tammany Hall. They were glad to employ his muscle in the "protection" of uncertain voters in local elections. Demonstrating a talent for strong-arming, Heenan was rewarded by a sinecure in the Customs Office, which gave him pocket-money, while Cusick set about the more serious business of promoting purses for fights. Deciding to start at the top, Cusick and Heenan published a defiant and insulting challenge addressed to the reigning heavyweight champion of America, John Morrissey.

Boxing, though illegal at the time, had the support of many *aficionado* politicians, wealthy businessmen, and other gangsters, described by a contemporary moralist thus: "A worse set of scape-gallowses could scarcely be collected, low, filthy, brutal, bludgeon-bearing scoundrels – the very class of men who have built up the Tammany Hall party in New York and to whose well-paid labours the party owes almost its existence." Eager to see the Benicia Boy fight, these scape-gallowses enabled Cusick to put together a large purse, and an even larger book of side-bets. Morrissey was contemptuous but unable to resist the challenge, and with the police properly squared, on 20 October 1858, in an open field near Buffalo, the two pugilists met before a large crowd. It was, in fact, Heenan's first major contest as self-appointed heavyweight champion of America. It was also his last, for, after managing to dance out of the embrace of the skilled but heavy Morrissey for nine rounds, Heenan began to tire. In the eleventh round Morrissey, still powerful and apparently untired, leapt out of his corner, and with a salvo of blows, smashed Heenan into unconsciousness and out of his title.

Yet amazingly enough, a few months later Cusick was again claiming the world title for Heenan. The claim was favoured, not by any subsequent fights in which the Benicia Boy had been successful, but by the fact that Morrissey had now retired from the ring to go into politics. As the prize-fighting game needed a champion, and as his defeat by Morrissey hadn't in the least diminished the Boy's flash, the fans of the illicit art were prepared to accept the illicit title. This time Cusick and Heenan were not going to take any risks. The Benicia Boy was available, but only for touring dates and theatres where he would fight exhibition rounds with his well-trained and gentle partners, for this way he was sure to win every fight. Such an exhibition was the one which preceded the meeting between Adah Menken and the man she was subsequently to describe as having played Anthony to her Cleopatra.

The details of the first exchange between the great lovers-to-be is unrecorded, but following their brief dressing-room encounter, Alexander Menken seemed to exhibit to Adah even fewer of those qualities which she required in a leading man. For his part, the strain of trying to manage his unmanageable wife, the pressures of his family, his increasing dependence upon drink, all rapidly made the marriage deteriorate rapidly. She wanted to go to New York and attack the highest citadels of the theatrical profession; he wanted to settle down in Cincinnati. Adah continued to advertise herself as Captain of the Dayton Light Guards (although she knew the episode was an embarrassment to the Menkens), and her ideas about costume were becoming more and more daring. Furthermore, the Benicia Boy had made a distinct impression upon her, and Cincinnati was no place for a Menken to play Cleopatra. She gave one more "elegant Poetical reading" to the Allemania Society, and then publicly declared her intention to return to the boards. After discussing the Menkens' incompatability with Rabbi Wise and other savants of the Jewish community, it was sadly decided that a divorce was the only sensible reformist solution. The couple were issued with a rabbinical diploma to that effect in July, and Adah left for New York. She was never to see Alexander Menken again; and why should she? By the laws of the people she had chosen they were no longer man and wife. So far as she was concerned, she was free of the Menkens, except for their name which she had made famous, and which she had no intention of changing professionally, whomever she might marry in the future.

In New York Adah at once began to look for a new manager, having by now learnt well that that function was a professional rather than a sentimental one. She went to see Frank Queen, editor of the *Clipper*. Queen knew everyone in the business and had been consistently friendly towards her. The *Clipper*, too, charted the courses of prize-fighters and other sportsmen, and Queen would be able to tell Adah of the present movements of the Benicia Boy who, like herself, was constantly on the look-out for profitable bookings. In March 1859 Heenan may have noted that Adah Isaacs Menken was in New York playing the Widow Cheerly in *The Soldier's Daughter*. Adah's old repertory piece produced little excitement, although she worked so hard on it that the *Tribune* commented that, like most western performers, "she wanted taming down". In any event, while in the *Clipper* office persuading Edwin James, then an associate editor of the

From the archives of the Nationalbibliothek in Vienna, this portrait shows Menken, off-stage, poised and thoughtful.

paper, to apply his talents and knowledge of the business to her interests and become her press agent, she ran into and was re-introduced to the handsome young giant with the charming Irish brogue and shy smile, whose reputation for taming ladies was somewhat greater than his record for beating champions.

Adah forgot, the moment she turned her devastating eyes upon Heenan, that Ed James had just agreed to represent her. As for the champion himself, he has been described as having been "never more than a twelve-year-old boy and anybody could impose on his feelings". The Menken had impressed him profoundly on their first fateful meeting in Cincinnati. Here, in New York, she seemed even more flamboyant, more voluptuous, altogether freer and much more forthcoming. Now she glided towards him, studying him without any pretence about the part she had in mind for him to play. How was she to know that the well-dressed champion of the world was as poor as the famous star of the southern and western theatres? How could she guess that the Benicia Boy, looking like Hercules with the profile of a Greek god, was just a big, good-natured, weak-charactered, Irish strong-arm man? She took shelter in those arms very soon after their predestined second meeting. Within a few weeks they were married, on 3 September 1859, by the Reverend J. S. Baldwin in Jim Hughes's roadhouse on Bloomingdale Road (now Broadway). The occasion was kept secret, for although Adah was head over heels in love with the Boy, she knew well that prize-fighters were an even more vagrant and scandalous class than actresses, and she had no intention of making her professional life even more difficult than it already was.

But it was an impossible secret to keep for very long, partly because everybody around Heenan and Adah knew about it and talked of nothing else, albeit in loud whispers; but also because Heenan, showing an attack that hadn't characterised his recent professional bouts, got Adah pregnant in the first round. The marriage simply had to be allowed to be known, regardless of the professional consequences. Jim Cusick had no objection to the publicity; he was seeking a match with a large purse between the Benicia Boy and Tom Sayers, the English champion, for the heavyweight championship of the world. Heenan would have to train for this fight in Europe, and both John Carmel and Cusick were adamant that Mrs. Heenan would have no place on the safari, for not only was she not well enough to travel so far, but there was also a dangerous likelihood that she would draw too much attention to herself and away from Heenan. According to Adah, her great unselfish love permitted Heenan to sail without her on 5 January 1860. In all these circumstances rumours inevitably leaked to various newspapers. The *Tribune* reported on 21 January: "Miss Adah Isaacs Menken... who was recently elected the captain of a military company in Dayton, Ohio, and who is at present playing at the Troy Theater, is the wife of John C. Heenan. The lady was... anxious to accompany her husband... but he objected." The story was picked up by other newspapers, one of which, Wilkes' *Spirit of the Times,* flatly denied that the marriage with Heenan had ever taken place. George Wilkes was much

An illustration of John Carmel Heenan and Adah Isaacs Menken, showing the pugilist's fists decorously hidden.

involved in the boxing business and had helped to arrange the fight with Sayers, and he maintained that Heenan had never mentioned any marriage to him and surely would have done if there'd been one to mention, which he entirely doubted.

When Wilkes' comments appeared Adah was working at the Gaiety Theatre in Albany with her sister, Annie Josephs. As soon as she saw the story she became hysterical, anticipating the comments that could follow upon her pregnancy becoming impossible to conceal. She wrote pleadingly to Wilkes:

Stanwix Hall, Albany, N.Y. January 25

George Wilkes Esq: Presuming you to be responsible for every line that appears in the columns of *Wilkes' Spirit*, permit me, as one deeply agrieved (sic) to address myself to you.

In your last issue, bearing date Saturday Jan 28th, there is an article copied from the *N Y Tribune*, stating the well-known fact of my being the wife of John C. Heenan. Of this I have nothing to complain; on the contrary,

I am proud and happy to be known as the wife of the bravest man in the world! But you or your "Itemizer" took the unauthorized liberty of adding: "This is incorrect. Heenan is not married".

I have no right to suppose, nor do I wish to, that *malice* prompted these words, as daggers to stab the reputation of the wife of the man for whom you have repeatedly expressed the warmest and most disinterested friendship. I can only suppose, and hope, it to be a *mistake* ... I beg that you will do me and John C. Heenan the *justice* to correct this grievous mistake which has caused me the deepest trouble.

Allen Lesser believes that Menken knew of Wilkes' financial involvement in the prize-fighting business. He quotes a letter he discovered (among many other rare documents), from Adah to one of Heenan's friends. In it she writes concerning Wilkes: "He is a bad man and no friend of John C. Heenan. Morrissey is the *supreme* in Wilkes' paper, but you know that Morrissey is not capital *now*, and Mr. Heenan *is*. Consequently he must pretend to be a friend of the American party in order to sell his paper. But take my word for it, he is not '*sound*' on the Heenan question."

Unsound as he may have been, Wilkes published an apology. By now the whole affair was too salty for New York newspapers to ignore. Adah's expert manipulation of the press began to rebound against her. She wrote to the *Tribune*, which published her reiteration "that she is the wife of Mr. Heenan". The *Sunday Mercury* came to her defence insisting that, "the poet-actress has indeed become Mrs. John C. Heenan, and if the accomplished Mr. Sayers conquers the precocious 'Boy', poetic tears will be shed". The *New York Leader* summarised the contest so far: "A very pretty dispute is going the rounds of the papers as to whether Captain Adah Isaacs Menken is or is not the wife of the Benicia Boy. The *Tribune* says that she is; *Wilkes' Spirit* denies the fact; the lady asserts it under her own hand, and everybody either does or does not know something about the affair. We believe we are the first to ask the important question in connection with it: Who cares?"

Someone in Cincinnati did. Two weeks later a letter appeared from Alexander Menken addressed to George Wilkes by way of the *Cincinnati Commercial*. Wilkes reprinted it in his own paper on 18 February:

My dear Sir: I see by the last number of your paper that you have published a letter signed by a woman calling herself Adah Isaacs Menken Heenan. In justice to myself and friends, I cannot permit this very delicate effusion to pass unnoticed. Allow me to inform you, my dear sir, that you were perfectly correct when you stated to your correspondent that John C. Heenan was not married, unless it be lawful in your State for a woman to have two husbands at one and the same time. The effrontery and *nonchalance* with which this woman sentimentalizes in her letter to you, in reference to your damaging her *reputation*, and the manner in which she tries to enlist your sympathies in her behalf, by alluding to your position as a son and brother, would be very amusing to me were I not so deeply involved in the matter.

And now, my dear sir, let me briefly state the facts in the case as they really exist.

On the third day of April, 1856, in the town of Livingston, in the county of Polk, and the State of Texas, I had the misfortune to be married by a Justice of the Peace, to this adventuress, since which time I have never been divorced from her; on the contrary have lived with her up to last July. I go into these particulars merely and solely for the purpose of setting myself right in the social circle in which I have introduced this person as my wife. I think this is due them in order that my position in regard to her may not be misconstrued.

I would say in this connection, that I have instituted proceedings in the proper courts which will rid me of this incubus and disgrace, and that this public exposé of private matters has not been sought by me – that I have borne disgrace for this woman, through the medium of the press and otherwise, "till forbearance has ceased to be a virtue". Even now I would not notice her, but her superlative impudence and brazeness, as evinced by her late letter to you, and through you on the public, in the most conspicuous way possible, renders her unworthy of my further charitable silence. In conclusion, permit me to say that I do not regret the phase matters have taken, as far as regards the separation of this person with myself, but I must remark, that as long as she is married to John C. Heenan, I would prefer she would make use of his name and discontinue mine, as I think, from recent developments, I would be "more honoured in the breach than in the observance".

Alexander Menken's final crashing condemnation and disavowal of Adah's Jewish divorce (surely more valid in the sight of God than any merely civic document) seemed about as terminal a calamity as could have befallen her. Here she was, alone in New York, an unemployed actress, a publicly branded bigamist, dismissed as an incubus by her first husband and about to be deserted by her second. And all as public as could be in a sham Puritan society which never forgot or forgave those who sinned and were caught. Wilkes, now an avowed enemy, made much of her shame in his paper, and the rest picked it up. The *Dayton Enquirer* revived the rumours about her night of intoxication and dreadful behaviour with its militia, denying that they had ever truly dubbed her an honorary Captain. The *Louisville Courier* stated that, in fact, she was married to neither Menken nor Heenan, but someone quite different, a citizen of Louisville (possibly to Kneass the composer). The Cincinnati newspapers conjectured aloud about what, if she was married to Heenan, she would now do about Menken. It was asserted that her poem *Karazah to Karl* was actually penned for Heenan while "enjoying an unnecessarily (so certain parties say!) lengthy rustication in this city about three years ago . . . Since that time, the 'Poem' has been written *expressly* for every paper which would publish it, and 'Come to Me' may now be taken, without doing violence to anybody, as a general invitation to 'go in!'". In effect they were saying with unconcealed lubricity, that Adah was anybody's. Parodies of her poem appeared, and the *Cincinnati Herald* published a drawing of Heenan on his knees to Adah:

> All punished and penitent,
> > Down on the knee
> I now bend, Adah, to
> > Avert an *adieu*.
> Oh, let not thine eyes, love,
> > Look black upon me.
> Because mine are forced to
> > Look black upon you.
>
> Forgive me, and never,
> > Oh, never again,
> I'll cultivate light blue,
> > Or brown inebriety;
> I'll give up all chance of a
> > Fracture or sprain;
> And part, worse than all, with
> > Tom Hyers' (sic) society.

The *Herald* was wrong about Sayers' name and Heenan's mood. When John Carmel left her that cold winter to sail for England and the world championship, he was completely unapologetic. So infamous was his behaviour that, in spite of the public shamefulness of her situation, she could still find some champions in the press. John Augustine (Gus) Daly praised her, expressing his opinion that she should be protected rather than vilified. Her old friend Frank Queen said she was one of the finest women on the stage: "she came to this city almost friendless, with nothing to rely upon but her own energetic spirit. The association of her name with that of John C. Heenan has made her the target for almost every newspaper scribbler in the country, who have severally married her to Tom Thumb, Jas. Buchanan, and the King of the Cannibal Islands . . . We trust that the scribblers have got to the end of their tether, and that they will hereafter assist, as they have heretofore endeavored to retard her, in her effort to support herself in a legitimate calling."

Even with her few gallant and daring champions Adah felt frighteningly alone. Playing whatever dates she could get, she wrote from Buffalo that the few notes of consolation she had received were "like water to a dying wanderer in the desert . . . I still strive to bear up and be strong of heart." Fighting fire with fire, she had composed a reply to Alexander Menken's damning letter, addressing it "to the press throughout the land":

> Sir: My attention has been called to a letter in your paper of the 18th inst., over the signature of A. I. Menken, unwarrantably obtruding his pretended grievances.
>
> Of the temper of the writer, or the tone of his letter, I have nothing to say; the propriety of its publication and the re-publication of the scurrilous attack upon me by the *Dayton Empire* and other obscure papers, I have a right to question.
>
> The charge imputed in the letter is a grave one – the crime of bigamy. If I am guilty, it is an offense against the laws of society, demanding severe punishment. Yet those laws are more generous than you have been as the conductor of the press; for the law indulges the presumption that I am innocent of the crime until proved by lawful argument to be otherwise.
>
> If the alleged marriage of Menken and myself was legal (which he has repeatedly denied), the divorce granted upon his application and by him shown me, should be my protection.
>
> But the press is not a proper place for the discussion of the question growing out of my former relation to Menken and my present matrimonial connection. When a proper occasion for the manifestation of the entire legality and morality of my conduct, as becomes a woman of honor, presents itself, it will be made public; until then I am entitled to the charity and silence of the press.
>
> The controversy you have sought and are persisting in with me is an unequal one. Your paper has an extensive circulation. It scatters its slanderous insinuations and charges broadcast over the country, while I am comparatively defenseless – am dependent upon the good opinion of the public, whose mind you seek to poison and embitter against me. Had you been acquainted with my antecedents, and known the trials and adversities through which I have passed to obtain whatever position I now enjoy in my profession, I think you would not have allowed the viper, whose communications you publish, to strike his fangs into my life's current.
>
> Menken may call me an "adventuress". He has been nourished by, and subsisted upon, the fruits of my professional labor, until I would no longer furnish supplies for his bacchanalian career, and such an appellation comes from him with a very bad grace.
>
> Whatever of controversy he may have with me should not interest the public. It is not the subject upon which the most hungry of itemizers should be allowed to feed, and I trust that I may be permitted, in future, to enjoy that exemption from newspaper attack which my present unprotected situation demands, and which all gallant men will award me.

Many editors, including Wilkes, were delighted to publish the Menken's defence of herself, enjoying hugely her direct accusation of Menken as having lived upon her, drinking up her earnings. But her account of her two marriages remained more than obscure to the average, untheologically-inclined reader. She had made the quite understandable error of assuming that a Rabbinical divorce automatically discharged her from a Texas marriage and, in her typically impetuous way, had rushed into a New York marriage without a thought for the possible legal complexities of her situation.

So here was Adah Isaacs Menken Heenan about to be sued for divorce by two husbands simultaneously; yet whatever her legal marital position might be, she needed work and if the only way she could get it was by exploiting her notoriety, well then, so be it. She now signed her poems "Adah Isaacs Menken Heenan", and would continue to do so until Heenan returned to New York in August 1860, after a surprising success in England. He had equalised with Sayers, who was eight years older than him and shorter. Now he cashed in on the unexpected success with a series of profitable exhibition bouts. Cashing in on Heenan herself, Adah got a booking at the Bowery where the rough audience was more concerned with her notoriety than her Thespian abilities. They gave her a rousing welcome as much for Heenan's sake as for her own, as a friendly critic observed:

"Benicia" was properly remembered in the enthusiasm. During the performance of her first piece, *Satan in Paris*, Mrs Heenan was frequently applauded, but when the curtain fell at the conclusion of the play:

There rose at once so wild a yell
It seemed as though each fiend that fell
Had shrieked the banner cry of "Hell".

The boxes and gallery joined in the shout, which was kept up until Mrs Heenan made her appearance before the curtain when the troubled element became calm and tranquil in breathless expectation of hearing a speech. But the actress was "too full for utterance" and retired amid a fresh outburst of enthusiastic cheers for Mr and Mrs Heenan.

When Heenan returned from England a reporter noted that among the crowds welcoming him was the unmistakable face of "the Jewish lady who was by some expected to reign Queen of the Lists, Miss Adah Isaacs Menken, who has claimed the distinction of being the wife of the great Heenan". The great Heenan, wealthy, successful, and well-liked for the moment, had no intention of risking his luck again on the back of Mazeppa's fiery steed. He was more than ever inclined to disown her, and, since she had borne and lost his child in secrecy, she had little with which to make claim upon his affections or resources. Now once again as "Adah Menken, the distinguished actress and authoress" she gave readings from Shakespeare and the modern poets at Hope Chapel on Broadway, and a lecture at Clifton Hall on *The Age of the Irrepressibles*, among whom she could surely have included both Heenan and herself. As for John Carmel, he left almost immediately for Chicago accompanied by a lady named Harriet Martin whose only claim to a footnote in history is that she was subsequently cited as co-respondent in the divorce petition which Adah brought against Heenan. But the sad and resultant scandal was to do none of them any good. Even exhibition bouts became difficult for Heenan to find, and soon he returned to England to take up the more secure and restful profession of bookmaker.

But now Adah's posture suddenly entirely changed. She had been writing in a depressed and piteous key: "In consequence of my poor health, and my grief, my success has not been good. I can not act now, all life and spirits gone", she had written from Rochester. In Buffalo, a two weeks' engagement had "proved the worst I ever had the misfortune to experience, and by the falsehood and duplicity of the managers there, I am left entirely pennyless". Notoriety no longer seemed to be working for her. She herself attributed her loss of luck to her association with Heenan: "Before I knew John, I was very ambitious, and my happiest moments were before the footlights." Now she hated "the heartless profession of exposing myself to the public". She even thought of deserting the theatre entirely, deciding to return to New York "for the purpose of seeking some employment and also to dispose of my theatrical wardrobe if possible. My present state of health does not admit of my continuing in the stage, and I am moreover completely disgusted with its toils and trials. But withal, I can work. I hate idleness. But I can only write for papers or books, or teach in a school. I can not sew or work as many women. I could read or lecture in public, at least I could do something, and I intend to." The loss of her baby had left her sick and depressed.

Then, suddenly, she observed indignantly that, while luck had deserted her, the capricious lady was favouring the husband who had been, up to now, such a liability to her. She decided with typical daring to cash in on John C.'s good fortune. So, as Adah Isaacs Menken Heenan, she took the booking at the Old Bowery Theatre for the week of 19 March. Giving up Mrs. Menken's pretensions to the classic and tragic, Mrs. Heenan aimed her shot at the heart and stomach of the public favouring them with a so-called "Protean" comedy in which she could play numerous parts in various costumes, all revealing, and many of them men's. *Carline, or The Female Brigand*, was the choice for the Old Bowery, and the coarse local audience loved it. She even got a good notice from the unfriendly *Wilkes' Spirit* who conceded that, "upon the stage she appears as an actress with a good figure, pretty face, and agreeable voice ... With her personal charms and talents, the perseverance she has exerted to become notorious might ... have made her celebrated." Others spared her the sting in the tail; the *Clipper* rallied to her, observing that she was "one of the most beautiful women now upon the boards, has a sweet musical voice, clear and distinct, and a pleasing, fascinating style in all she says or does. It is not to be wondered at", the *Clipper* concluded, "that she at once crept into the favor of the Bowery *habitués*, and was nightly the recipient of their most earnest applause". The critic of the *Saturday Evening Gazette*, A. Wallace Thaxter, went backstage to meet Mrs. Heenan and was appalled to find that she was a chain cigarette smoker. Notoriety was, obviously, undermining her moral character completely. William English, a competent theatrical hack, put together a new farce for her called, *Heenan Has Come!* She played it in Providence, Rhode Island, with great success. The *Philadelphia Mercury* two weeks later reported that, "Mrs. Benicia Boy was the sensation here this week ... a bouncing voluptuous-looking Jewess, with a well-developed figure, which she takes delight in exhibiting, a profusion of dark curls, and wicked black eyes". Sick and sad Adah might feel from time to time, but her problems kept the box office busy. Her Mrs. Heenan performance continued, peaking with the relative success of Heenan's fight with Sayers; whereupon the Old Bowery booked a return appearance. Adah gave them *Satan in Paris* and it played to a packed house yet again.

Heenan's British victory (in which even Queen Victoria had expressed interest) had made him an undoubted winner and, as such, the American press and public favoured him. Adah was now the loser and, according to the general rules of the game, could expect little support or mercy. Heenan on his arrival in New York was given a reception at Jones's Wood near Seventieth Street, the occasion on which some people said they had seen Adah Menken, although it seems very much out of character for her to attend a social occasion where she was certain to be embarrassed, for Heenan remained non-committal on the question of whether or not she was his wife. As the *Charleston Mercury* reported: "We will not test the truth of the gossip respecting the marriage of the Benicia Boy. Thus far he has held back and sought no interview with his Adah ... Heenan takes the matter as a good joke on a bad subject." But Adah was hardly one to be ignored quietly, and when she was evicted for non-payment of her bill at the Westchester House on the Bowery, she hired Hope Chapel and offered the public a defence of herself. She accused Heenan of shutting up "every avenue by which she could honestly gain her bread, and driving her down to the whirlpool of sin through the forgetfulness of ghastly shame and blasted charity!" The press thought she was overdoing it, and that a lady "violated good taste" by such an exhibition. After all that had happened between her bout with Menken and her knock-out by Heenan, and all the salacious copy the newspapers had made of it, it seems extraordinary that Adah should now be condemned by them for not being genteel. But she was concerned only to make her side of the story public. The *New York Illustrated News* listened and concluded that, "the moral is perfectly plain. Either these people are lawfully married or not. If lawfully married, the champion is only carrying out a *charge* fixed on his 'profession' - total indifference to the finest ties which bind society and crush scandal; if not lawfully married, we should like to know in what the charge materially differs, *all* the facts being as they are?"

On 5 October the facts concerning her debt to Westchester House became public through a suit which the hotel brought against Heenan. But Adah didn't mind the publicity at all, for the bill was described as being due "for board and lodging furnished to Mrs Ada I. M. Heenan as the wife of the defendant, at his and her request, between the months of December, 1859, and July, 1860". It would seem thereby that Heenan, before deserting the pregnant Adah, had installed her in the Westchester, and would he have booked her in as Mrs. Heenan if she had not legally so been? But Heenan contested the suit vigorously, his lawyer describing Adah as, virtually, a prostitute. "I will prove that other men, with this same lady, entered her own name at this same house as John Doe and lady, and that they occupied a room; probably the same as Mr. Heenan is alleged to have occupied. I will prove the character of this frail, fair woman, and that she had her name entered upon the books of this and other houses as the lady of John Doe or Richard Roe, or any who might have money enough to pay for that particular purpose."

It was the nadir of Adah's career to be thus openly accused of what the public had always believed was the first and natural vocation of actresses. Her liberal and enlightened beliefs, together with her valid and perfectly honest relationships with many distinguished men in her own and adjacent professions, were now dragged through the filth of the gutter. And to make matters worse, before she could ascend the witness stand and, with irresistible Portia-like clarity and passion, cast her detractors themselves down into the mud, the case was settled out of court. She wrote letters to the press arguing her position, expertly refuting the calumnies against her; but she was unable to neutralise the impact made by that dreadful court speech. The press added the Dayton affair together with Alexander Menken's letter and what had been said in court, and deduced from it all that Adah Isaacs Menken Heenan was a fatal, deadly and lewd woman.

Adah, not surprisingly, grew a little paranoid under the pressure. She assured an associate, Stephen Masset, an actor and humorous monologist, that Heenan was watching her house day and night, seeking evidence to substantiate the lewd charges against her. His Tammany Hall associates and rough-neck friends were a danger to her very existence. "My life was twice attempted", she insisted to Masset. "Since Heenan declares me to be the most dangerous woman in the world, whenever a woman's husband neglects her she fancies that I have charmed him, body and soul."

It was insufferable to Adah to be regarded so cheaply, and in high dudgeon one midnight she called for the police to take away "two frantic deserted wives" who had come to "demand the return of their lords". It sounds an unlikely story, but it indicates how persecuted Adah was feeling. Certainly the after-effects of her pregnancy and the loss of her baby boy in June were affecting her health. "I am confined to my bed today – very ill from fright and excitement, to say nothing of my neck being nearly broken and my arm wrenched off", these latter bruises the result of being jostled by the morally indignant who now, she said, persecuted

Part of a letter from Menken to Stephen Masset. Text reads: "Dear Stevey, You are a dear good little fellow to send me my breakfast. I have been in the deepest trouble since you left. See my letter in the Herald this morning, it can only give you a very faint idea of how horribly I was assailed by Heenan's Counsel. Heenan himself, yesterday, watched my house all day. I have no idea what his intentions were. No good, you may depend."

her ceaselessly. Masset and Queen were the only men she could still regard as friends in spite of the rumours that she was keeping a stud of wealthy lovers.

Queen tried hard enough, but now even he was unable to persuade theatre managers to risk affronting the public by engaging Adah. Then the Stadt Theatre in the Bowery agreed to employ her to entertain the German immigrants who constituted the bulk of its audience and who were unlikely, because of their ignorance of the English language, to be too aware of the Menken's notoriety. But Adah's courage was, for the first time, failing. She wrote to Masset: "I am almost despairing today. I have been out trying to get music, etc., for my dances tomorrow night and have failed all, for I am sure that I will not be able to go on with it. I have no wardrobe – nothing to make an appearance in. What is the use of trying to do anything? I am more unhappy than ever." And yet, in the event, she not only was able to go "on with it" but was successful enough with the audience to be retained at the Stadt for nearly a month. By which time she had regained aggressive confidence enough to be able to undertake work in a Broadway music hall; or so she thought. But the humiliation of the coarse audiences' jeering drove her from the place after a few performances; like a thief in the night she left for Jersey City.

There in Jersey, in a cheap wretched room Menken set herself to compose a statement in which she would address herself no longer to false human beings. She no longer had any defences, nor would she seek them. She had no desire to attack her enemies. She was a victim of love, and now, in the rediscovery of the submissiveness of her childhood, she forgave her persecutors, offering her vulnerability to her God in the following suicide note:

> I feel called upon to make an explanation of the rash step I have taken in defiance of all law, human or divine, because I know that many things will be said of me, some good and very many bad; and perhaps blame attached to those who are innocent. *God* forgive those who *hate* me, and bless all who have one kind thought left for a poor reckless *loving* woman who cast her *soul* out upon the broad ocean of human love, where it was the sport of the happy waves for a few short hours, and then was left to drift helpless against the cold rocks, until she learned to love *death* better than *life*.
>
> Because I am homeless, poor and friendless, and so *unloved*, I leave this world.
>
> Because I have forgotten to look up to the *God* of my childhood prayers, and ceased to remember the counsel of my dear old mother – and because one of *God's* grandest handiworks – one of His glorious creatures lifted up my poor weary soul to see the light of his love, and the greatness of his brave heart, until his sweet words of truth and promise, drank out *all* my life – absorbed all of good and beauty, and left me alone, desolate to *die*. I am not afraid to die. I have suffered so much, that there can not be any more for me.
>
> I go prayerless, therefore *pity* and not condemn me.
>
> My worthless life has long since left me and gone to dwell in the breast of the man, who by foul suspicion of my love and truth for him, has thus ushered me up to the bar of the Almighty, where I shall pray for his forgiveness for the cruel and wrong he has done the weak and defenceless being whose sin is her love for him, as my death proves. *God bless him*, and pity me.
>
> ADAH ISAACS MENKEN
Jersey City
12 Mo. 29th D.

Adah thus carefully constructed her suicide scene. In the course of it she, with only her other selves as appreciative audience, played out the stricken deer hunted by cruel men and their savage hordes to its pitiful end; and so symbolically passed away Mrs. A. I. Menken Heenan. From her ashes would arise two new and powerful female phoenixes; one of them a poetess who, like her mentor and model Whitman, cared nothing at all for the barbarians who had destroyed her frailer self; the other, a self-confessed theatrical Bohemian, determinedly voluptuous, fatal and flashy, temperamental, tempestuous and a terror to all men. The loser, Adah, was washed away by her own tears. The winner, the Menken, was now loosed upon the world of New York.

Menken. A Sarony portrait.

Five

Enter the Menken – as Poetess to a Puritan

THE LITERARY EDITOR of the New York *Sunday Mercury*, Robert Henry Newell, met Adah Isaacs Menken Heenan at the lowest point in her life and career. He was a sensitive, gentle, ironic and conventional intellectual, and Mrs. Heenan was hardly his type. Even when she opened in *Mazeppa* in New York his attitude towards her was still patronising and satirical, although he had, by now, developed amused and friendly feelings for her as a warm if outrageous bohemian personality; of course, her physical attractions could not be denied. His newspaper published on 4 March 1860 one of her poems of despair, *Fragment of a Heart*, which she signed *Infelicissimus*, "the unhappiest". Newell had added a note to the poem which had surprised him by its power and sincerity, attributing this "almost insane" quality to Adah's genetic origins. "We may state that the lady is a Jewess, and almost insane in her eagerness to behold her people restored once more to their ancient power and glory. Her best poems have been founded on this vigorous sentiment, as we may term it, and the present 'prose-poem' is strongly tinctured with it."

Adah at this time clearly identified her longed-for personal restoration to high status with that of the lost "ancient power and glory" of the Jewish people.* Indeed, her troubles now seemed to her constantly to confirm the prophetic and tragic Jewish destiny which she had fully embraced while under the religious instruction of Rabbi Wise. The posture gave her a despairing courage of sorts, though the next poem she wrote, *The Dark Hour*, was full of foreboding.

The melancholy poetic pose was fashionable and though many critics observed that Adah's writing was awkward and uneasy at times, her thoughts and sentiments appealed. Allen Lesser considers, "the poems she wrote during this storm and stress period of her life, more self-revealing than those which any other female American poet had ever dared publish, (and) disclose her growing bewilderment, her indignation, and finally the crushing sense of humiliation that

---
* See poetry appendix for *Hear, O Israel!*

followed. With almost hysterical rapidity these poems flowed from her pen throughout the year (1860), each more disillusioned and bitter than the one preceding, each more keenly alive to the spiritual agony she suffered."*

Certainly Adah's writings in this phase dramatise the cruel and harsh victimisation of women in mid-nineteenth-century social life. Women could recognise the truths contained in her writing, even if they attributed the extremity of the Menken's experience of them, to her moral laxity.† Men might laugh at her poetic postures (as they yielded to her theatrical ones), but they were forced to recognise that there was a challenging reality in what she wrote about. Intellectuals of both sexes, increasingly concerned with the countless social injustices to women, had to acknowledge that Adah Menken was expressing those unequal and miserable aspects of their time and society. It wasn't necessary to pretend that Adah was a major poet in order to acknowledge that she was a distinguished protester of women's rights. Her matter was significant enough to compensate for her stylistic limitations. In any case, how many "poets" were there writing at that time with much distinction?

Even the respected Mr. Newell's poems were scarcely more than mediocre. But whatever his opinion of his own verses, Newell was very aware of the more absurd aspects of Adah's style, and yet he was apparently coming to respect the attitudes which she protested so courageously. He was happy to be seen about town with her, and to be taken for her intellectual mentor and literary companion. Often he was seen with Adah at Charley Pfaff's tavern, much frequented by the literati about Broadway. Edgar Allan Poe had been an *habitué* of Pfaff's, and now Henry Clapp, founder of the high-toned literary paper the *Saturday Press*, ruled in the Bleecker Street hostelry where he was known as "The King of Bohemia". There Clapp sat in the presiding chair at a long table, anticipating by many years the literary cabal a group of New York writers was to establish as the Algonquin Round Table. In Clapp's group were William Winter, the theatre critic; George Arnold, poet and satirist; Fitz-James O'Brien, the very spirit of Bohemia and a personal associate of Poe's, a heavy-drinking soldier-of-fortune, killed in 1862 fighting for the Union. There, too, in the group, could often be found Walt Whitman, the anarchist poet, and other visiting dignatories of the literary world, such as Emerson and Howells.

If Clapp was the reigning king of the Pfaff's group, Whitman was their Pope. Newell disapproved of Whitman and would have nothing to do with him, but when Adah wrote her essay *Swimming Against the Current*, on the poet and his work, expressing her immense admiration for *Leaves of Grass* and support for its anti-establishment content, Newell, with great fairness, published it, while stating openly that he rejected entirely Menken's "eulogium of that coarse and uncouth

---

* See appendix for typical examples of Menken's high-styled "spiritual agony", *Drifts That Bar My Door*.

† See *One Year Ago* in the poetry appendix.

creature, Walt Whitman". Perhaps Newell was jealous of Adah's admiration of Whitman's philosophy; perhaps he did not know that his developing feelings for Adah were not in the least threatened by the homosexual poet. "Look at Walt Whitman," Menken wrote, "the American philosopher, who is centuries ahead of his contemporaries, who, in smiling carelessness, analyzes the elements of which society is composed, compares them with the history of past events, and ascertains the results which the same causes always produced and must produce ... He hears the Divine voice calling him to caution mankind against this or that evil; and wields his pen, exerts his energies, for the cause of liberty and humanity!"

Adah was right enough about Whitman's future and many contemporary critics were not. Identifying herself with him as one who "had been drowned in the current of life, because they swam against the stream", she felt that Whitman and herself were, like Poe, "starved to death by an ungrateful people". She prophesied that "in the next century, their words and schemes will become understood", and that to them "marble statues will be erected". To the establishment intelligentsia of the time her words were as wild as her free verse, so strongly influenced by Whitman, for it is an extraordinary fact of literary history that Adah Menken was one of the first writers to follow Whitman whole-heartedly, her poetry perfectly exemplifying the freedom and dangers of that rolling American mode.

Even Newell, unsympathetic as he was towards the Whitmanesque, wrote that he could not but admire "the bold and defiant spirit in which the lady spurns all the conventionalisms imposed upon the generality of writers by the literary tone of her age", and though he criticised her for "savoring too strongly of oddity", he had to conclude that "the picture is full of vigorous effects".

Yet although the literary Menken was finding acceptance with a few intellectual outcasts, she felt lonely and sad. John Overall wrote to her: "Why are your letters so sad? Forget the world – laugh at poverty. Be glad and happy with your heritage of genius." But though Adah now quite accepted and often gloried in her Bohemian status, she was unable to do so in whole-hearted joy, for one of her selves longed always to be accepted by the establishment of literature.*

Lesser notes that at this time in her life, "the figure of death appears over and over again in Adah's poems. The death of her child and later of her mother, both within a few months of each other, left wounds that were slow to heal and led her to seek consolation in spiritualism." Her introducer to this common obsession of theatricals was her friend, the so-called "Queen of Bohemia", Ada Clare. The other Ada was also short-cropped but with blonde hair; she was as dashing in her dress as Menken, also smoked cigarettes in public, and scorned conventions even more blatantly than did Menken. Clare insisted upon her right

---

* See poetry appendix for *My Heritage*.

to live her own life in her own free way, a true forerunner of the modern emancipated woman. She was about the same age as Menken and, though unmarried, proudly presented to all her illegitimate son, whom she publicly announced she had got by the famous pianist and composer, Louis Moreau Gottschalk. Clare was intensely Parisian in her manner and style and brought to Pfaff's the atmosphere of Montmartre, often arriving with her small boy introducing themselves, challengingly, as "Miss Ada Clare and Son". Adah was deeply impressed by Clare's dash, courage and style, and eagerly accepted her invitations to séances. Together they found in the touching optimism of spiritualist beliefs, support through the depression, despair and loneliness which inevitably followed their moments of high-style theatrical challenge to the social norms. Adah wrote that "the belief that the spirits of the dead are permitted to return to us ... and that they bring with them the hopes of a future life, and the assurances of God's eternal goodness", brought her a trust in life which human beings, certainly men, never justified. Together Adah and Ada, supported by one another and the spirits of the past and the future, declared war on male-dominated respectability.

The friends had much in common. They were both Southerners, had borne children which their lovers would not acknowledge, advertised their passions publicly, and had savoured suicide, on which subject Clare had published an essay. The Menken embodied her feelings and thoughts on her own suicide in her poem *Answer Me*;* and their sentiments and conclusions on the experience agreed. It took more courage, they both believed, for a woman to live, and be herself, than to die, a victim and sacrifice of the male-dominated society.

Clare had gone to Paris, enjoyed a season in that fashionable hell, and returned transformed. Menken had descended to the colder and infinitely more hellish room in Jersey City, but she had bounded back more glamorous than ever. From Clare she learned to present, always, a bold and fascinating front to the public, demonstrating that the old frail and submissive Adah was dead for ever, lost to an "uncoffined and unburied Death", a "Death that left this dumb, living body as his endless mark". Adah had returned from a voyage "down, down, down to the soundless folds of the fathomless ocean". She had risen reborn as the Aphrodite the male world wanted her to be. As such she would:

... gloss my pale face with laughter, and sail my voice on with the tide.
Decked in jewels and lace, I laugh beneath the gaslight's glare and quaff the purple wine.
But the minor-keyed soul is standing naked and hungry upon one of Heaven's high hills of light.

So, laughing wildly and quaffing the purple wine, the Menken drew up the

---
* See poetry appendix.

seemingly infinite resources of her personality to, once again, assault the highest citadels of the theatre. She fascinated Frank Queen into paying for a new wardrobe, she took on an aggressive theatrical agent, Thomas Allston Brown. Ed James was re-invigorated with confidence in her future and rejoined her as press agent. Between them they fixed a deal; a date for Menken in Portland, Maine, to be followed by a tour.

The now miraculously revived Menken attacked and again attacked. Restraint was abandoned and abandonment was unrestrained. Any and all publicity was acceptable. In March she played Milwaukee in her old piece, *The Soldier's Daughter*, and this time the press was wild about her, the *Sentinel* calling her a second Lola Montez, and observing that "her style of acting is as free from the platitude of the stage as her poetry is from the language". Her poems and articles were distributed freely to be reprinted in the newspapers of the towns in which she played. Supported by her fame and her notoriety equally, her performances drew expectant crowds and they were not disappointed. Once more there were dinners in her honour, and cornet bands and local dignatories serenaded her. The theatre-managers booking her were delighted at the queues which formed for tickets at any price. The Detroit *Free Press* noted happily that "the palmy days of theatricals were revived last evening, and for the first time in years the house was crowded from pit to dome. Not only were seats occupied by sitters wherever they were to be found, but standing places were in demand and difficult of access." And when they saw Adah perform, those great-hearted audiences roared their approval. "To say that the audience was immense would do justice to their numbers, but to say that they were enthusiastic, would hardly express the furore. The beautiful Adah carried them by storm", observed the thrilled critic of the *Free Press*.

Menken brought the same excitement with her to Albany, Chicago, and then back to Detroit, just as the news of the surrender of Fort Sumter came through. The citizens celebrated the great victory by crowding to the theatre to see Adah. So great an audience in the circumstances surprised even her, and she commented to her agent Brown on the "fine business notwithstanding the great political excitement".

But now the Civil War, so long threatening, was upon them all. Many actors decided to go to Europe, believing that the American theatre would simply cease to exist for the period of the emergency. Adah, too, thought of England. "I feel confident that we can manage to get off to England next season", she wrote to Brown. "I am very anxious to go and feel certain that I should succeed there. I have some good pieces and good wardrobe, and that is something, you know." But for the time being she continued her tour, having put together herself a play based upon the life of the great Lola Montez with whom she was now often compared, and whom she increasingly took as one of her personality models. Adah dreamed of going to Europe and emulating the Anglo-Irish adventuress who had ruled the King of Bavaria and caused a revolution. For the play she adopted Montez' striking Byronic rebellious aristocratic style, keeping it (on and off-stage) for life. But, for the moment, Brown was unable to arrange anything in Europe for her, and, somehow or other, theatres were continuing to draw the public in spite of the war. Menken added plays with martial content to her repertoire, and fought off queries regarding her Southern origin by distributing freely copies of her patriotic poem *Pro Patria* wherever she played. As to the Heenan and the Menken scandals, she now took no trouble to deny them. Let them fill the newspaper columns and the theatres. She was above all innuendoes; she found that the notorious position was a well-paid one, and not entirely uncomfortable once you gloried in it.

Menken's theatrical style was developing rapidly. She used uninhibitedly the infinite changes of her remarkable personality, multi-faceted, the facets so much more brilliant than real life. No longer did she attempt imitations of even the greatest ladies of the theatre. Now she ignored any style other than that which the Menken was making her own, that of Protean comedy. In the military comedy-drama, *The French Spy*, she provocatively displayed herself in several close-fitting uniforms. In *Black-Eyed Susan* she played a sailor-boy with a "pathos and deep feeling" that "would stir to emotion the hardest heart". Her improvisational daring brought an entirely new quality on to the American stage. This refreshing and always surprising informality, often appearing as instinctive and intuitive (as it frequently was), enabled Menken to throw together an extraordinarily extensive repertoire very quickly; for the essence of her technique lay in amusing and quick-witted mime and improvisation, playing off the audience; thus she turned her inadequacy as a student of fixed lines into a positive asset. It might be devastating and infuriating to her fellow Thespians to find themselves confronted by constantly changing lines, business and stage positions, but what did it matter? The audience's eyes were hypnotically fixed upon the Menken, and the confusion of her colleagues was neither here nor there, for the public were paying to see Adah; she alone was the star. It was something new in the theatre, very American, passionate, friendly, close to the footlights and directed straight at each individual citizen in the audience, with a display of sex and temperament which, in its freedom and unselfconsciousness, had never before been seen by audiences used to third-rate imitators of the stiff, formal, and painfully dignified European styles of performance, or to exhibitionists of the crudest type. Menken was evolving into one of the first of the great musical comedy soubrettes, those flashing ladies whose vigour and power of personality was of that rich human ore from which the solid gold of the great American musical was, eventually, to be extracted.

Robert Henry Newell was a good enough critic to realise that the Menken was contributing *something* to the theatre, even if his personal tastes were too conventional for him to actually like it. He wrote of the disturbing lady later:

Menken as William, the love-sick sailor-boy, in Black-Eyed Susan.

"Miss Menken had the keenest mind I ever encountered in a member of her sex. Indeed, few men were her mental equals, and she could discourse fluently on matters pertaining to literature, the sciences and the latest news of the world in which we live. She was a learned theologian, and I have heard her hold long, erudite talks with Dr Henry Ward Beecher, the Rev Jonathan Flaherty and other divines of note, in which she more than held up her end of the conversation. Her erudition, coupled with her great beauty, made her the rarest of her sex." But it was Adah the poetess and intellectual Newell most admired. When he heard that the brash showman Captain Smith had approached her with the suggestion that she should play Mazeppa, he thought the property absurd and the project obscene. Adah should, in his opinion, be elevated out of the theatrical world, with its dubious characters and low morality, into the literary and political society in which he functioned by right of birth and of talent. For Newell was a true Victorian bourgeois, a Puritan and a gentleman, and while it was not inconsistent with all these qualifications to want an Adah Menken, it was necessary that she should be transformed before being possessed by a man of such special virtue and quality.

In his unfinished autobiographical novel *Didaschelle*, Newell expressed his belief that Adah Menken could become one of the great women of the time, provided she accepted the guidance of the right strong, masculine hand. In spite of herself Menken could be saved, and inspired to "some supremely unselfish achievement". Tortured by his Pygmalion-like ambitions for her, not realising that this was a role she always played for herself, afflicted by a growing longing for her, Newell found himself courting an infamous actress. It was the most difficult and traumatic situation in which a conscientiously Puritan intellectual could find himself. As for Adah, her experience of divorce had brought her to the public statement that marriage was not for her. From now on she would live, a free soul, like her friend Ada Clare; her own woman, giving herself freely to those she loved, in her own time, and on her own terms. But the Bohemian was not the whole of Menken's character at any point in her life. There was always in her a poor would-be middle-class girl from New Orleans, who wanted to be accepted by middle-class society. After the romantic episode with Alexander Menken, and the passionate error of her casting of the big Irishman to play her Anthony, surely the intellectual gentleman Newell might well be right for the husband part, in spite of all she had said and written on the institution of marriage.

Adah Menken's third marriage, to Robert Henry Newell took place on 24 September 1862, licensed under New York City Board of Health requirements, and presided over by the Reverend J. C. K. Milligan and a few very close friends of the couple. Newell immediately carried Adah away from the corruptive influences of New York to his home in Jersey City. There he offered her the strong masculine hand which, in his opinion, was all she needed to lead her to the pure waters of the Life Intellectual. He advised her that her present engagement at the New Bowery Theatre was to be, he felt, her last in the professional theatre. She was now a properly Christian married woman with all the duties and responsibilities which that entailed. Now he revealed his secret and sacred conviction that the place for such a woman was in the home; there she should remain, loving and servicing her husband in various ways, though she might, in her spare time, read or even write poetry. The scene which followed the revelation of Newell's plans for Adah's future is not difficult to imagine. Reportedly it terminated with "the bride escaping by a window and going to New York, declaring that she could not live without her Bohemian associates".

The week-long marriage was, of course, extensively reported and sniggered over in the press. Newell could not have known that the submissive and vulnerable

Adah had died sometime before in the same dreary town to which he took her for their honeymoon. The new Adah acknowledged yet another of her silly old mistakes in the matter of choosing leading men; wives were never her most successful performing roles, she pointed out.

Great Expectations *with Menken as Pip*, at the Louisville Theatre.

Six

Enter Adah I. Menken – the Southern Star of the West Coast

IN NOVEMBER 1862 Adah Isaacs Menken Heenan Newell was far away from all her husbands, playing in Baltimore, at the Front Street Theatre. The venue was well-named, for it was near enough to the war for the Confederate cannon to be heard. The city was under martial law, all public buildings guarded, with Union soldiers everywhere. Theatre business, as it often is in wartime, was ebullient, and Adah, with her "form divine" well-displayed, and the comic songs and dances of her Protean roles, was exactly what Baltimore needed to keep its spirits up and its thoughts off the approaching thunder.

Adah was playing a number of her now well-established pieces, so that the public could expect new amusements nightly in Front Street. Baltimore had a reputation for being a vigorous and vital city, uninhibited so far as its political and other entertainments were concerned. It was the raffish town in which poor deranged Edgar Allan Poe had been caught up in the macabre comedy of a local election in 1849. In the Fourth Ward Club, a Whig "coop" used for holding vagrants and itinerants for voting purposes, at the back of an old engine-house on High Street, Poe had drunk a final toast before being found, "rather the worse for wear ... in great distress" in the rain-soaked gutter near Ryan's Fourth Ward poles. In Baltimore he had died, soothed from the terrors of delirium tremens by his other addiction, laudanum, and calling repeatedly for Reynolds, the South Polar explorer on whose experiences Poe had based his story of the horrifying symbolic white death journey of Arthur Gordon Pym.

Menken gave an occasional thought to the shamefully neglected Southern genius whose work she respected so highly and whose memory was revered by the Bohemian circle at Pfaff's. There Poe's disreputable friend, O'Brien, had regaled her with tales touched with the master's own grim brush. Though her fate in Baltimore was the reverse of Poe's, his story and the closeness of the Confederates reminded her constantly of her Southern rebellious nature. Meanwhile, as the pretty sailor-boy William in *Black-Eyed Susan,* she was not only greatly stimulating the men in her audiences, but also exciting numerous ladies, who were "removed from the theater in a fainting state". All this was making "my business *immense*", she wrote to James. "It is really true that we must turn people away. Tonight is the 13th of 'Mazeppa' and the house last night was crowded. Such a run of a piece was never known in Baltimore." And yet a shadow was over her. Her inner self was disturbed, even though her percentage of the gross box office receipts was bringing her more money than she had ever before received. On her benefit night a group of locals came on stage after the final curtain, and presented her with a fifteen hundred dollar diamond bracelet, "the greatest present ever got up in Baltimore, and no humbug about it either". It all added to her conviction that, "some day I am going to be the greatest artiste in the World".

13 December was the last day of the Battle of Fredericksburg, a dreadful defeat for the Union, costing the lives of twelve thousand men in a failed effort to hold back Stonewall Jackson's army. The trains into Baltimore were loaded with the wounded. While Adah triumphed in the theatre, horse-drawn ambulances made a miserable cortége down Front Street on their way to the army hospitals. The weather was wet and cold, and Adah's conflicted thoughts and the exhaustion of her nightly performances had produced an unceasing neuralgic pain under the eye. Eventually she felt too ill and disturbed to go on stage: "ill-natured and too unpleasant even to write to anyone", she wrote to someone. For two weeks she retired to her hotel suite allowing no visitors. She drew the curtains and read voraciously, anything that would take her mind away from Baltimore and the conflicts raised in her by the terrible war. When she eventually agreed to see some of the distinguished visitors who insistently called upon her, she was as faint and languid as if she were playing Camille. Even when the manager of the Front Street Theatre arrived to offer her a new contract as an incentive to return to the theatre, she seemed scarcely interested. Desperate at the loss of the greatest box office draw he had ever had, the defeated producer rose to leave; whereupon the Menken's managerial self took over and told him, categorically, that her client would only be available for a bigger percentage of the receipts than any artiste had ever before been paid. Stunned but relieved to be making a deal after all, he agreed to Menken's demands. He would also redecorate her dressing-room at the theatre in any style she required. Perhaps she would like yellow silk since, looking around her suite and at the dressing-gown and the slippers she wore, it seemed to be her favourite colour. No, stated Adah with her usual perverseness. She would require the room to be done out in Confederate grey. It was the only demand she made which caused the management to hesitate. Was it a wise décor to choose in present circumstances, with Baltimore virtually in the hands of the Union Army, and military police constantly on the look-out for Secessionist sympathisers? Adah loftily said she always took full responsibility for her own décor, and that, furthermore, she would not go on unless it was grey. The manager

conceded, bemused and anxious at the star's sudden excess of Southern loyalty. It was rumoured that she had once published an attack on Abraham Lincoln and, though he tried hard not to notice it, there seemed to be a Confederate flag half-unfurled in a corner of the room. But perhaps it would all be ignored. With a sigh of resignation he caved in on all points. But he shuddered again when he saw that the Menken had livened the grey of her newly-decorated dressing-room with pictures of the Confederate heroes Davis, Lee, Bragg and Van Dorn.

The new scandal of Mrs. Menken's not-so-secret political sympathies revived newspaper interest and public curiosity. As soon as the box office re-opened at the Front Street Theatre, queues formed. Was the Menken reacting politically to the urges of her sentimental and family associations with the South? Or was it her genius for publicity, and her addiction to it at any price? Speculation was rife about her true political position, when one of her more regular callers was suddenly arrested as a Confederate spy. It emerged that he had been under surveillance for some time and that Adah Menken had frequently met with him. The military police called on her at the theatre, noted her décor and at once arrested her. She described the scene to James:

> On Monday I was arrested and brought before the Provost-Marshal for being a Secessionist. Of course I did not deny the charge; but I denied having aided the C.S.A. They wanted to send me to "Dixie" but would not permit me to take but one hundred pounds of luggage. Of course I could not see that. So after a great deal of talk they concluded if I would take the "oath" to let me off. This I refused most decidedly ... I tell you, Ed, I gave them "particular fits" ... I am to report myself to Provost-Marshal Fish in 30 days. If I have continued my unlawful ways I can take my choice between the "oath", or going across the lines without any clothes.

Menken's daring genius for publicity was behaving dangerously in a city largely sympathetic to the North. But she happily reported, "it has done me a great deal of good and helped me to knock Mr. and Mrs. Barney Williams (*a popular act which was drawing business away from Front Street*), 'higher than a kite'. I am now playing to crowded houses, and that in *Mazeppa*, too, which you know had an awful big run here before. But there seems to be more excitement about the piece than ever."

In her remarkable letters to Ed James* concerning business, publicity and other such down-to-earth matters, we hear the voice of a Menken grown entirely pragmatic in the theatrical facts of life. There is an occasional reversion to her moralistic prophetess-like note: "to feel a pure, true and eternal faith in one of

---

* The Menken James correspondence passed on James' death, into the possession of the wealthy theatre Gilsey family of New York, who first allowed Robt. F. Roden access to them. They were subsequently studied and quoted extensively by Allen Lesser, both in his unpublished thesis on Menken, and in his published life, *Enchanting Rebel* (1947).

San Francisco, Cal.
Jan 13th 1864.

My dear Ed:

Do not believe that I can forget. I am busy every moment of my life. Lately I have bought a new horse, and it has taken much of my time to train him. But I now am happy to say that he is brilliant and talented. My health is excellent. I am now playing "Mazeppa" to crowded houses. My "Brookwood" ran 12 nights. The enclosed ad. of Greenback please hand in the office. Give my warmest regards to Frank. I receive all the papers you are so kind as to send. God bless you for your words to so unworthy an object. I shall send you some pictures in a day or two.

Your faithful
Adah.

Letter from Menken to Ed James, dated 13 January 1864. Text begins: "Do not believe that I can forget. I am busy every moment of my life."

God's humans is a thing to lay down a life for"; or, "to be true is not the common thing; it is not born in a man and being new according to its intensity becomes overpowering". But the practical touring theatrical did not allow the prophetess too many scenes. "You know," she wrote to James, "that nearly everybody we are acquainted with would laugh at this letter and think it a capital joke that an actress, one notorious for reckless carelessness in all truth and feeling, should write so." From which one may reasonably conclude that Mrs. Menken's principal concerns at this time were neither spiritual nor patriotic, but were for the sheer business of staying successful in the theatre; which meant ensuring, by any means possible, that Mr. and Mrs. Barney Williams did her trade no damage.

In February 1863, although the weather was awful, Baltimore was still flocking to see the greatest star to have visited them since the unnoticed Poe. By now the Menken owned an enormously enlarged and improved wardrobe, several horses, much jewellery and, for her, an unusual amount of cash. But stripping nightly in a draughty theatre in such weather, even with Adah's iron constitution, was a certain way to catch a bad cold. She kept the show going for five days, then a high fever abruptly ended the amazing Baltimore Menken season, and the battle with Provost-Marshal Fish. After a month in bed at her hotel, a strangely frail Mrs. Menken quietly left Baltimore for New Jersey. There at Long Branch, a quiet seaside resort, she settled down to rest and contemplate for a few quiet months; but though one needs peace and warmth to effect a recovery from pneumonia, one need not totally neglect one's affairs in the process.

Adah had, throughout her Baltimore season, kept in touch with Frank Queen, her agents Brown and James, and other friends, particularly writers who could publicise her doings and adventures. All of them knew that she wanted to move on, either to England or at least to California, where distance from war and sunlight reflecting on gold were compensatory attractions. She sent her playbills and reviews to her business friends, instructing them to pass the material on to the English and Californian press. Gossip columns and itemisers were already murmuring that the Menken was about to appear in California, "for an engagement of one hundred nights at Maguire's".

The theatre of Tom Maguire was the principal San Francisco date and, through James, Adah had been negotiating. Maguire wanted her, certainly, but, she complained bitterly: "They seem crazy to have me out there, but they don't want to pay any money. How is that? I don't see it." When she returned to New York from Long Branch, the columnists speculated on her state of health; rumoured that she had been booked into London at Astley's; observed that she looked frail and out of sorts; concluded she was broke and about to sell even the horse which she rode in *Mazeppa*; "which looks", decided one columnist, "like retiring from the equestrian business". But it was all nonsense, for Adah's energy and appearance were as vibrant as they had ever been. Fortunately, before her

The California Theatre, San Francisco.

agent Brown inconsiderately left her to join the Union army, he brought Maguire to heel. The coast showman agreed to pay her "by far the greatest terms ever given a star in California". Under her San Francisco contract she would receive one third of the nightly gross receipts and fifty per cent of all matinees and Friday nights! The New York columnists who had recently advised that she was retiring from the business now, just as eagerly, reported her amazing deal.

But Adah was, for the present, unconcerned with New York publicity. All her thoughts were for California. She had her repertoire to organise; new material to arrange (Daly was late with the delivery of a play); she had to make arrangements for horses to be ready in California; and endless fittings for an entirely new wardrobe. She was also already looking far ahead, to London, constantly spurring James and Queen on to encourage interest in her there. And now her equipage for the successful Californian tour which would project her towards London and the great theatrical world beyond America, was almost complete. She felt, however, that something was missing, something a lady still needed when about to venture among the wild men of the West. When Robert Henry Newell approached her, begging for a second chance at their marriage, Adah realised what she needed.

A husband; and if Newell was prepared to be understanding rather than demanding, if he accepted that she was a free soul, a great star, and at all times her own woman, why should he not take on the role? Apparently he qualified at this, his second audition. The passage to the Atlantic side of the Isthmus, first stop on the long journey to San Francisco, was booked in the name of "R. H. Newell and wife".

Newell and wife left in plenty of time, on a hot morning in July, to catch the boat. New York was in a state of uproar. The armies of the North and the South under Lee and Meade had just met at Gettysburg, and the resulting carnage had shocked both sides of the divided nation. A Confederate force of thirty thousand had surrendered to General Grant at Vicksburg, Mississippi, and the people of New York wanted the war to end. Mobs protesting against the Draft Law marched through the city, looting shops along the way. The depleted police force was powerless, and Third Avenue had become a battlefield. The *Tribune* office was burned, and the rebellious, the unemployed, and the criminal took over entire blocks of the city up to Central Park. The Newells passed through a street where a man who may have been a Southern sympathiser, but who was certainly black, hung by the neck from a lamp-post. Ruffians had to be whipped away from the carriage, and the Newells arrived at the port with no time to spare. Later Newell heard from journalist associates that the mob had held the city for four days, attacking negroes, looting, burning and fighting the small hard-pressed police force. Martial law had been declared, more than a thousand people murdered, thousands more wounded, and property damage had run into millions.

The voyage to the Isthmus was quiet enough, though enlivened by fears of the Confederate privateers who were rumoured to be searching, like revenging sharks, for Northern victims. There was a blackout on board for security, but Newell and wife were (according to his later account) unconcerned with anything except their eight-day second honeymoon. By the time they arrived at the hot, raffish and unattractive little tropical port of Portobello, Newell was exhausted, though his wife luxuriated in the heat, seemingly impervious to the insects, her Creole blood welcoming this return to exotic climes.

The crossing of the Isthmus accompanied by eight trunks containing Adah's new wardrobe, proved even more exhausting for the unfortunate Newell. Always correctly dressed, he was bathed in sweat and uncomfortable on the wooden seat of the old carriage of the narrow gauge train en route to Panama. Yet Adah waxed poetic over the jungle they were passing through, with its deep green mysterious luxuriance, its strange sounds and horribly humid heat. Later she was to give exciting accounts of the rites of the savage jungle headhunters of the area, but Newell was more factual in his account of the journey:

> Rain fell constantly, and the party was always soaked to the skin. Tents erected at night provided little protection, as the rain fell in such great

quantities that it soon soaked the canvas and poured through it. Those who have never visited tropical places cannot imagine the density of the rain nor the discomfort it causes.

There is a disagreeable, sickly-sweet odor in the tropical forest caused, I believe, by rotting vegetation. Swarms of mosquitoes, flies, gnats and an infinite host of other flying and crawling creatures make these forests no place for the fastidious.

We saw no person other than members of our own party on the journey. Nor, contrary to what we had been warned, did we encounter any vipers. The greatest discomfort was encountered at the City of Panama, on the shores of the Pacific, which we reached after an overland march of more than fifty miles through the rain forest.

This city, believed to be one of the oldest in our Hemisphere, lacks every modern convenience. We were quartered in an ancient hostelry much used by the adventurers seeking gold in California and silver in Nevada. The food is inedible, a combination of Spanish and local Indian dishes which are boiled for long periods in the greases of tropical plants and lose all individuality and flavor. Streets in the City of Panama are narrow, winding and filled with a stench of decay less tolerable than the odors of the forest.

Spanish is the only language spoken in the City of Panama. Miss Menken is fluent in the tongue, and was greeted everywhere with warmth. But there are few divertissements in the City of Panama, and the wait for the *Palace Queen*, the steamer that was to take the party to San Francisco, became tedious. The *Palace Queen* arrived at the harbor eight days behind the date scheduled for her arrival, her Master offering no excuses for his tardiness nor apologies for the inconvenience suffered during the interim by his passengers.

The delightful sea-voyage second honeymoon was far away. Then Newell had sighed: "Cares drop away at sea", and Adah had been the World's Delight and all his. Now in the stinking heat of the appalling tropical city, Adah's moods grew more than normally changeable with the high humid temperature, while Newell's low-key temperament fell into profound depression. She wrote to James: "I have made many sacrifices for Rob, but he is a boor and can't recognise all that I've done for him." She left unclear the nature of these sacrifices, although, sweating in the dreadful humidity of their awful hotel, poor Rob himself began to look as if he was principal among them.

The final stage of the Newell's journey, the voyage on the *Palace Queen* to San Francisco, was observed by a Colonel Benjamin H. Jefferson, who wrote to his wife his personal conclusions about the present marital status of Newell and wife:

At some meals, Miss Menken enlivened the saloon with her presence, and all found her a jolly companion, full of salty wit. Mr Newell never came to the table with her. At other times he came to the saloon alone, and was a gloomy fellow, speaking no more than civility demanded. I saw Miss Menken with reddened eyes walking alone on the deck two or three evenings, and felt sorry for her.

Perhaps, as is said, she is no better than she should be, but I felt sorry for her. Newell is a surly brute, and must have been overbearing and cruel, or why else would such a gallant woman weep? Her frequent displays of good spirits were remarkable, when one thinks of the harsh treatment she was forced to endure.

Gerson concluded, in his always imaginative version of Menken's life, that Jefferson had been got at by Adah, ever a fast solicitor of a strong male shoulder to weep upon. Certainly, by the first week of August when the *Palace Queen* bore them through the Golden Gate, the Newells' second honeymoon was entirely forgotten.

San Francisco was well aware through bills and posters, of the impending descent of the goddess. David Belasco, the great impresario-to-be, then aged ten, remembered seeing them, for portraits and photographs of Adah were on display everywhere. Charles Warren Stoddard, then aged twenty, an idealistic young poet, who was to be mad about the goddess all his life, excitedly described the portrait of the Menken on display at Tom Maguire's Opera House:

A striking picture, it was, far out of the common run in that day: a head of Byronic mold; a fair, proud throat, quite open to admiration, for the sailor collar that might have graced the wardrobe of the Poet-Lord was carelessly knotted upon the bosom with a voluminously flowing silk tie. The hair, black, glossy, short and curly, gave to the head, forehead and nape of the neck a half-feminine masculinity suggestive of the Apollo Belvedere.

When Newell and wife landed on the quay, the waiting crowd applauded. The Menken, a local columnist reported, was "a vision in yellow". She carried a yellow parasol and, on her head, "a fantastic creation of flowers and feathers bound firmly by a band of black lace that passed under her chin". The San Franciscans gasped at her *chic* and applauded again. Burly, elegant Tom Maguire came forward and greeted her as if she were a queen. No one seemed to notice Mr. Newell. The billing in San Francisco quite clearly was to be, "the Menken and ... some husband or other".

In the mid-1850's San Francisco discovered respectability. The half decade that had passed since the gold rush had brought insanity and colonisation, but had also seen the evolution of a middle-class of business men with families and established interests to protect. The Vigilance Committees which had asserted law summarily with fast necktie parties, rail-rides and tar and feathers, were good enough for rough miners, but once a San Francisco gentry existed a more regular form of law and order was required, and could be paid for. By 1855 schools were being built, libraries and hospitals endowed, and murders were down to little more than six hundred for the year. In the next five years life rapidly grew civilised and comfortable with excellent and respectable hotels and restaurants for the industrialists made rich by shipping, lumbering, fishing and ranching. When Adah Menken arrived most men still carried a pistol, but they hardly ever used it. Tom Maguire's Opera House had brought culture to San Francisco; and Joe Lawrence's literary journal the *Golden Era*, was the headquarters of a Californian literary intelligentsia, more expert with their pens than with their revolvers. San Francisco also had a Metropolitan Theatre where Italian opera and classic drama were staged, always a sure sign of cultural apotheosis in American cities. Tom Platt's Music Hall was anticipating a Californian industry of the future with a show of "Stereoscopian" pictures. Certainly there was still the Barbary Coast with its saloons, gambling halls and brothels for all classes of clients; but there was also the Unitarian Chapel on Geary Street where the great preacher Starr King preached fundamentalism along with loyalty to the Union. There were many Confederate sympathisers in the State, but provided everyone's first loyalty was to California, the rest of their politics were regarded as relatively unimportant. The style of the West had much in its raffish chivalry to remind Adah Menken of New Orleans, except that the Western capital was vibrant with energy and activity and its climate much better. From the moment that she arrived there, Adah protested that without knowing it, she had, in her heart and soul, forever been a San Franciscan. And San Franciscans loved it, recognising her, at once, as one of their own.

Menken as Mazeppa.

Seven

Enter the Menken – into the *Golden Era*

MAGUIRE GAVE a great reception at his Opera House for the Menken (and husband). Leading personalities of San Francisco, from the most Bohemian to the extremely conservative, were invited, and so fascinated were they all to meet the extraordinary and notorious actress that hardly an invitation was refused. At the reception it was observed that the Menken was a hearty eater but drank practically nothing. She was, indeed, the embodiment of high style, charm, gentility and culture, and the citizens of San Francisco took to her on sight. As a result, *Mazeppa* was sold out for its entire run before the first night, and Maguire at once exercised his option on the Menken's services, extending her engagement for a further month.

Maguire gave the Menken the greatest publicity campaign which had ever been devoted to a theatrical event in the history of San Francisco. To support her he put together what he advertised as, "the finest corps dramatique ever having an organization in this city". The men who were to surround the Menken were all performers with local followings; Frank Mayo, Louis Aldrich, Charles R. Thorne Jr. and W. Stephenson, with Edwin Booth's elder brother Junius Brutus Booth who looked as Roman and senatorial as he sounded. Maguire had engaged these gentlemen without making it clear to them that the unquestioned star of all the season's productions was to be Adah Isaacs Menken, and that the repertoire would consist of her two Protean vehicles, *Mazeppa* and *The French Spy*. When the actors discovered the situation they protested, under the leadership of Junius Brutus, at the frivolity of what they described as "circus plays". Such vehicles offered them none of the opportunities their followings expected of them. Madame Menken, with all due respect to her notoriety, hardly had the status to justify them submitting their talents to such treatment. Adding insult to injury, more attention seemed to be given to Adah's horse and rehearsing it to be a fiery untamed steed, than was offered to any of the distinguished supporting artistes. Maguire and Adah used their respective talents to calm the rebellion, which eventually settled down to a contemptuous occasional mutter, almost totally silenced by the unending free food and drink Maguire provided, and the generous salaries he paid. The actors went into rehearsal, and all proceeded well enough until, Junius Brutus, playing the villainous count, almost lost an ear in an under-rehearsed duelling scene. With a rather coarsely common oath Booth threw down his sword and announced that he was exiting from the production. Adah, who had by now tamed her horse, at once applied her talents to persuading Booth to return. She found him packing his things backstage; within a short time she led him back, as docile as any of her stallions or husbands. After the taming of Junius Brutus the company offered the Menken no further opposition.

Backstage through the two weeks of rehearsal, watching and reporting the Menken "tame that mean mob of 'actors' at Maguire's to something like discipline", was a tall, good-looking man with hair to his shoulders, named Cincinnatus Miller. He introduced himself to Adah as a journalist "doing some small newspaper work". She thought him more attractive than the general run of newspaper writers and was not at all surprised to discover that his background was the romantic one of a rider for the Pony Express. Miller well appreciated her skill in taming horses and men, and gave her full support in his articles. According to him there was no one else on the stage: "the poor little woman had to carry the whole load of 'forty thieves' on her lone little shoulders". The Menken was so impressed by Miller's appreciation of her qualities that she rewarded him with her friendship, and, some say, the suggestion he change his name from Cincinnatus (not her favourite city) to something more memorable, such as Joaquin Miller, the *nom-de-plume* under which he was to become famous.

Maguire's *Mazeppa* publicity had concentrated upon "the great sensation scene of the flight of the wild steed and his helpless rider up the rocky passes". But he had also put the word around, encouraging the laying of enormously high bets that the Menken might not dare to strip fully before the wild, frighteningly manly, San Franciscan audience. Quietly he himself backed her to strip for considerable sums, and after a little business discussion together, Menken and Maguire agreed an adjustment of her costume. As a result, for the first night of *Mazeppa* at the Opera House, Menken discarded her flesh-tights. She wore a white blouse that totally revealed her "lone little shoulders", and a pair of shorts which showed her legs high above the knees. So much of a woman had never before been publicly revealed in San Francisco, outside of a Barbary Coast cathouse. Here it was and citizens could enjoy it, with their wives beside them; for it was art. The young poet Stoddard, totally in love with the Menken, embodied the highest of local feelings in the matter, describing her as if she were the Venus de Milo: "Garments seemed almost to profane her, as they do a statue", he wrote in muted tone. "She was statuesque in the noblest sense of the word. It was impossible to think of her as being fleshly, or gross, or as even capable in anywise of suggesting a thought tinged with vulgarity. The moment she entered upon the scene she inspired it with a poetic atmosphere that appealed to one's love of beauty, and satisfied it. She was the embodiment of physical grace. She possessed the lithe sinuosity of body that fascinates us in the panther when in motion. Every curve of her limbs was as appealing as a line in a Persian love song. She was a vision of celestial harmony made manifest in the flesh – a living and breathing poem that set the heart to music and throbbed rhythmically to a passion that was as splendid as it was pure."

The critics were also excited by the Menken. They approved her "vigorous originality", and recognised that her Mazeppa was "the matchless and inspired realization of Byron's sublime ideal". Everyone agreed with the evaluation, although hardly anyone had read Byron. Most of the thirty thousand art-lovers who packed the Opera House to capacity over the sixteen nights of its run, came to see a beautiful, daring and half-nude woman, and considered the price they paid for the pleasure, a bargain. By the end of her first run, more than half the population of the city had seen *Mazeppa*. Maguire, with showman-like judgement, now decided to change the programme. The "forty thieves" were annoyed at having to re-rehearse; they rebelled and were placated with food, drink and money, as actors normally are. But the Menken was happy to agree to the additional work for, although her share of the receipts of those first sixteen performances was said to be nearly ten thousand dollars, she needed a few less exhausting evenings to recuperate. She was also convinced, as was Maguire, that they could, after an interlude of alternative material, bring back *Mazeppa* and play to packed houses all over again.

For the second sixteen nights of her season, the Menken played *The French Spy* and *Black-Eyed Susan*; but although the costumes she had designed for her numerous roles in these vehicles were close-fitting and, from a normal point of view, sensational enough, after the revelations of *Mazeppa* the audiences were disappointed. She now offered them her Lola Montez piece (Montez had only recently died in 1861 in poverty-stricken paralysis in San Francisco), and her jolly and daring play *An Unprotected Female*. And although San Francisco languished for Mazeppa and nudity, the theatre was still filled night after night, except for that of 22 September, which was the Jewish Day of Atonement, when the Menken went, not unobserved by the fascinated fans, to the city's small synagogue to pray. On that day she always fasted, she said, and maintained the practice in subsequent years. Perhaps the tragic atmosphere of that day of days for Jews appealed to her theatrical personality; or perhaps she sincerely felt that the confessional element in the ritual was good for her soul. The same week she caught another appalling cold, and went down with a similar neuralgia and fever to that which had put a sudden stop to her successful Baltimore season in the preceding year.

It was Newell's opportunity, he thought, to get Adah out of the theatre. Backed up by several doctors he warned her solemnly that she was reducing her life span by continuing to perform. Sooner or later the resultant exhaustion would expose her to fatality, for even such a horsewoman as she could not expect to tame the Pale Horse of Death. But the Menken insisted that she must return to face her fate as soon as possible. Byronic postures had become part of her nature, and as she rested, pale and lovely, like the tragic heroines of *Camille* and *Fazio*, Mazeppa could hear the murmur of the voices of dead poets calling her back, and the frustrated audiences in the distance champing at the box office, and clinking their money uselessly. She closed her eyes and sighed, loving it all. Newell, enraged but totally defeated, decided that it was time for him to return to New York, and when he mentioned that possibility it seemed as if Adah had hardly heard him. Without opening her eyes, she murmured something to the effect that they were both free souls and must fulfil their separate destinies. By December Newell had returned to New York and the Menken was back playing *Mazeppa* to capacity in Maguire's Metropolitan Theatre in Sacramento.

The Western press, feeling very sophisticated and modern, was advising its readers that, from now on, "prudery is obsolete". Yet there were still some complaints about Menken's performances. The *Bulletin* was shocked at the number of ladies present, though it charitably decided they were there only for censorial reasons, "determined to know if the performance was a proper one for them to behold". Apparently it wasn't and some of them, members of a Reform Group, subsequently complained that the Menken's style belonged more to the wild old times of the Forty-Niners, than to a respectable society where many days often passed without any murders at all. But in spite of the prudes, the Menken was awarded an unparalleled theatrical success so far as box office receipts and publicity were concerned. When she returned for Christmas to San Francisco to begin a month's run of *The French Spy*, the audiences in the self-consciously sophisticated great capital of the West were avid for her. As a reward she offered them *Rookwood*, largely written by herself and, in action, similar to *Mazeppa*, having both a stripping scene and a dangerous equestrian sequence. While quite as revealing as *Mazeppa*, her parts in *Rookwood* were not so exhausting; in spite of which, her horse fell on the first night, injuring itself seriously and having to be shot. But the Menken hopped adroitly out of the way of the beast's fall, to a great gasp of fear and admiration, followed by the deafening applause Westerners reserve only for the greatest of horse-lopers. Maguire was worried that training another horse would mean closing down and losing business for a few nights, but Adah merely changed the script a little and managed to go on performing with an untrained horse for both her shows. "My health is excellent," she exclaimed to James. "I am now playing *Mazeppa* to crowded houses. My *Rookwood* ran 12 nights." But she was to have her greatest success of the new San Francisco season with a jolly if sometimes rude Protean musical play, largely of her own construction. *Three Fast Women*, one of the American theatre's first musicals, presented Miss Adah in six parts; she was delicious little Florence Squires, the heroine;

Louisville Theatre!

COR. FOURTH AND GREEN STS.

Last Week!

OF THE

IMMENSELY SUCCESSFUL

ENGAGEMENT OF THE

BEAUTIFUL AND EXTRAORDINARY ARTISTE

MISS ADAH ISAACS

MENKEN

WHO HAS ADDED

ANOTHER LAUREL

TO HER ALREADY

WORLD-WIDE REPUTATION!

BY HER ARTISTIC RENDITION OF HER

GREAT PROTEAN CHARACTERS

IN THIS, THE GREATEST DRAMA OF THE DAY, BEING A

FAMOUS EXTRAVAGANZA

WRITTEN BY MISS ADAH ISAACS MENKEN, entitled the

THREE FAST WOMEN

NEW FEATURES, NEW CHARACTERS,
NEW SONGS, NEW CONUNDRUMS,
NEW JOKES, NEW DANCES.

Playbill from the Louisville Theatre, 1860s.

Lovely Nancy, "an organ girl with the song of *Bully Lager Beer*"; Montagu Fitzherbert, "a fop young Moses, with song *On the Cliff House Road*"; Tom Bowline, "a sailor with a hornpipe"; Rosebud, "a minstrel"; and Harry Scarlet, "a sporting duck". San Francisco loved the piece which burlesqued their own city's Barbary Coast with its whores, criminals and gallants, and they were amazed and delighted to see that the great tragedienne and equestrienne could also play a black-face minstrel, smoke a cigar, crack local jokes in the Western style, and show lots of deliciously pretty leg. They continued to pay the Menken to shake it until she left at the end of April, bringing a sad ending to a great theatrical era in which, according to Gottschalk, Ada Clare's snobbish lover, a true musical artist could not earn a thousand dollars in five months, while "on the other side, I regret to say it, the circus flourishes, and Miss Adah Isaacs Menken, after having driven all the people crazy, has carried away with her fifty thousand dollars. You will easily understand that the chaste muse, sister of Apollo, can only go astray before a public which is enthusiastic at the nudities of Mazeppa."

The Menken's success in Californian theatrical history was rarely to be equalled until the invention of Hollywood. She had been substantially supported, perhaps even partially created, by the local literary paper, the *Golden Era*, and its energetic editor and contributors. They helped stimulate the excitement surrounding her with puffs, reviews, articles and poems, including her own. They first dubbed her "the Menken", and backed her as if she was a favoured Presidential candidate. Since they were no ordinary collection of provincial hacks, but a group whose future distinction was already clear in their style, manner and the impact they were having upon readers, their support was invaluable.

The *Era* group had a style and approach, a muscular energy and sinewy humour which came directly from the vigorous society for which they had elected themselves to speak. They embodied in their writings the vitality of the Golden West, qualities which were entirely American, owing little to, and caring less for, the starched formality of the East Coast and Europe. Relatively free of self-conscious literary attitudes, they were far warmer-hearted, generous and tolerant than the Puritan eastern literati, from whose influence they were cut off by horrendous distance, for a trans-continental railway was still many years away. Joe Lawrence's group were effective arbiters of what went in San Francisco. The paper was successful and Lawrence's offices impressive, even luxurious. Joaquin Miller found them to be, "the most grandly carpeted and most gorgeously furnished that I have ever seen". There Lawrence and his "brilliant satellites", all of them young and determined to make their names, already constituted a literary establishment quite unlike the minority Bohemian group at Pfaff's. The *Golden Era* spoke for the new, modern, forward-looking society of California, and the causes it espoused could be relied upon to win support from all except the stuffiest of the self-styled local gentry.

Newell was well-known to Lawrence as Orpheus C. Kerr, the satirist of the

Civil War, and called on the editor soon after arriving. But he at once discovered that being husband to the Menken was his principal literary interest for Lawrence and his brilliant satellites. They included Frances Bret Harte who signed himself "The Bohemian"; Charles Warren Stoddard, the poet (who became more famous as Twain's secretary); Ina Coolbrith, poetic mother-figure to the group who ended as a librarian in Oakland; Prentice Mulford, who later betrayed his early Bohemian associations by writing for the Purity League, and who drowned himself after discovering that his wife had posed in the nude for several artists. Other *Era* contributors were Gilbert Densmore, W. S. Kendall, Fitzhugh Ludlow, Charles Henry Webb and Mrs. Hitchcock. But the most distinguished *Era*

Bret Harte.

associate (though they did not know it at the time) was Sam Clemens, who was about to become Mark Twain. Charles Farrar Browne was at that moment, the most individually celebrated of the group, having already created himself Artemus Ward, the corn-cob wiseacre of the Cleveland *Plain Dealer*, and as such the originator of a great tradition of American ironic humour and stand-up commentary still very much alive in our own time.

Lawrence described the Menken's arrival at the *Era* office: "'How do you do? I'm Adah Menken,' the Goddess said, as she paused in the entrance to our ink-stained office. At least a dozen of us were sitting around the room. We leaped to our feet, but none had the grace to reply to this vision of rare beauty in white." Artemus Ward later agreed that "she was pretty enough, but it wasn't until she started to talk that I paid much attention to her. A talking woman is no rarity, but this one made sense!" Flashing her beauty, wit, her Creole mystery, and her New

York sophistication, Adah was obviously the queen the group had been waiting for, though Ina Coolbrith and Mrs. Hitchcock felt they detected dangerous intimations of earthquakes to come. But no San Franciscan male is bothered by an occasional tremor, and the kind induced by Adah were entirely welcome. She at once became one of the boys in the backroom, with them all madly in love with her, aspiring, sooner or later, to positions more profoundly satisfying than those of "brothers". But Adah could always handle literary men. Flattering their talents and appealing to their minds she, most of the time, kept their lusts at bay. And once she was accepted as the muse of the group and had composed her sonnet *Aspiration* for the *Era*, she could no longer be treated as an ordinary woman in any respect: for none of them, they all agreed, could compose a better classic fourteen-liner:

> Poor, impious Soul! that fixes its high hopes
>   In the dim distance, on a throne of clouds,
> And from the morning's mist would make the ropes
>   To draw it up amid acclaim of crowds –
> Beware! That soaring path is lined with shrouds;
>   And he who braves it, though of sturdy breath,
> May meet, half way, the avalanche and death!
>
> O, poor young Soul! – whose year-devouring glance
>   Fixes in ecstacy upon a star,
> Whose feverish brilliance looks a part of earth,
>   Yet quivers where the feet of angels are,
> And seems the future crown in realms afar –
>   Beware! A spark *thou* art, and dost but see
> Thine own reflection in Eternity!

Dante Rossetti was later to regard the sonnet as the best of Menken's poems. Meanwhile the *Golden Era* group was solemnly advised by it that here was a lady of no mean literary proportions, in spite of her incredible figure, and they were literary gentlemen enough to respect both. But it was hard. Joaquin Miller wrote: "Who of those days does not remember that graceful yellow figure in a single garment of silk?" But when her literary friends called on her in the luxurious suite (which Maguire had had specially re-decorated) in the fashionable Russ House, and found her, "lying on a yellow skin, robed in a yellow piece of silk, with her head to the fire like an Indian", it was difficult for them to keep their sanity. And then when Adah, her astounding eyes full of tears, told them of her hatred of the theatre, of the torture of her work, the pain she frequently felt but always concealed, the sacrifices she made for her public, they all felt (more or less) profoundly for her (one way or another). Afterwards some of them ironically wondered whether the fortune she made doing the hateful work was not some

Dante Rossetti, one of Menken's celebrated admirers.

kind of small compensation, even for having to bear the scandalous rumour which never ceased to circulate about her. Bret Harte dared to ask her whether it was true that she had lived with a general in Texas, "as his adopted daughter". She denied the *canard* she herself had started, but added, laughing at Harte's earnestness, "It was General Jackson, and Methuselah, and other big men."

The Menken's poetry was much more impressive to the San Franciscan literati, than it had been to the cynical New York intellectuals. Miller was particularly moved by the image in *Resurgam* of the Menken dying, "with my fingers grasping the white throat of many a prayer" - actually, a very poorly realised image, since one hand may only effectively grasp one throat at a time. Still, the *Era* was more than content to reprint several Menken articles and poems, and with such an out-put she quickly became a significant contributor. But maintaining the spirit of San Francisco, she never allowed her cultural distinction to spoil her fun. By now, effectively free of the restrictions of an eastern-type Christian marriage to a Puritan literary gentleman, she went riding or sightseeing in her opulent carriage with Lotta Crabtree, a young actress who had just made a successful appearance at Gilbert's Melodeon and who admired and imitated her, as she had followed Ada Clare. Always quick to take up challenges, Adah, wearing men's clothes from her wardrobe, accepted a bet from the actors of the company, to visit the Barbary Coast brothels and gambling houses. Though she smoked a cigar as she did so, it is reasonably certain that no one mistook her for a man. She returned some two thousand dollars richer in gambling gains, and proudly told the admiring company that she could easily have trebled it with cash offers had she been prepared to forget that she was a literary lady and an artiste. The experience appealed to her, and she subsequently often visited the faro houses, sometimes accompanied by Artemus Ward, in whose curious invented dialect it amused her to converse.

Ward's attitude towards the Menken was quite the opposite of his general feelings towards women, as embodied in his sketch, *Woman's Rights*: "'The female woman is one of the greatest institooshuns of which this land can boste. It's onpossible to get along without her. Had there bin no female wimin in the world, I should scacely be here with my unparallled show on this very occashun. She is good in sickness – good in wellness – good all the time. O, woman, woman!' I cried, my feelings worked up to a hi poetick pitch, 'you air a angle when you behave yourself; but when you take off your proper appairel & (mettyforically speaken) – get into pantyloons – when you desert your firesides, & with your heds full of wimin's rites noshuns go round like roaring lyons, seekin whom you may devour someboddy – in short, when you undertake to play the man, you play the devil and air an emfatic noosance.'"

The "roarin lyon" Menken gave a party for Ward and her *Golden Era* boys, delighting them all by performing typical Ward monologues in a perfect imitation of his stage accent. Newell attended the celebration, but soon left. Mrs. Newell, an actress who stripped, was now a well-known gambler, a horse-racer and the constant companion of a gang of charming but somewhat riotous and Bohemian young men. He found the situation unbearably depressing, and embodied in his poem *Aspasia* both his fascination and frustration with Adah. The original *Aspasia* was the *hetaira*, the woman companion, concubine, bed-partner, and intellectual friend of Pericles and Newell should have known that such a woman was always too committed to intellectual and personal freedom ever to become a perfectly devoted wife. As a *hetaira* she enjoyed an extraordinary licence and power to exploit and manipulate men in male-dominated societies. In Athens, Aspasia's house was the centre of the best literary and philosophical society, often visited by Socrates; and there in San Francisco, before his troubled eyes, Newell's wife was fulfilling a similar role, quite incompatible with that selected for her by her husband. He admired her, adored her; but he sadly realised that Aspasias are never the exclusive property of any man. Never a distinguished poet, the painful experience produced the best of his verses:

> This is her Court in the Kingdom of Night,
>   Princes are bending before her;
> Nobles and warriors wall her around,
>   Ready to serve and adore her;
> Even the sage breathes the incense of love
>   Cast by her majesty o'er her.

What is the sternness and strength of a man,
    Barbarous, monkish, or knightly,
When the Imperial Passion commands,
    Ruleth it ever so lightly?
Naught but a tottering wall of defence,
    Rendering weakness unsightly!

Beauty may dwell in the statue of stone,
    As in the living Circassian;
But in the beautiful sculpture of God
    Is there what no man can fashion –
Life that is light bringing blindness to men,
    From the high altar of Passion.

Here is the priestess and here is the queen,
    Fairest the light can illumine;
Worshipped by man in the highest estates
    Granted on earth to the human.
But to her altar and unto her throne
    Cometh no form of a woman.

Woe to the maiden, or mother, or wife,
    Tempted by pity to name her!
Even a thought of the sisterless one,
    Charity given, would shame her;
Mothers may speak of the motherless one,
    Only to shudder and blame her.

She, in Philosophy's fathomless spring,
    Bathed her unsatisfied spirit;
Yearning for that which is not of the earth,
    Taking what seemed to be near it,
Ere to her youth came the voice of the world,
    Warning her spirit to fear it.

Think of her then, in her womanless court,
    Maidens with sisters and mothers!
Think of her, lonely, with hundreds around,
    Maidens with fathers and brothers!
Think of her, truthful and pure in herself,
    Lost by the falsehood of others!

Under the branches whose blossoms are fire,
    Gathering thrones in her glances –
Queen of the lilies that nod to the rose,
    Catching its colour by chances;
Treading a universe under her feet,
    Lo! where the goddess advances!

Newell, clearly, was still mad about his own wonderful *Aspasia*, but it was proving more and more difficult to take her home to his mother and sisters. The theatre's gain was, he sadly concluded, the Newell family's permanent loss.

The Menken found the worship implicit in poems dedicated to her, perfectly normal and acceptable. But Adah, the passionate, voluptuous, Creole woman wanted something else from her men, something she had hoped to get from the giant Heenan before she discovered that he housed a pygmy. For though in the '60s a woman might be a determinedly free soul, within her still lived the traditionally-induced masochistic creature embodied in the romantic stories of lady novelists published by the *Ledger* and the *Waverly Magazine*. Oddly enough Newell, writing as Orpheus C. Kerr, had shrewdly perceived the presence of this Jane Eyre quality in the psychology of the women of his time, and had written of it: "Long and patient study of womanly works teaches me that woman's genius, as displayed in gushing fiction, is a power of creating an unnatural and unmitigated ruffian for a hero at whose shrine all created crinoline are impelled to bow. Such a one was that old humbug, Rochester, the beloved of *Jane Eyre*. The character has been done-over scores of times since … The great difficulty with the intellectual women of America is, that they will persist in attempting to delineate a phase of manly character which attracts them above all others, but which they do not comprehend. … Their *Rochester* hero is harder to understand than Hamlet, when he falls into the hands of our school-girl authoresses. He looms rakishly upon us, a horridly misanthropic wretch, despising the world with all the dreadful malignity of chronic dyspepsia, and displaying a degree of moral biliousness truly horrifying … His behaviour to the poor little heroine is a perpetual outrage. Alternately he caresses and snubs her … yet is he loved dearly by the virtuous little heroine all the time."

Kerr may have got it right, but Newell was unable to deliver. He tried to apply the "caress and snub" formula to Adah, but she seemed indifferent to either approach from him. And now she was receiving expensive gifts from men she could hardly describe as intellectual companions; they were rich and powerful and made no secret of the nature of their ambitions for her. Adah had tried, throughout her life, to keep her self-made rule of one lover or husband at a time but, it seemed to Newell, that the applicants were now too numerous for her to be able to maintain the system much longer if, indeed, it had not already collapsed. Specifically a valuable golden ruby ring seemed to him to be significant evidence of an actual or anticipated infidelity. Though Adah steadfastly maintained that she was never for sale and followed only her own inclinations, Newell's melancholic "chronic dyspepsia" grew acute, and Adah found his depression quite unbearable. On 24 September 1863, she wrote at length to Ed James about her general situation:

> If you have a sister, never permit her to marry a "gentleman". I am in tears. I have not been in bed all night, and my new gown of Imported French

Silk (the green one that I promised to give your niece when I come home) has a rip in it that can't be mended.

All the sports like me. That's a consolation. Last week I gave a complimentary benefit to St Francis Hook and Ladder Co. They presented me with a beautiful fire belt and serenaded me with the finest band in the State and finished up with "Three Cheers for Adah". I was so choked up that I couldn't thank them as I wanted to.

I am writing again, which is my only salvation. Joe Lawrence is publishing one of my poems next month. I'm not satisfied with it, but he won't let me make any more changes in it. He says I'll ruin it if I keep altering words and commas, but I am still the perfection-seeker who has never known true happiness and who will, I fear, never know it.

I miss all of you. There is no zest in the air here, and I think of the falling leaves at home. I'd like San Francisco better if the women didn't throw their ugly noses so high in the air when they pass me on the streets. But I don't care. There is a crowd of sports outside my house to cheer me every day when I go to my errands, so I can't ask for more than that.

She signed the letter *Infelix*, "the unhappy", the name she habitually adopted when in poetic or depressed mood. Considering that she was, at this time, receiving the highest salary ever paid to a theatrical performer, it is clear that the conflict between being "a free soul" and remaining Mrs. Newell was becoming intensely distressing to her. Again she wrote to James: "You know not what a dark, heavy cloud casts its shadows over my life. With all my professional success there is not a day of my life that I do not pass the fiery ordeal of tears and prayers. It is now only eight o'clock in the morning. I am in tears. I have not been to bed all night. I cannot, in this letter, tell you all the cause, but suffice it to say that I married a 'gentleman'! ... Perhaps you do not know what that word means as I do. It means a far superior being to either of us, and who occasionally condescends to tell us what low, wicked and lost creatures we are." She does not explain whether she had "not been to bed all night" with or without her husband, but it is known that the *Era* group kept extremely late hours and Adah was never one to leave a party early. In either case her melancholy was real enough.

On one occasion, riding with Joaquin Miller to Seal Rocks, she exhibited an extraordinary range of emotions. As their horses galloped over the sand she said, according to Miller: "I was born in that yellow sand once, sometime, and somewhere; in the deserts of Africa, maybe." It was an improbable and startling revelation, meant to be taken as a poetic truth only. Miller was deeply impressed. The Menken continued talking, "as I had never heard woman before and never shall again, of the color, the lion-color, the old-gold color, the new-gold color, the sun, the light, the life in the moving mountains of sand about us". It was impressive but a little over the top, and Miller's customary humour suddenly returned to him. "It was my first lesson in color. And if I owe anything to anybody at all for my kind of crude work with the quill I owe it to Adah Isaacs Menken and that occasion." Later Menken offered him yet another numbing demonstration. She suddenly threw herself on to the wet sand, sobbing, leaving Miller to hold the horses. She offered no explanation of her tears except that, "I had to do it". Then, before leaving the beach, she threw her wet handkerchief into the sea, crying: "Good-by, gray old grandfather, good-by". By now all satirical inclinations in Miller were stunned into silence. He felt that he had participated in a truly profound, if inexplicable, experience of the poetess.

Newell observed correctly in his *Aspasia*, that the *hetaira* is short of female companionship. Apart from Miss Crabtree the Menken found few ladies in San Francisco with whom to be companionable. She invented a meeting with Lola Montez, her great model and idol. Ada Clare did, however, have the temerity to appear in San Francisco while the Menken was reigning. Somewhat down on her luck, she sought the great new star's assistance. The Menken graciously introduced Clare to the *Golden Era* as "a lady journalist", but after her own efforts for the paper the other Ada was hardly a great attraction. But Clare did revive Adah's interest in spiritualism. Together they visited Emma Hardinge, a well-known medium who, stimulated by generous gifts from the Menken and the dedication of a poem (previously inscribed to Stephen Masset), effected communication with Adah's mother, for apparently her own mother does speak to an *hetaira*.

The Menken was not too sure these days of the value of Ada Clare's friendship. After her final quarrel with Newell she advised Clare not to be seen in public with her. "You have your reputation to establish in this place," she said with gentle consideration, "and to be seen with me might hurt it." After that the usually generous Menken remained unhelpful until she herself was ready to leave San Francisco. Then, not wanting to be followed by anyone whose talents would be dangerous to her reputation and myth, she strongly recommended Ada Clare to Maguire. Following Menken's advice he cast Clare as Camille to Frank Mayo's Armand. The production was a total failure; which saddened the Menken a little when she read about it while enjoying her own incredibly successful tour of silver-rich Nevada.

Tom Maguire owned other Opera Houses in Nevada, and offered Menken attractive enough guarantees to make it worthwhile for her to play them, in spite of the dangers of the rough lode towns in which the citizens were richer in silver than they were in cultural taste. Towns like Gold Hill and Washoe were still little more than villages of rough wooden huts with a few clapboard houses for the wealthy, and numerous saloon bars and "houses of entertainment". But the shambling untidy villages were built over some of the richest lodes of precious metals discovered since '49. Blasting and the vibration of heavy wagons bearing ores to the noisy stamp-mills, made them attractive to the Royal Menken. They

The interior of Henry Wood's New Theatre, Broadway, illustrating the splendour of the surroundings.

were full of actual or potentially millionaire working miners with fortunes entombed in claims with names like *Wake Up Jake*, *Gouch Eye*, *Let Her Rip*, and *Root Hog or Die*. They could well provide reasonable compensation for the crudity and inconvenience of the tour. Arriving "with two immense cigar boxes full of clothing" as a heavily witty local writer put it, the nude Menken was announced, in advance, to be the most exciting thing to hit Washoe since the first old sweat picked up the first nugget. The *Gold Hill Evening News* was impressed:

SHE HAS COME! – The Menken was aboard of one of the Pioneer coaches which reached Gold Hill this morning, at half-past eleven o'clock. She is, decidedly a pretty little woman, and judging her style we suppose she does not care how she rides – as she was on the front seat with her back turned to the horses. She will doubtless draw large houses in Virginia, with her Mazeppa and French Spy, in which she excels any living actress. On the occasion of her arrival, her husband, Orpheus C. Kerr, occupied a decidedly lively and conspicuous position on top of the hind boot. He was dressed in a black moustache, a plug hat, and a gray blanket, and looked either like a troubadour or a Georgia major, just returned from the war. He also rode backwards, which particular fact confirms our previous opinion, to wit, namely: that there is something more than ordinarily contrary in these children of mirth, adventure, and bare-back equestrianism. (We announce this fact, because Orpheus was one of the Captains of the Mackerel Brigade, of the skeleton regiment, William Brown, commanding, on the Potomac river.) We hope Orpheus will not neglect to call on us while he is in Washoe, because we have a book which has his name in it. Welcome to the Menken and Orpheus.

Maguire arranged for L. F. Beatty, his local manager, to open the box office from 10 to 4 daily for several days before Menken's first show on the night of Wednesday, 2 March 1864. Miss Menken would, that evening, the advance publicity advised, astound local citizens with "her world-renowned characters in the Thrilling, Musical, and Spectacular Drama in Three Acts of *The French Spy!*" She would be supported by a travelling company of sixteen artistes, and "a splendid Orchestra, under the leadership of Hubert Schreiner, with numerous auxiliaries". Seats were $1 and $1.50, and private boxes $5 and $10 each, a considerable increase on normal prices. Mr. Beatty found twenty local young enthusiastic amateur ladies and gentlemen to form a *corps de ballet* (a hair-raising thought), and Washoites were warned: "they should prepare to be astonished at a rare exhibition of mental and physical development, an intellectual muscularity, when this petted child of genius drops down among you for compared with them limbs and that bust, all the 'feet' in your Territory are as nothing".

Every seat in the house was sold for all five nights devoted to displaying to Comstockers the Menken in her famous Protean role in which she played Henry St. Alme, Hemet Carmauly, and Mathilde de Merio, all with gusto. As a mark of respect, mockery and so as not to entirely lose business, the local music hall mounted a burlesque version of *The French Spy* with a locally popular actress, Mrs. Beatty, in the lead. The production was far less restrained and stylish than Menken's show, but the locally patriotic *Union* newspaper insisted that it was in some parts superior to the Maguire production and that the soldiers drill in it was "a masterpiece". But the competition had no damaging effect on the business of Menken's show, except to publicise it unintentionally.

Then, on Monday, 7 March, "the shape artist" as local journalists rudely called Miss Menken, appeared in her great *tour de force*, *Mazeppa*; the Opera House was packed, with many standing and hundreds turned away. The local critics, especially young Sam Clemens (now calling himself Mark Twain) and Dan De Quille (whose real name was William "Joggle" Wright), were, according to the *Humboldt Register*, over-impressed by the Menken. The *Register* invented the term "Menkenized", and under that title wrote that "the local of the *Enterprise* is awfully spooney in his comments on Menken's performance. He had better take some of Mrs. Wilson's soothing syrup and get to bed earlier of night". But the local of the *Enterprise* was not the only one to be Menkenized. Most of the men

Mark Twain, 1835-1910, a dedicated follower of Menken's performances.

were and not a few women, some of them ladies. At the end of the run Menken was presented with a silver brick, "of the market value of $403.31 and stamped as follows: 'Miss Adah Isaacs Menken from friends of Virginia, Nevada territory - March 30th, 1864'." A local mine was named the "Mazeppa Mountain Ledge", and, for a while, a whole mining area was dubbed "The Menken". The Menken Shaft and Tunnel Company was formed and issued stock certificates bearing the picture of a naked lady bound to a galloping stallion; its owners presented the Menken with fifty shares in acknowledgement. Their par value was $100 each; a year later Menken was said to have sold them for $50,000.

Among the male attention the Menken attracted was Tom Peasley who owned the largest saloon in Virginia City. After her show one night Peasley, in his capacity as chief of American Engine Company 2, announced that Miss

Menken had been unanimously elected a member of the Company. Menken accepted the honour (and the silver belt which went with it) graciously. She spent a good deal of time at Paisley's and a following crowd watched her play expertly at faro, noting with admiration her experienced gambler's tactics and *sangfroid*. Undoubtedly the Menken enjoyed the Washoe wild western atmosphere; there were fights over her, and once, when she considered herself insulted by some drunken heckler, she stopped the show and harangued the audience into silence.

Mark Twain and Dan De Quille working for the *Territorial Enterprise*, constantly puffed the Menken, the young Clemens being much taken with her and writing home that "she is a literary cuss herself . . . She has a beautiful white hand, but her handwriting is infamous; she writes fast and her chirography is of the doorplate order – her letters are immense. I gave her a conundrum, thus: 'My dear madam, why ought your hand to retain its present grace and beauty always? Because you fool away devilish little of it on your manuscript'."

Clemens drank, flirted and quipped with the Menken, and certainly he observed that she had other physical attractions apart from "a beautiful white hand". Later, when working in San Francisco, he wrote an ironic but flattering account of the Menken's tour, which he titled somewhat heavily, *A Full and Reliable Account of the Extraordinary Meteoric Shower of Last Saturday Night*. He can be observed in that piece battening down his admiration with heavy irony: "About this time a magnificent spectacle dazzled my vision – the whole constellation of the Great Menken came flaming out of the heavens like a vast spray of gas-jets, and shed a glory abroad over the universe as it fell! (N.B. I have used the term 'Great Menken' because I regard it as a more modest expression than the Great Bear, and consequently better suited to the columns of *The Californian*, which goes among families, you understand.)."

But while young Twain and De Quille were "awfully spooney" over the Menken, the *Union* became the local Thunderer, dubbing Maguire's "a Hippotheatron", and the Menken's performance "a scandalous, obscene exhibition, a defamation of a historical character whose ghost might well exclaim: 'To what base uses may our name be turned?'" The same indignant reviewer praised the Music Hall's latest burlesque, the painfully titled, *Alta Skeesicks Blenken*. It was a tiny local battle between tiny local newspapers, but kept things alive for the run, and became quite rude when the *Union* observed that the *Enterprise* champions were cooling on Menken. "Guess Dan has discovered that she wears drawers", they scandalously concluded. But all publicity was excellent for Menken's business. Having been insulted in her time by experts, the callow local reporters and editors were as gnats upon the rump of a tigress.

After her twenty-nine-day Washoe season Menken accepted her silver bar, the silver belt of the engine company, any other silver proferred, and exited to the almost drunken adieu of the *Enterprise* that, "Miss Menken played a variety of characters, and she was better in all of them than each that preceded it, if possible, which hardly seems reasonable to believe it, yet nevertheless was so," possibly the worst-written rave-review she ever received, and commented on by the *Humboldt Register* as "a sentence remarkable for its felicitous wording and corresponding beauty". Washoe settled back into its daily boring routine of picking gold or silver rocks out of mud, suddenly empty and undramatic; as a local poet put it:

> Menken, adieu! No more shall lusty "boys"
> Applaud Mazeppa, till hoarse throats grow hoarser;
> No more shall they, mid lights and horrid noise,
> See that *fine* form outspread upon a courser!

Many were the tall stories which, western style, were built up around Menken's Nevada tour. The best of them was retold by Gerson, who describes local miners building an exterior platform stage for Menken to perform on, and then at the end of her performance: "there was bedlam, the most extraordinary scene ever to take place in the history of the American theater. Someone threw a chunk of silver onto the stage, narrowly missing the star. Others delightedly followed the gift-giver's example, and a shower of precious metal crashed onto the rough-hewn planks. Adah, for the moment solely concerned with the prevention of mayhem, retreated to the rear of the stage ... A line quickly formed, and men came onto the stage one by one to make their offerings to the Goddess. Each was given a warm embrace, and others in the audience were so stirred that they raced off to their lodging houses, shacks, and tents, where mattresses were upended, treasures were dug up from secret hiding-places, and the pile of silver on the stage rose higher. Adah's kisses became correspondingly warmer, and the audience howled gleefully when one sheepish miner handed her a heavy ingot ... For the next forty-eight hours Adah was inundated with silver. Men brought her ingots, chunks, and even bags of silver dust."

It is a perfect example of myth-making though Adah's Nevada Strike from performing, gambling and gifts was indeed considerable. She herself modestly denied that it was as much as a million dollars. Newell estimated it at $150,000. James favoured $100,000, and Gerson insists that while in Nevada Menken received, "more for a single performance than any actress in the history of the theater". Unsurprisingly she left by coach for San Francisco looking tired, according to a fellow traveller, and somewhat frowsy without her stage make-up.

Mark Twain's description of the Menken in performance at this time (written when he was somewhat less "spooney" and more critical) under the title, *The Menken – written specially for gentlemen,* is a living, satiric but thoroughly convincing account of the Menken in full theatrical flight; and is certainly the best contemporary description extant of *Mazeppa* in action:

When I arrived in San Francisco, I found there was no one in town – at least there was no body in town but "the Menken" – or rather, that no one was being talked about except that manly young female. I went to see her play *Mazeppa*, of course. They said she was dressed from head to foot in flesh-coloured "tights", but I had no opera-glass, and I couldn't see it, to use the language of the inelegant rabble. She appeared to me to have but one garment on – a thin tight white linen one, of unimportant dimensions; I forget the name of the article, but it is indispensable to infants of tender age – I suppose any young mother can tell you what it is, if you have the moral courage to ask the question. With the exception of this superflous rag, the Menken dresses like the Greek Slave; but some of her postures are not so modest as the suggestive attitude of the latter. She is a finely formed woman down to her knees; if she could be herself that far, and Mrs. H. A. Perry the rest of the way, she would pass for an unexceptionable Venus. Here every tongue sings the praises of her matchless grace, her supple gestures, her charming attitudes. Well, possibly, these tongues are right. In the first act, she rushes on the stage, and goes cavorting around after Olinska; she bends herself back like a bow; she pitches headforemost at the atmosphere like a battering ram; she works her arms, and her legs, and her whole body like a dancing-jack; her every movement is as quick as thought; in a word, without any apparent reason for it, she carries on like a lunatic from the beginning of the act to the end of it. At other times she "whallops" herself down on the stage, and rolls over as does the sportive pack-mule after his burden is removed. If this be grace then the Menken is eminently graceful. After a while they proceed to strip her, and the high chief Pole calls for the "fiery untamed steed"; a subordinate Pole brings in the fierce brute, stirring him up occasionally to make him run away, and then hanging to him like death to keep him from doing it; the monster looks round pensively upon the brilliant audience in the theatre, and seems very willing to stand still – but a lot of those Poles grab him and hold on to him, so as to be prepared for him in case he changes his mind. They are posted as to his fiery untamed nature, you know, and they give him no chance to get loose and eat up the orchestra. They strap Mazeppa on his back, fore and aft, and face uppermost, and the horse goes cantering upstairs over the painted mountains, through tinted clouds of theatrical mist, in a brisk exciting way, with the wretched victim he bears unconsciously digging her heels into his hams, in the agony of her sufferings, to make him go faster. Then a tempest of applause bursts forth, and the curtain falls. The fierce old circus horse carries his prisoner around through the back part of the theatre, behind the scenery, and although assailed at every step by the savage wolves of the desert, he makes his way at last to his dear old home in Tartary down by the footlights, and beholds once more, O, gods! the familiar faces of the fiddlers in the orchestra. The noble old steed is happy, then, but poor Mazeppa is insensible – "ginned out" by his trip, as it were. Before the act closes, however, he is restored to consciousness by his doting old father, the king of Tartary; and the next day, without taking time to dress – without even borrowing a shirt, or stealing a fresh horse – he starts off on the fiery untamed, at the head of the Tartar nation, to exterminate the Poles, and carry off his own sweet Olinska from the Polish court. He succeeds, and the curtain falls upon a bloody combat, in which the Tartars are victorious. *Mazeppa* proved a great card for Maguire here; he puts it on the boards in first-class style, and crowded houses went crazy over it every night it was played. But Virginians will soon have an opportunity of seeing it themselves, as "the Menken" will go direct from our town there without stopping on the way. *The French Spy* was played the last night and the night before, and as this spy is a frisky Frenchman, and as dumb as an oyster, Miss Menken's extravagant gesticulations do not seem so overdone in it as they do in *Mazeppa*. She don't talk well, and as she goes on her shape and her acting, the character of a fidgety "dummy" is peculiarly suited to her line of business. She plays the Spy, without words, with more feeling than she does Mazeppa with them. I am tired of writing now …

Thus concluded the young Mark Twain. He had spent a fair amount of time "whalloping" around after the Menken, and was fair "ginned out" himself.

Entrance to Astley's Theatre in 1820.

for her, as lacking in interest as was last year's hit to the New Yorkers. She stayed at home writing sad poetry, saw a few faithful friends, rejected several marriage proposals (and other arrangements), spent money, designed new costumes, had many fittings, drank a little more than was her habit, and ate a good deal, for her normally hearty appetite tended to wax rather than wane when she was depressed. It made the fittings particularly annoying and frustrating, since, somehow or other, her dressmaker was stupidly making everything so much larger than it ought to be. She felt certain it was time to leave for Europe.

Adah could not understand why James, Frank Queen, and the other friends she had consistently bombarded with requests, demands and appeals that they pursue a London booking for her, had come up with nothing. Surely some sort of

A portrait of a fatter Adah Menken, taken in Vienna at the end of her theatrical life.

an offer must have been received from London? Surely Edward Tyrrell Smith, the English theatrical Smith, and possibly an even greater showman than the gallant Albany Captain who had first promoted *Mazeppa*, surely his theatre, Astley's, with its great past history of horse-shows, *must* be interested in booking her? Eventually James told her that Smith of Astley's had, in fact, made her an offer. Adah was overjoyed. She knew it! He had to, for it was her fate. Her destiny, she knew, had a London success ready and waiting for her. What were the details? Then James gave her the bad news. Smith was offering a miserable hundred pounds a week, and in no way would he discuss the kind of percentage deals to which she had become accustomed. A hundred pounds, James calculated for her, was about five hundred dollars. Adah was at first stunned, then shocked, she sobbed that it cost her more than that to feed her horses. James sadly felt that he had failed her; Adah agreed with him. She turned her face away, and James unhappily left her.

Eight

Enter Menken – as the Belle of London

WHEN THE MENKEN returned to New York she discovered that fame elsewhe[re] doesn't mean too much to its citizens. A foreign genius whose gimmi[ck] fails to catch the interest of that city's itemisers must yield to an inventor w[ho] introduces a revolutionary concept, such as parting hair on the right side rath[er] than the left. Adah may have had the greatest success in California's theatric[al] history, but how long and how distinguished was that history anyway? New Yo[rk] was interested in California for its gold, not for its cultural genius. What lit[tle] notice had been paid to her western adventures could scarcely make Adah a h[ot] favourite after a whole year's absence from New York; for like all great cosm[o]politan citizens, New Yorkers believe that anyone who is absent from them th[at] long has either lost their talent, their senses or their money. The Menken, it w[as] true, had come back silver-rich and was living in some style in a six-thousan[d] dollar brownstone house purchased, presumably, with her earnings from som[e] activity or other. But that in itself did not make her exciting. Of course *Mazep[pa]* was remembered, but it was now an old story in a town in which exciting ne[w] stories happen (or if they don't, are invented) every day of the week. And as f[or] the once highly debated question of whether Adah was Mrs. Menken, Mr[s.] Heenan or still Mrs. Newell, all that too belonged to last year's scandals. She w[as] recognised at Pfaff's with her old associate Ed James and Alderman Joe Brice, [her] legal friend, and frequently she was kissed on both cheeks and greeted effusive[ly] by associates from that rapidly dimming year-old past of fame and fortune; bu[t] the *habitués* of café society rapidly returned to their current preoccupations.

The Menken would have been happy to see less of Alderman Brice, but h[e] constantly bored her with his anxious opinion that her divorce from Newell unde[r] California law was questionable in New York State. He considered that, particu[larly] in view of her unfortunate history in these matters, it would be advisable t[o] file again for divorce under the law of the State. She instructed him to proceed[,] but the matter offered her little interest and no stimulus; last year's husband wa[s]

For some days the Menken remained, totally incommunicado, in her brownstone house. Then an instruction arrived for James to book *Mazeppa* into Baltimore, the former scene of her triumph. Adah was convinced that city would show her fidelity, a quality found more often in provincials than among the stale and cynical citizens of treacherous, self-conscious, cosmopolitan cities like New York. James thought Adah might have something there, and complied with her sudden imperious instructions.

But in March 1864, dear old faithful Baltimore was war-weary, preoccupied with such trivial issues as the promotion of General Ulysses S. Grant to the command of the Union army, which boded ill for a border-city with divided loyalties. The supporters of the Confederate General Robert E. Lee were still hopeful that his genius for command would, somehow or other, bring a victory of sorts, or at least an honourable stalemate to the conflict. But Grant was a cold, silent, steely and implacable opponent; his appointment was bad news in Baltimore. Furthermore, so many local sons had died, on one side or the other, that there was no longer that war-time feeling of euphoria which keeps box offices busy. The *Mazeppa* advance business was exceptionally bad. On the fourth night of the show there were no more than fifty people in the house; her managers and colleagues begged Adah to call it a day. But the Menken now had good reason to believe that, strongest among the gods who never failed her, was Publicity. All it required was the appropriate attention-catching tactic and Baltimore would forget its worries and flock to *Mazeppa* again. She brooded on the question and finally made a decision without seeking the benefit of Ed James' experienced judgement. Somewhat ostentatiously she now visited Singer's fashionable restaurant and rather loudly, told Mr. Singer that she was expecting a stranger; had anyone been asking for her? Singer replied in the negative, but offered her a good table. A performance of agitation followed which drew the attention of the restaurant's guests. Pale and distraught Adah made an important exit after begging Mr. Singer to send her a message immediately the strange gentleman should arrive and ask for her. Talk started immediately. Was the Menken involved with a new lover of scandalous distinction? Someone said that she had been seen in the company of officers. The question was though, as one wiseacre put it, "Which Army?" The Menken's Southern origins were as well-remembered by Southern sympathisers, as her *Pro Patria* lines were by supporters of the North. Mr. Singer was consulted on the question. Did he know anything about this stranger that Miss Menken was so agitated about? He knew nothing, he said, except that she had told him the man would have a strong Southern accent; that told some enquirers a whole lot. When Adah returned in the evening, she was even more agitated that the mysterious gentleman with the strong Southern accent had not yet appeared. And now speculation was rife. The notorious Southern belle was openly establishing contact with important Confederate elements. The rumour was picked up by a local journalist who, spying on her, noted that the Menken spent that supper-time alone but at a table set for two. She consumed an extraordinarily large steak, her eyes fixed on the entrance of the restaurant. A waiter, being well-tipped, advised that he had heard her offer Mr. Singer a hundred dollars not to mention that she was consuming steak while waiting for the Mysterious Stranger with the Southern accent. Mr. Singer refused the offer, and her agitation caused Miss Menken to speak even louder than usual, louder certainly, than was suitable for someone playing the French or any other kind of a spy off-stage. Adah waited at Singer's until closing-time, drinking peach brandy and nibbling cherry bonbons. When she left she told Mr. Singer, loudly, that she would return the following day. In the event of the expected message arriving before, would he please, please she begged, at once send it to her. Important events may very well depend upon it, she declared. By the time she returned to her hotel that night, the rumour was circulating in Baltimore that the Menken was negotiating peace (or something) with her highly placed Confederate contacts.

Adah slept well that night, confident that the newspapers the next day would raise again the speculation which had brought so much business to the box-office the last time she was in Baltimore. Surely there was another military Fish to take the bait; certainly the local press would put two and two together, and revive the whole exciting charade of Menken the Confederate spy. And it worked. While she was happily consuming a late breakfast of veal chops the next day at Singer's, a squad of Union soldiers arrived and took Miss Menken into custody.

At army headquarters Adah discovered that Fish was now a Brigadier-General and intended to question her personally. This he did, and naturally, without the Southern courtesy and chivalry which Adah expected from military gentlemen. Fish was none too pleased to be involved in yet another *contretemps* with the actress for, whatever happened, such embarrassing situations are not helpful in winning wars. When her charm had no effect whatsoever on Brigadier-General Fish, the Menken adopted her haughtier style. That seemed to make him colder and less gentlemanly than ever; whereupon she grew bewildered and vulnerable. But Fish was well-named; his nature was cold and scaly, and he was quite unresponsive to warm-blooded creatures like Adah. She grew incoherent and nonsensical in her responses to his endless questions. Finally, either because he was thoroughly annoyed with her, or because national security in Baltimore was too dangerous to make jokes about or take chances over, Fish prepared a report on her Confederate past and the present rumours, and told her flatly that she would be sent to Washington under an armed guard. Now Adah was truly upset. It was shattering to meet a man who was so totally unresponsive to her, so immovably grim. Tearfully she explained that she was booked for a run of *Mazeppa*. Fish replied, drily, that the exigencies of war disregarded non-military engagements, and summarily dismissed all present.

Although the "armed guard" turned out to be not at all threatening, and was much more amenable to Adah's charms (for she dressed modestly but enchantingly for the journey), the War Department in Washington seemed rather busy, quite unsympathetic, totally unconcerned about the run of her show, and immovably convinced by Fish's report that her presence in Baltimore was "not in the national interest". It was a dreadful experience and, worst of all, because of the stupid inhibitions attached to "national security", she received virtually no publicity from the entire adventure. All that happened was that the advance on her salary (a percentage) was consumed by the consequent losses on the show. Eventually she returned, unnoticed, to New York, a little poorer and greatly depressed. Later in Paris she strengthened the story (which much amused Dumas Père), telling how she had been incarcerated in prison until General Grant, one of her greatest admirers, hearing of her plight, personally ordered her release, inviting her to visit him at his headquarters so that he might deliver a personal apology on behalf of the army, congratulate her for her patriotism (as conclusively demonstrated in her famous poem *Pro Patria*, of which she gave him a signed copy), and expressing the hope that when peace came there would be an opportunity for him and Mrs. Grant to attend a performance of *Mazeppa*. The Parisians were unlikely to know that Grant was famous for never saying a word unless it was absolutely essential, and for being a self-conscious Puritan. As for Mrs. Grant, she was a domineering appallingly cross-eyed lady who wouldn't have been caught dead in the presence of a half-nude actress.

By the time Adah had returned to New York she had unalterably made up her mind. With or without an engagement, she would mobilise her resources and leave the ungrateful country which seemed quite unaware of the sacrifices she had made to entertain it. She would go where her destiny called her, to England. She arranged to leave her palace at 458 Seventh Avenue, the beloved brownstone upon which the silver she had mined on her western tour had been lavished. Ed James' wife Hannah (a firm friend since Adah had sent James back to her from the pursuit of yet another lady), would make sure the place was kept cleaned and aired. Ed himself could attend to outstanding business in New York; Alderman Brice would pursue the divorce action against Newell. Unnecessarily he advised her that, for the time being and until further notice, it would be better to avoid getting married again. She assured Brice that marriage would never again enter her plans. Hurriedly she put together a modest wardrobe and, with only twenty-eight pieces of luggage and her black servant, Minerva (Minnie, who had adopted the surname Menken), she set sail for Plymouth, England, on 3 April 1864.

As befitted a great star, Adah booked the best suite, tipped well, and was treated like royalty, being paid court by captain, officers and most of the other first-class travellers, including a charming gentleman, most elegantly dressed, very handsome, and wealthy, who spent much of his spare time gambling, which he did with a great deal of Western-style dash. This Captain Barkley, like the rest of the gentlemen on board, paid her flattering attentions. But her mind was firmly set upon her plans for London, and though she noted that the captain might well turn out to be a charming escort should there be time for such diversions in the metropolis, for the time being she gave him no hope of ultimate intimacies.

The Menken's plans were focused upon making her London début in the great Drury Lane Theatre, and she chose a small but respectable hotel near it, Bunyard's Private Hotel, in Norfolk Street, off the Strand. A successful appearance in Drury Lane would confer upon her theatrical distinction of the highest order, and she lost no time introducing herself to Edward Stirling, the manager of that establishment. But not only were the Menken's terms absurdly high by London standards, said Stirling; Drury Lane was *not* a suitable venue for Protean pieces, for its traditions were classical. Well, Adah was certainly not about to attempt Shakespeare in a town where quite a lot of people were familiar with the actual lines the dramatist had written. Stirling then, very politely, recommended as a more suitable date for her, Astley's Amphitheatre in the Westminster Bridge Road, not knowing of the approaches from America which had already been made to Edward Tyrrell Smith, the Astley manager, with such insulting results. Astley's, he pointed out, had traditionally specialised in "horse-dramas"; indeed *Mazeppa* had been produced there, sometimes successfully, sometimes not, as far back as 1831. True, for the past couple of years the theatre had tried to change its traditional character, having received a face-lift under the brief management of Dion Boucicault, who had removed its circus ring and put in stalls, potted plants and artificial fountains. But the present manager, Smith, was a highly experienced and adroit showman; he had himself once been the lessee of Drury Lane, the Alhambra and Her Majesty's, had managed a travelling circus, a tavern, a wine-merchant's, dealt in paintings, acted as land-agent, bill discounter, and had been a newspaper owner. He had once operated the infamous Cremorne Gardens, where pleasures of every kind were cheaply available, knew gambling casinos well and had run night-clubs and wax-works. He had even stood for Parliament, being defeated by Samuel Whitbread, the great brewer. Once, when business was slow in his tavern, he had filled it by putting his barmaids into bloomers. Smith was used to great ladies of the theatre too; he had once offered the great Rachel top billing in a circus. The Menken agreed about Smith's qualifications and was happy for Stirling to write to him. Stirling did so, but Smith replied briefly: "Thanks. Menken can go to Drury Lane or to the Devil. She won't do for me. She was kicked out of America." It seemed rather final, but Stirling knew his old Drury Lane associate too well to take it seriously. He suggested that Menken call on Smith, flying all her colours. She did so and there must have been instant recognition between them, for she left the office with a contract which Smith later described as "wicked and preposterous".

For London and Smith it was certainly an astounding deal. Under Menken's contract, she would receive half the nightly receipts; the cost of grooms and equestrian directors would be paid by the management; a stage-box would be reserved throughout the season for her personal visitors; and a star dressing-room was to be suitably prepared, decorated and appointed. Astley's would provide a first-class full supporting company, and the production would be mounted in the highest style. The Menken must certainly have been looking her best that day, and her presentation of her triumphant American theatrical business, enormously impressive to him; or Smith desperately needed a great new attraction for Astley's, which, to tell the truth, had never quite made the transition from amphitheatre to theatre successfully. Some said that the deal was clinched when Adah put on (or took off) her Mazeppa costume for Smith. Whatever else happened, the instinctive and impetuous showman in Smith recognised at once in Adah a sensational theatrical property, and he signed. *Mazeppa* would open in late September or early October. August and September would be spent in a pre-production campaign worthy of the partnership of Menken and Smith. He at once arranged for her to move to the Westminster Palace Hotel, near to Astley's and convenient for daily and highly publicisable rides on the Mall and Hyde Park. Her suite at the Westminster would include a large reception room for the accommodation of the paragraphists and journalists to whom she agreed to make herself more than ordinarily available. To get interest started, Smith at once released the following paragraph:

> Miss Adah Isaacs Menken, the popular young American Actress, is now in London. Every fine afternoon she appears among the aristocracy in Hyde Park, either mounted on her famous black mare and escorted by a groom in full livery, or else airing herself in an open carriage with a liveried coachman and footman complete. Her equipage is much admired by the fashionables.

After a few days another paragraph appeared:

> The public watch Adah Menken, day after day, driving up the Mall with her team of ponies. Duchesses, even if they are young and beautiful, pass unnoticed when La Belle Menken is in sight. Apparently impassive, and casting glances at no one except the little "tiger" behind her, she sweeps along the Mall, the "observed of all the observers".

The London campaign of La Belle Menken now under way, Smith set about personally advising certain theatre critics that they must be prepared for a most unusual, modern and American entertainment in Astley's new production of *Mazeppa*. The public, too, was advised of the unusualness of the production by posters showing a possibly naked personage bound to a wild steed, a little dimity around her/his loins and a small moustache being the whole of the rest of his/her discernible clothing. The poster read: "Unprecedented success of Miss Adah Isaacs Menken as Mazeppa". As Miss Menken was neither the mad white horse or the ravening wolf in the picture, it followed that she must be the near-naked,

London flocked to the portals of Astley's, lured by playbills such as the one above.

moustachioed figure. The mid-Victorian respectable London middle-class reacted immediately as calculated. Their self-appointed champion, a bad playwright, H. B. Farnie, editor of a leading musical and theatrical paper *The Orchestra*, though he cultivated a reputation in café society as an inveterate lady-killer, now assumed a righteously indignant and unfamiliar posture:

> There is a depth of degradation in the drama which England has not yet reached, and which she, hopefully, never will; however common may be that degradation beyond the seas. It would be needless to allude to anything so distasteful were we not menaced with an invasion of impurity against which we cannot but protest. A notice has been circulated through the newspapers of London – our own journal among them – that an American sensation actress, a Miss Adah Menken ... is to appear at Astley's in the equestrian play of *Mazeppa*. We do not know the nature of this performance in which "Mazeppa" is played by a female, but we read what a New York contemporary says of similar exhibitions on the other side of the ocean.
>
> It is to be hoped for the sake of decency, and for the sake of the reputation in which Mr. E. T. Smith stands, that the exhibition at Astley's is far from

anything of this degraded order. We repeat that we know nothing yet of the actress's merits or the character of the piece, and, therefore, do not attempt to anticipate the event. But there have been imported many corruptions from America already, corruptions in language, in religion – or, at least, that superstition which does duty for it – in art. It would be the more painful, therefore, to have to point out to a London manager that the public morals are not yet so sunk as to tolerate a performance which would be hooted everywhere, save in a Yankee audience, or among their kindred spirits in a Sepoy community.

Farnie's somewhat chauvinistic and slightly racist broadside would have left your average actress in a state of shivering terror. But the Menken replied with what many of her writer-friends later considered to be a masterpiece of calculated moralistic journalism:

Westminster Palace Hotel
August 24th, 1864.

Sir

In your leader last week on "The Morals of American Art", you associate my name with what an American journal terms "the naked drama", and express the hope that Mr. E. T. Smith will not degrade Astley's by an exhibition of indecency. As I am about to appear at that establishment such an observation is calculated to do me serious injury, and I am sure you will allow me a few words of explanation, as you confess you know nothing of the "merits of the actress, or her piece". To begin with the play is Lord Byron's *Mazeppa* and I impersonate the hero; but my costume, or rather want of costume, as might be inferred, is not in the least indelicate, and in no way more open to invidious comment than the dress worn by Cerito Rosati, or even the grotesque garbs employed by ladies on the London stage.

I have long been a student of sculpture,* and my attitudes, selected from the works of Canova, present a classicality which has been invariably recognized by the foremost of American critics. I may add that my performance of *Mazeppa* had a most prosperous career in America, and, as is usual in such cases, my success created a host of imitators, and some of these ladies, I hear, have adopted a style of drapery inconsistent with delicacy, or good taste.

"Mazeppa", like any other speciality, is easily vulgarized. Let "La Sylphide" be scantily dressed, or ungracefully acted by an indifferent artist, and what will be more offensive? The critics found no fault with Mrs. Charles Kean's embodiment of *Ion*, and the young ladies who exhibit their well-formed limbs in the Haymarket or the Strand burlesques (notably in such parts as *Cupid*, or *Ixion*) are not accused of indelicacy. At any rate do me the

---

* A frequent claim of Menken's based upon a short and obscure association as a model with a mediocre Ohio sculptor named Jones, who also gave her lessons in the art.

favour as a stranger, to suspend your opinion of my representation, and after you witness it I am quite willing to abide by your criticisms.

>I am, sir,
>   Yours very truly,
>   Adah Isaacs Menken.

In the next issue of *The Orchestra* Mr. Farnie stated that he was "more than pleased to have Miss Menken's frank and explicit statement". Other papers and journals copied both Farnie's attack and the Menken's reply and all of London's Bohemians and celebrities now wanted to meet her. Free with her invitations for champagne and supper in her Westminster Palace Hotel suite, Adah rapidly established her own salon, particularly cultivating, as ever, journalists and writers who were, after all, both soul-mates and an unending source of puffs and interviews. A somewhat *risqué* poem dedicated to the Menken was circulated. Some thought that the verses were by a famous poet madly in love with her:

> Covering half thine ivory breast
> Which, O heavens! I should see,
> But cruel destiny
> Has placed a golden cuirass there,
> Keeping secret what is fair.

Whoever the poet was, Smith was his publisher, for it was he who paid for the leaflets to be printed and distributed in generous numbers.

Smith and Menken's secret about the degree of her nakedness in *Mazeppa* was becoming increasingly open, and the newspaper speculations grew correspondingly more frequent. "The lady Mazeppa looks on the walls nearly as nude as her wild steed and certainly not half so well-clothed as the wolves and vultures who follow him on aldermanic thoughts intent." What an "aldermanic thought" regarding the Menken might be, they were too genteel to specify.

Smith arranged other innovations for the projected first night of *Mazeppa*. He developed his advance booking system, encouraging seat touts, and was able to predict confidently that there would not be a seat available for some days before the first night on 3 October 1864. Those eager to catch the sensation of the theatrical age were advised to book well in advance, and should not assume, whoever they were, that they might turn up casually at the box office and find seats available. Smith anyway, detested the casualness with which smart people took the theatre for granted, assuming that there were always seats to be had for the asking. He believed that theatrical occasions should be attended with ritual, knowing well that increased respect would bring increased business, and, hopefully, justify the increasing of seat prices. If he was to get into profit quickly on the costs of the *Mazeppa* production, bearing in mind the insanely generous deal he had given the Menken, all the stops would have to be pulled out. He must use the whole of his show-business wisdom and experience in a great campaign to make his investment into a London star. So the endless puffs continued for, "Miss Adah Isaacs Menken, who has earned well deserved laurels in California, the Colonies and the United States" must be discussed endlessly. Additional large posters, more generally distributed than usual, added to costs, but Smith had gone *banco* on Menken. The constant selling of the nude element was essential; on the other hand, the moral sensibilities of the English public must not be too affronted, as Mr. Farnie had reminded them. So Smith made it clear that, "great curiosity is at its height respecting the part being performed by a lady, but the English Public will judge and appreciate the character in this Classic Drama, represented by a Heroine (in a Classic Dress) who has performed it hundreds of nights". The statement attached to the large posters demonstrates Smith's skill in playing it both ways simultaneously, as had the somewhat androgynous figure on the fiery steed of Tartary. The "Heroine (in a Classic Dress)" would be supported by respectable professional artists and "a grand stud of horses, two hundred soldiers and ballet", not to mention "a cataract of real water and precipices". Smith was now committed for more money than even he, chancer as he was by nature, liked to think about. The Menken had to succeed, for both their sakes.

She did. From the opening setting, in which blue light revealed her in a close-fitting black velvet costume, to the astounding stripping scene and the illusion of totally naked flesh that followed, La Belle Menken delivered to the audience all and more than it had paid for. Whatever the critics might say, *Mazeppa*'s London first night was an unquestionable and smashing success. After the final curtain Smith made to lead his star forward from the wings to take the applause of the audience. But it wasn't a moment the Menken was inclined to share. "For heaven's sake, man," she whispered loudly, "stop fussing!" and leaving Smith in the wings she advanced confidently to centre stage to take her curtain call on her own. She threw the audience kisses in that fresh, naïve, charming, typically American way, radiating the energy of the New World and the vibrancy of its mighty show-business life. And yet, pulsating with brilliant personality, La Belle Menken still projected that absolutely essential quality of the star, the goddess made human, the irresistible allure of female vulnerability. It was, she said afterwards, the greatest curtain call of her career, and "no one may ignore it".

AN EX(BUS)HORSE-TIVE ARGUMENT.

Mazeppa:—"Now, just you bang that 'bus door smarter to-night, or the old hoss'll never get a good start."
Carpenter:—"All right, Miss. Cue's "wild career."   [*N.B.*—*The noble steed is an old "Favourite."*

Punch *was particularly scathing about Menken and cartoons like this one, which appeared in a short-lived Victorian magazine called* Fun, *were not rare.*

Nine

Enter La Belle Menken – the delicious corruption from America

IGNORED LA BELLE Menken was not. There were many laurels to add to her crowning wreath, provided she picked her way carefully through the critiques and reviews.

> John Oxenford of *The Times*: "The lady's costume is certainly not one that Queen Elizabeth would have recommended to her maids of honour, but certainly, also, it is not a whit more objectionable than those of the female Highland boys and mythological beauties who are now accepted as matters of course."

> E. L. Blanchard in the *Daily Telegraph*: "While it must be admitted that a considerable amount of a symmetrical figure is somewhat lavishly displayed, there would be an affectation of prudery in denouncing as an offence to decency what has not only escaped censure, but has provoked unstinted admiration at other theatres."

> *The Era*: "Miss Menken retains, of course, the tight fleshings which have been properly worn by previous 'Mazeppas', and for the usual dark brown half-bodice she has substituted loose folds of white linen which descend only slightly towards the knee, but leave the upper limbs no more delicately exposed than those of ballet and burlesque ladies who have seldom been accused of impropriety."

> *Punch* had reviewed the Menken in adverse (and appallingly bad) verse:
>
>> Here's half the town – if bills be true –
>> To Astley's nightly thronging,
>> To see "the Menken" throw aside
>> All to her sex belonging,

> Stripping off woman's modesty,
> With woman's outward trappings –
> A bare-backed jade on bare-backed steed,
> In Cartlich's old strappings!
>
> "Who lived to please" – no need on us
> That stale excuse for thrusting –
> There *is* a way to please one-tenth,
> The nine-tenths by disgusting.
> Your shame why let these bills, wherewith
>   You plaster London's wen, ken?
> "Bring forth the horse!" Yes, Mr. Smith,
>   But don't bring forth the Menken!

Subsequently Mark Lemon, *Punch*'s editor, decided to take up a Queen Victoria-like unamused position, and a further note appeared: "Mr Punch acknowledges the receipt of a pamphlet containing tolerant notice and vulgar puff of a Jewess who is attracting the least respectable portion of playgoers by an exhibition not quite so disgraceful as the pictures that invite them, but sufficiently vulgar and indecent to deserve such patronage ... He has no more to say upon an odious subject out of his jurisdiction."

H. B. Farnie, the great lover and custodian of public morals, joined Mr. Lemon in protecting the purity of the London public from the degradations of the "vulgar Jewess". He wrote in *The Orchestra*: "The applauding shouts that go up from an over-crowded house at every bold movement of the semi-nude actress prove that an insensitive public could stand a great deal more if it were there, and would like it to be there only too well ... We wonder if a lady – a lady in the true acceptation – would go a second time? ... The attraction ... lies undoubtedly in its impurity. People expect the voluptuous pictures scattered about London, and the voluptuous verses printed on the playbills, to be realized by the American actress, and they go for that purpose."

But even if there was, so far, a shortage of locally inspired "voluptuous verses", the "quick-witted" doggerel London prided itself on coining was not at all harmful to business:

> Lady Godiva's far outdone,
> And Peeping Tom's an arrant duffer;
>   Menken outstrips them both in one
> At Astley's – now the *Opera Buffer*.
> Poor ballet-girls! Of what avail
> Your pirouettes, once so refreshing?
>   You'll be compelled to take leg bail
> Unless you throw aside the fleshing!

The *London Review*: "Strictly measured by a dressmaker, or weighed in a pair of scales, her scanty costume would not perhaps prove more airy than that sometimes worn by daring ballet-dancers, but much depends upon the style and the way of wearing it. Miss Menken's figure is good and muscular, and as Mr. Smith has engaged her figure, she keeps to her contract in showing it. On horseback she looks like Lady Godiva in a shift ... the respectable audience ... of course go to see the spectacle and not Miss Menken's figure."

The Illustrated Times: "There is a sufficiently lavish revelation of feminine symmetry to warrant spectators in pronouncing the exhibition as extraordinary. The new appearance ... attitudinizes with great effect. Planche, in one of his wittiest extravagances, says of the *Poses Plastiques* that 'they are an endless exhibition; that their termination cannot be anticipated,

Since every day they're less inclined to clothes;
Group follows group, each has its brother,
Trying, the wags say, to outstrip the other.'"

The Queen, a highly respectable paper for ladies, was awfully put out: "It is not a sign of advancing refinement when a female horse-rider can attract by her being apparently put in a hazardous position and emulating the muscular power of a man. Verily the nineteenth century, though boastful of its delicacy, countenances some very coarse proceedings."

But on 22 October, after time for due consideration of the Menken–Mazeppa affair, the impeccable *Illustrated London News* published the following encyclical, as replete with inaccuracies as it was with good quotes for both Miss Menken and her London producer, Mr. E. T. Smith, and well worth reprinting in full for its encapsulation of who and what the world, at this stage of her game, thought Miss Menken was.

Dolores Adah Isaacs Menken was born in New Orleans, Louisiana, in the year of 1840, of French and Spanish parentage, and is of the Jewish religion. Her father, of whom we can learn very little, was exiled from France for political offences, it appears, and died during the early infancy of the subject of our memoir. Her stepfather, one Josiah Campbell, was a graduate of the Edinburgh University in Scotland, and a surgeon in the U.S. army, stationed for many years at the regular barracks of Baton Rouge, Louisiana. He was a gentleman of some attainments, and skilled as a surgeon and physician. He was the first to perceive that Adah was a gifted child, and he undertook her education with a love and patience which continued until his death, in 1855. In these years of study Adah mastered many languages, besides becoming thoroughly versed in the classics and mathematics. When only twelve years of age she translated Homer's "Iliad". After her stepfather's death the family became reduced to straitened circumstances. Her

COMPANIONS OF THE BA

SIG. MARIO.   MDLLE. PATTI.   MDLLE. NILSSON.   DION BOUCICAULT.   CHARLES READE.

GLADSTONE.   DISRAELI.   DEAN STANLEY.

SPURGEON. A. SWINBURNE. A. DUMAS.
           LONGFELLOW. TENNYSON.
MACKONOCHIE.   BISHOP OF OXFORD.

This Victorian cartoon of fashionable Le Havre, published August 1868, featured many of the luminaries of the period including Menken. The actress, seen to the right of the picture was described as clad "by way of variety" in "a costume for the seaside instead of the usual baseless fabric which leaves her reckless behind the scenes".

mother being of a poetic and erratic nature, could but poorly battle with the world alone. Adah knew she must do something, and, childlike, thought of the stage. By energy and perseverence she soon became a *danseuse*, having the exceeding good-luck to have had the benefit of the best masters of the French and Spanish schools. Her first appearance before the public was made at the French Opera House, in New Orleans, at the early age of fourteen years. She was *premiere danseuse* there for one whole season, and was admired and petted by the French population, and upon the occasion of her farewell benefit received many presents. She subsequently joined the Montplaiser Troupe, and went to Cuba, appearing at the Tacon Theatre, and attracted much attention there, and at various places of public amusement. She afterwards resolved to give up the stage and turn her energies to literature, and commenced by studying German, and reading classical authors with the best of masters. Music and painting were also among her studies. During this time she published a volume of poems called "Memories", under the signature of "Indigina", which gave promise of some fame to the youthful authoress, and induced her to speculate in a newspaper, which, with all due respect to the lady herself, was about as bold and daring a feat as that which she is now practising on the boards of Mr Smith's theatre at Lambeth. We are not informed whether her literary bantling was healthy or not, but we opine otherwise, for the lady returned to her native city and again became an actress, and, if American editors do not throw the hatchet as of old, it is no "American" to say she had plenty of admirers. The stage amused the fickle lady for a short time, but it was again abandoned, for she betook herself to Cincinnati, and became the principal contributor to a Jewish paper there. In April, 1859, she met John C. Heenan. Her marriage with the prize-fighter has been commented on by nearly every newspaper in the world. She was divorced from pugilist wedlock on the third day of April, 1862, in the city of Woodstock, McHenry county, State of Illinois, America. The sympathy of the American public, it is said, was greatly with Mrs Heenan. There were three sessions of the court before her cause was triumphant. This *trial* was closely followed by another – viz., the death of her mother; after whose demise she commenced her personation of Mazeppa at Albany, New York. This was in 1863. Her subsequent career in California stamps her performance of Mazeppa as really surprising, and although we do not go the length of some commentators in our praise, we are free to admit, from what we have personally witnessed of it, it is a surprising attempt. Talent is of no nation, and wherever we find it we are amongst the first to cherish and encourage it. We tell "the Menken", as she is affectedly styled across the Atlantic, that she decidedly has talent of a very high order. The novelty of a woman lashed half-naked to a wild horse, hurrying up rocks and down precipices, may attract for a temporary period, but she can do much more. We are of opinion that Mrs Heenan can *act* as well as *ride*. Let her have an original character similar to that in which Miss Bateman made her *début* – ten to one she will then fairly earn and retain an enviable fame. We are writing advisedly, and whether we offend or please, the public will never find man, woman, or child elevated above their proper level in the pages of this journal. Whatever praises may have been lavished on Mrs Heenan by the admirers of her foolhardiness and the panegyrists of her person, some value will ever be attached to the correct judgment of a critic who does not suffer himself to be led away by the momentary impulse of feeling, or dazzled by the too brilliant effect of womanly beauty; who is as ice when discharging a public duty, and even in the midst of the loudest peals of approval can stoically point out a little to censure as well as much to applaud. Mrs Heenan possesses qualities which have been individually the privilege of very few, and which, perhaps, collectively were never before, nor ever can be, united in so extraordinary a degree in one person. Mr E. T. Smith deserves well of the British public for engaging such an *artiste*. With such a one Astley's this season must prove a most successful speculation.

Final approval of La Belle Menken came from an anonymous cockney curb-side jingle-writer who, knowing well dirty old London's secret inclinations behind its moralistic face, jingled away merrily:

> Behind a cab-horse,
> Beyond Charing Cross;
> To see Miss Mazeppa
> Ride on a wild horse.
> *Rien* on her figure
> As everyone knows –
> She should have rough music,
> Wherever she goes.

Miss Menken didn't mind. Her style of riding required "rough music"; in fact she loved the London tune. As she had suddenly realised, she told her countless new friends and admirers, she had always been, in her deepest self, a Londoner.

While Adah Menken, like all artistes, needed endless love and admiration from the public, and expected its professional voices, the journalists and reviewers, to express that love constantly, experience had taught her that some critics, protecting their reputations for being different, would have to resist conceding how great a star was A. I. Menken. But she knew the celebrity-creating machine better than any of them. Menken realised very well that an H. B. Farnie was, in his small way, a performer like herself, with an act to maintain. The absurdity of his comments on the "impurity" of her *Mazeppa* and its danger to a city in which the population of prostitutes of both sexes available between Pall Mall and Leicester Square nightly was several thousands, was hardly to be taken seriously. Paris had the gay and naughty reputation, but London's middle-class *Punch*-reading gentlemen were serviced by an incredible number of brothels, bordellos and houses of assignation, which catered for genteel erotic tastes, ranging from homosexual flagellation (a favourite with cultural roots deeply established in England's magnificent public school system), to the purchasing of very young girls, guaranteed virgins; for virginity was still considered by many gentlemen to be a sure cure for syphilis, and the importation of young girls was a major trade with Ireland, the English industrial areas and the Continent. St. John's Wood, an expensive district nowadays much populated by sheiks and dominated by a great mosque, was, in the sixties, a charming enclave of little villas, many of them housing kept women.

Adah knew well that in all middle-class societies the crime of vice lies not in committing it, but in being caught doing so. True, she quite openly exploited the erotic with her notorious "strip scene" and her pseudo-naked ride, but she did also sing, dance and perform in a uniquely personal way; she also wrote not much worse poetry and occasionally better prose than many respectable professional literati. Furthermore, she consistently protested, with vigour and courage to the dimly awakening awareness of a few of the most intelligent and talented women in the world, that their status and treatment in a totally male-dominated society was that of an entirely exploited sexual slave-class. Adah always reserved the right not to conceal her religion, whether she was born to it or had perversely adopted the least popular of monotheisms. Of all the tirades and prejudices expressed by the more snobbish gentlemen of the British press, the enmity of those like *Punch*, who dismissed her, not for her work, or for her eroticism (there were other stage-ladies who offered similar spectacles), but for being "a vulgar Jewess", offended her most. On the other hand she found Farnie, one of whose own plays she knew to have been denounced as "the most vulgar, the most debased and the most deplorable work yet presented to the British public", both funny and preposterous in his role of custodian of the morals of middle-class society. She recognised that he was merely protecting his own rear from the boots of other more highly-bred moral bullies, and responded by offering *The Orchestra* a poem in praise of Adelina Patti. Farnie published it without for a moment suspending his campaign to defend London from the depraved incitements of Menken's voluptuousness.

Adah also accepted that E. T. Smith had his profits (and her share of them), to make, by whatever publicising means was most effective with the English public. When during the week of the Cattle Show, he suggested additional matinees and advertised them to visiting farmers as their only opportunity to see "the saucey wench in tights", she was quite undismayed. It was not her concern if Smith decided to encourage the public to believe that her *Mazeppa* was a bordello charade. She considered his adverts to be full of typically English humour, not too dissimilar from the bad jokes in *Punch*:

> Important Notice to Invalids: A double-bedded room at Astley's Theatre at 7 o'clock. Dr Samuel Emery (*Menken's supporting actor*) in attend-

ance to prescribe. Boxes, to cure all complaints, can be had at the office. Miss Menken's Cream of Tartar Blister draws the million at 8 o'clock. All cured and sent home by 11 p.m.

Menken knew that such vulgar notoriety came along with more acceptable compliments such as the *Mazeppa Waltz*, played by the Guards Band at Crystal Palace and quickly picked up by the street musicians; and the *Mazeppa Galop*, an immediately popular dance, as well as a comic pantomime satire on her called *The Cream of Tartar*. She collected avidly the popular jingles and such comic songs as *The Latest News*:

> Here you are! Here you are!
> Morning papers, just come out –
> Great sensation! Conflagration!
> Latest death through crinoline!
> Adah Menken in *Mazeppa*
> Sweetest woman ever seen!

All this, and the jokes of the music-hall comedians were an essential part of what theatrical fame was (and is still) about. Yet Menken longed for acceptance by the English she admired, the poets, writers, artists and Bohemians who made London, for her, the great cultural centre of the world.

At Astley's it was understood that Miss Menken was to be informed in the interval if "anyone was in the house" on any particular night. She would then issue invitations to whoever among the visitors she felt, either for reasons of social or cultural prestige, she ought to meet. Backstage at Astley's, after the performance, she received the chosen in the parlour of her dressing-room suite, where there was a glass of champagne for almost anyone who was, had been, or might, in the future, become someone. It was an expensive form of public relations which she had utilised effectively in America, and which, she thought, could do her reputation no harm in London. Her serious salon, however, was to be conducted in her suite at the Westminster Palace Hotel. To the Westminster were invited only those whose talents she admired, the intellectuals whose acceptance she never ceased to crave.

Rumours circulated about wild nights in the Menken's suite but, although many of the distinguished men who visited her would have had no objection whatsoever to becoming lovers, Adah was far too skilled in such matters to allow intimacies normally to proceed beyond the point which she considered to be perfectly acceptable between Bohemian friends. A fellow actor, James Fernandez, had the temerity to take a bet to pinch her thigh in the course of the performance one night, in order to assess whether or not it was padded (a common practice among actresses with skinny legs). He received, in the middle of the scene, a

THEATRE ROYAL, ASTLEY'S.

13 Night _Saturday_, 2nd day of November 1867

Miss Menken's Engagement

	ACCOUNT.						
	DOORS.						
3	Private Boxes				3	13	6
	Seats in ditto						
2	Transfers from ... to				1	2	
46	STALLS		5/-		11	10	
	Transfers from Upper Circle	3/6					
	,, ,, Pit	4/-					
	,, ,, Boxes	3/-					
12	,, ,, Balcony	2/-			1	4	
87	BALCONY		3/-		13	1	
11	Transfers from Pit	2/-				2	
	,, ,, Upper Circle	1/6					
13	,, ,, Boxes	1/-				13	
123	BOXES		2/-		12	6	
	Transfers from Gallery	1/6					
16	,, ,, Pit	1/-				16	
22	,, ,, Upper Circle	-/6				11	
208	_child to Stall_ UPPER CIRCLE	1/6			15	12	6
	Transfers from Gallery	1/-					
15	,, ,, Pit	-/6				7	6
102	PIT		1/-		5	7	
13	Transfers from Gallery	-/6				6	6
819	GALLERY		-/6		20	9	6
	BOX OFFICE.					133	3	6
2	Private Boxes				4	4	.
15	Stalls				3	15	.
34	Balcony				5	2	
	Boxes				13	15	
	Less Commission					12	16
	Total				12	16	145	19	6

W. H. Swanborough

The popularity of Menken's performances at Astley's is confirmed by the above revenue account.

sharp blow from her neat little whip. It was a caution for which many gentlemen in the audience would have paid dearly, but in the Palace (as her hotel was called), there was never any necessity for her to resort to such chastising devices for those who broke protocol. The invitees there were all fellow-artists, amused and curious enough to attend the lavish parties which were the nightly court of La Belle Menken.

It was a costly performance but the Menken was always entirely reckless with her money. She felt that generosity and extravagance were obligatory upon the artistic *noblesse* among whom she considered herself to be a royal personage. The preface to a pirated edition of her poems in 1888 commented that, "with all her faults she was a noble creature; her generosity was unparalleled. She squandered money recklessly... The attachés at the theatre, men, women, and children, were her beneficiaries, and even in the streets she would thrust handfuls of silver, or rolls of bills, in the hands of strangers... No one cared less for money and had her income been a thousand dollars a minute, she would have been poor at the end of an hour." Allowing for the understandably warm exaggerations of an editor and publisher pirating her work without having to pay royalties, the image projected is not entirely a theatrical fiction. The successful artist often does, like a compulsive gambler, offer the beneficences of the Bitch Goddess back to her as a votive and a challenge. Her best-beloved will always be protected by her, believes the true chancer, feeling himself to be the special darling of Lady Luck, one whom she will never entirely desert. Menken had this compulsion to gamble with her good fortune. On the other hand, she was shrewd enough to know that luck never suffered from being well-supported by the important and influential people whom, she believed, she was making into her friends.

By December, when due to an advance pantomime booking, E. T. Smith had to wind up the *Mazeppa* season, Adah had personally met, drunk with, talked to, been propositioned by, laughed and formulated grand future plans of one sort or another with an amazing number of those who mattered in London life. The show was still doing extraordinarily well considering the length of the run, though business was faltering a little. Smith had, on Menken's suggestion (for she had, once again, become involved in spiritualist experiments, this time with the infamous fakers, the Davenport Brothers), added to the bill one Signor Sigismund Redmond, a "spirit conjuror", who, when tied in a sack and locked in a chest, was still able to produce a cacophony of invisible tambourines and bells. But *Mazeppa* was running its course in spite of a little assistance from the spirits. Adah didn't mind too much. The season had brought her what was, for those times, an unprecedented and unequalled income of which, in spite of her extravagances, she still had a good deal in hand. Estimates varied greatly, but her earnings were conservatively assessed to have been no less than five thousand pounds, and some said as much as ten, for her six-month season. Many insisted, knowingly, that she had earned the same amount and more, by quietly bestowing special favours upon non-literary gentlemen who were never part of her Westminster Palace salon. It seems unlikely, for Menken was earning more money than even she could spend; furthermore, she knew very well, from her long and varied experience of the vicissitudes of theatrical ladies, that once one began whoring, it was difficult to keep the clients at bay, and the public's respect. In any case, she had started an affair with the gallant gambling gentleman who was to become her last husband, the handsome Captain Barkley. But for the present the liaison was conducted with the greatest discretion, for too obviously serious an affair with one gentleman would have discouraged too many others. Menken knew that men lose their spring without a little of the eternal hope left burning in their breasts. So, for the time being, Captain Barkley was to be seen as simply another admiring occasional escort.

It would have taken a very high level of whoring indeed to equalise Adah's earning capacity at this time as an actress, approximately a hundred pounds an appearance, when the future Dame Madge Kendal was playing Ophelia for ten pounds a week at the Haymarket, and the great Ellen Terry was considered highly paid at a flat hundred pounds a week. Adah was no Cora Pearl, avid for money for its own sake. She needed lots of it to spend, but had always believed that if an artiste was forced by miserable circumstances to prostitute herself, she had better make sure that she did it secretly.

Mazeppa was always a demanding role and Adah longed for a rest from it. From time to time her understudy, Ada Murray, was allowed to take over, but only at matinees, with, incredibly, an actor disguised as Menken substituted for the final sequence. One can only assume that the matinee audiences had become either too small or too drunk to notice such details. Now she wanted to make a short visit to Paris she told Smith. She wrote to Ed James, two days after *Mazeppa* closed on 17 December; "I assure you, I was very near 'used up'. I have really, however, only a few days, for I commence rehearsals of the new piece next week after Christmas. It is fondly expected by my manager that I open about the middle of February. But I shall wait a little longer if I can. I should like to run off to Paris two weeks for a 'lark'. I'll try it."

Menken would carry with her to Paris introductions to important people from her friend Charles Fechter, the matinee idol who was a star in France, America and England. His imperious disposition and her "Cleopatra in crinoline" character had hit it off together from their first meeting, and it was, of course, rumoured that they had had an affair. If they did, it is a pity there is no material available concerning it, for it would have been tempestuous and amusing. Through friend Fechter she hoped, in the course of her short "lark" in Paris, to meet Gautier and Dumas Père, his good friends, and to assess the possibilities the Paris theatre had to offer her. In the meantime, John Brougham, an American actor and a copious if undistinguished dramatist, was working on a piece devised as a vehicle for her. Called *The Children of the Sun*, it would incorporate the most

Menken, described as "Cleopatra in a crinoline", when searching for Swinburne (who was avoiding her).

successful elements of *Mazeppa* while being less exhausting as a role. Smith had seen the first draft and was very doubtful about it. While Brougham re-wrote it, a lark in Paris was just the thing to keep the actress occupied. Personally Smith thought a more sensible procedure in the New Year would be to exploit the enormous London success of *Mazeppa* by touring it in the provinces. Why bother to put together an unproven new piece when the wild steed of Tartary was waiting in the wings to bear them both into snow-storms of bank-notes? Adah departed for Paris happy to leave boring business decisions in Smith's hands.

In Paris Adah soon discovered that the Théâtre Porte St. Martin was interested in booking her, but not until autumn. "I am flooded with people and letters and still urging on my wild career", she wrote to James, reporting a long interview with Théophile Gautier who, she said, had agreed to write a play for her after they had worked together on a suitable synopsis. The play never materialised, and meeting Dumas Père also was to be a pleasure deferred, but Gautier sensibly advised her to seek the support of Dante Gabriel Rossetti in London for the publication of her poems. Deciding that Paris was definitely a lark to be renewed extensively Menken returned to London refreshed and ready for *The Children of the Sun*, to discover that, through the pantomime season, a whole crop of imitation Mazeppas had sprung up like toadstools.

The cheaper theatres and music-halls were all offering *Mazeppa*-style entertainments, starring ladies who had no cultural or poetic hesitation whatsoever about stripping, and they all purported to be Menkens, only more so. One called herself Adah Inez Montclain; another simply insisted that she was the "London Adah Isaacs". The Pavilion, Whitechapel, produced a cockney Mazeppa, and the City of London Theatre advertised, "The Beautiful Menken, together with her celebrated steed, Ada". There was also a "Rose Menken" who was doing quite well. E. T. Smith and Adah Isaacs Menken issued a solemn warning to the public: "Managers are cautioned to be on their guard against individuals describing themselves as 'The Beautiful Menken', whose unparalleled success in her classical delineation of 'Mazeppa' has induced unscrupulous imitators to adopt the title everywhere accorded the greatest living exponent of the poet's ideal." Apparently imitators were also taking over the business she had created all over America. She wrote to James warning him: "I presume some of the army of 'Mazeppas' have captured you. Let them beware! If they are worthy of my steel, let them remember that I wear a sword – and can use it too! ... one new Mazeppa here, Charlotte Wyette, a stock actress, made a dreadful failure. She was so intoxicated that she fell down in the last act. None of the papers took notice of her but to comment on the disgrace of her state. She is now at the lowest theatre in London, worse than a Lager beer saloon."

The Menken-Mazeppa vogue had passed into that distressing, but inevitable phase of success, of which endless imitation is the dreadfully unprofitable proof. John Brougham's vehicle was desperately needed. A reading was arranged and Adah wrote: "My good friend, the great Fechter is to be present at the reading of my new piece, and is to make suggestions suited to my talent. I can not tell you how kind F. has been to me. He has conducted all my Paris engagements, and made me out a great creature to the French press. Chas. Dickens has also aided me with advice and encouragement as to my appearance in Paris." *The Children of the Sun*, in spite of Fechter's suggestions, was still a poor piece, and in the end Adah and Smith opted for the provincial tour.

The tour was to open in Glasgow where the company manager John McKenna advised her against kicking over the traces too violently. He wasn't too sure of the local citizens' response to Menken's bare legs. She pointed out that she revealed not much more than they did in their kilts and went on regardless. She also pointed out that she had had great triumphs in Albany where the Scottish element was strong, and she had always found that Celts responded strongly to the poetry of her work. Nevertheless, Glasgow was restricted to a tentative week, but Menken's assessment proved right after all. The *Glasgow Herald* saw "in her graceful acrobatics evidence of careful study and cultivated taste". A further week was played to the appreciative Scottish city. And then on to Liverpool, where the Menken left her card and photograph with the Lord Mayor. The local amphitheatre was crowded, the public adored her, business was excellent but the press proved unfriendly except for the *Daily Post* who recommended Menken's figure, beauty and talent to all, assuring ladies, "that they had not the least occasion to look knowing or agitate their fans". But the local literary paper, *The Porcupine*, was appalled that the citizens of Liverpool should so lack self-respect "as to fall to an adroit appeal to their baser instincts". *The Albion* was even more upset. It had never liked Americana anyway, and the Menken was beyond everything:

> America has sent us many things for which we have had little reason to thank her – Spiritualism, Mormonism, Barnumism, Davenportism, and a host of outrageously bad actors, but *La Menken* surpasses and transcends all in utter worthlessness.
>
> It bodes an evil day for society in England, when it must be recorded that the theatre has been crammed to suffocation every evening during the past week by crowds of well-dressed people, a great number of whom had evidently gone with the hope of gratifying a prurient taste, and gloating over a nudeness passing the bounds of propriety, heralded beforehand, but in which propriety has no existence ... The exhibition is as low as it can well be.

Still, the heavy cash-box from the front office offered Menken and her managers some compensation, and the show galloped on to Birmingham. There the press were disappointed that Adah wasn't naked enough, for, as a rest from *Mazeppa*, she played her other standard pieces, *The French Spy* and *Black-Eyed Susan*, in the latter wearing trousers, which shocked some locals as much as bare legs. While in Birmingham she sat for the famous photographer Napoleon Sarony, who briefly kept a studio there before moving to New York (where he again photographed Menken). For him she flashed her thousand dollar sable coat and other costumes in stylish poses. It all helped Mr. Swanborough, who had booked her into his theatre, to make up heavy losses he had sustained in the past, producing high-class dramatic entertainments; so the Menken had the satisfaction of contributing to local culture both ways round.

The tour went on to Leeds, the best and surest date of all. There financial success was unparalleled, with every evening house and matinee packed to capacity. But again some of the newspapers were rude about one thing or another, and now the Menken seemed unusually bothered by them. When McKenna pointed out that it mattered little what the critics said, for the business was excellent, Adah, edgy and bored, fired him, terminated the tour, and returned to London, and the latest "Prince in her Life" whom she had left there.

A drawing of Astley's. c. 1840s/1850s.

Ten

Enter Mrs. Newell – with a Prince of Gamblers

Menken's only serious lover throughout her first London season was the gallant "Captain" James Paul Barkley, the elegant, handsome, wealthy, and somewhat mysterious Southern gentleman who had first turned his cool, imperturbable, gambler's gaze upon Adah as she took the air on the deck of the transatlantic liner bearing her to her European destiny. Menken was convinced that, like her model Lola Montez, the divine plan for her involved Europe, probably with close liaisons, if not actual morganatic marriages, with princes. She was thrillingly aware of the possibilities of an affair with Barkley, and highly attracted by his looks and style, very much those of Bret Harte's gambling gentleman Jack Hamlin, a typical Western hero-figure, with an approach both strong and tender, cool and passionate, a natural wooer, but always with the threat of a derringer in his coat-tail. But for the moment the Menken's destiny had no great part to offer even an apparently immensely wealthy sporting gentleman in her present production plans. He was, though, much on her mind, and the normally restrained Menken scholar Lesser permits himself some unusually imaginative liberties based upon his interpretation of some of her enthusiastic letters mentioning the gallant Captain. Lesser feels convinced that their affair began, in spite of Menken's wise counsels to herself, on board ship. He may well be right, for Menken was a firm believer in, and sometimes even a seeker after, what the French call with gallic excitement and science, the *coup de foudre* style of love-affair, the stroke of lightning which ignites an instant flame of passion. Lesser waxes romantically:

> At first she had made him keep a proper distance, but each day as they walked sedately around the deck she had felt her resistance weakening. James Paul Barkley was his name, and his sharp features and soft brown hair, the southern drawl in his voice, haunted her every moment she was away from him. Once she moaned and talked in her sleep until her maid-companion

woke her to ask if anything were wrong. Afterward she lay awake thinking about him, wondering if she really was falling in love again.

The next night as she stood at the rail with Barkley, watching the water rush past the prow of the ship, she learned the answer. He was talking about himself, about the boyhood he had spent in Tennessee. When the war broke out, he had helped recruit a company for the Confederate Army and been commissioned a captain for his efforts. During a skirmish with some Union scouts one night, a ball had broken his leg. After the wound had healed he had gone off to California to make his fortune. Mining stocks, he grinned, had paid off better than prospecting or gambling with cards and now he was a rich man.

In the silence that followed, his hand sought hers. This was the moment to go, she told herself, to utter a pleasantry that would break the tension and permit her to escape. Instead she waited, her muscles rigid, the blood pounding in her veins like the throb of the ship's engines. She felt herself drawn to him, held so tightly she could hardly breathe while his ardent words wove a spell of enchantment about her. For a moment she held his strong face in her hands, her dark-blue eyes fearfully searching his. Slowly her lips yielded to his kiss, and then as she gripped him in a frenzy of passion she knew.

It was nearly dawn when she left his cabin. As she tiptoed down the corridor to her own room, she smiled inwardly at the irony of a situation that forced her to be discreet. She who had always flouted conventions now feared them lest they rob her of the man to whom she had pledged her life. He had asked her to divorce Newell and marry him, but she had firmly refused. Their love was the only bond she would recognise; this time there would be no marriage to crush it under the weight of rigid social forms.

Well, such magic did happen in the long days and nights of transatlantic dream-time, and a passionate, full-blooded affair was certainly something Menken needed at this moment, for nothing would have made her feel more inclined to success than a good sharp *coup*. But Barkley was under strict instructions to keep himself in the background in London, and though he could be in attendance at her salons and dinner-parties (for there was safety in numbers and their secret could be deliciously shared in public), he was to be very discreet. Nevertheless, he took rooms adjacent to hers in the Westminster Palace Hotel, and though he kept himself out of the gossip-columns, it must have been well-observed that the wealthy American gentleman was a serious contestant for the star's intimate attentions. But then, who wasn't? The Menken was beseiged by the famous, the wealthy, and the aristocratic, and she conducted herself with such refreshing American spontaneity that it was generally assumed that she maintained as large a stud of performing males as she did of horses.

Only one of her associates suspected the truth of the depth of her involvement with Barkley; her "brother", and oldest friend, agent, publicist, and fixer-general, Ed James. James was trying hard to get to England, where he might share in the heady atmosphere of Menken's success for which he had worked so hard for so long with so little return, apart from friendship and the occasional "sisterly" kiss. He was hoping to come over for the *Clipper* to report the American pugilist Joe Coburn's forthcoming title-fight. Coburn had, apparently, called unexpectedly on the Menken, and discovered her with Barkley, whose presence was perfectly explicable, of course, even at breakfast, in Bohemian circles, if explanations were called for from a lady who generally observed the principle of never excusing, and never explaining her behaviour. Still, it *was* somewhat suggestive, and it seemed likely that Coburn would report his observations to James. For some reason, the Bengal Tigress Menken felt a wife-daughter type of fear that James might suspect and disapprove of the affair. She over-explained the situation, and instantly told James all by so doing:

> I am very much afraid that Joseph (Coburn) misunderstood me in speaking of a certain gentleman that he met at my rooms. I have since believed that J.C. thought there to be an undue intimacy existing. I only joked J.C. about the gentleman but as he did not return to see me and did not write, I think he made the mistake I allude to. He may even have said something in his letters to you of it. But I assure you it was all a mistake on Joseph's part. Of course I intend to tell him so but as that is very uncertain I thought I would tell you.

Menken realised at once that she had given the game away, and felt, even at such a distance, the sullen disapproval of her "brother", whose good thoughts were always essential to her. James' silence worried her, and soon she was writing to him again:

> I can not imagine why you are so slow.
> Have you a new Love? "Be off with the old love before you are on with the new" is an adage to be remembered by you. Besides I am not to be thrown off at all. I still adhere to first principles.

The letter is interesting, for it demonstrates, perhaps, the old observation that a man may only have a close friendship with a woman who is a former lover. Had Menken and James been lovers in the early days of their association? We cannot know, but affairs between starlets and elder Pygmalions are not exactly uncommon in the politics of show-business. Menken certainly now carried on as if nervous of losing the friendship of a most important old lover. When she finally heard from James, warmly, that he would be arriving imminently and longed to see her, she rhapsodised:

> I shall see you on Thursday, Friday, or Saturday, and then if you are tired of kissing the picture you shall kiss me. How will that do? But you need

not give up the picture, for you can kiss that as often as you like, and you can only kiss me once.

Now that James had come to heel he was, of course, awarded the little tame circus dog role again: one kiss and a new photograph to gnaw upon. But one may presume that he was well-used to the Menken's style by now, and accepted it. What is puzzling, in view of the fact that he knew her well enough to realise that she did not tend to go in for long periods of sexual abstinence, is his disapproval of this particular lover.

Now Ed James knew the American world of gamblers and other sports extremely well, and in spite of Menken's assurances to him that "you cannot imagine how J.B. likes you. He has been looking for a letter from you very anxiously", and her constant attempts to make the two men friends (Barkley being not at all disinclined), James continued surly and suspicious, keeping for the first time in their long relationship, distant from Menken. The reasonable conclusion must be that James knew much more about the gallant, handsome, extravagant captain, than did Menken, and considered him to be "not sound". Barkley may have been a respectable "broker" and "bond-dealer" for the moment, able to lavish jewels upon James' great creation, the Mazeppa of the Western World, but a gambler is always a gambler and, in the end, they are all losers. James made no secret of his conviction that, however suitable Barkley might be as a principal courtier and elegant bed-fellow, he was not to be regarded by his adored "sister" as anything more serious than that. For James knew to his great cost that always within the reckless Bohemian Menken lived on the little romantic middle-class girl from the South-West, Bertha Theodore, who still believed that true love should lead to marriage, in spite of the fact that one might mistake the path two or three times in a few years of searching for it. Menken too, knew very well little Bertha's silly romantic propensities, and apologised for her to James:

> I'll tell you how it is, old fellow, sometimes I am afraid I neglect you, and for that my conscience will not let me sleep the "sleep of the just". I hope you will try to justify any little seeming neglect on my part; for I mean to do everything that is right, pleasant and proper. But know what hell is said to be paved with. I believe that I am a very large shareholder in that pavement. I would like to sell out. But so many wretches have invested largely in the same stock that I fear it will be rather difficult to find a victim.

The language, James might have observed, reflected the ideas of the con-man upon whom she was wasting herself. To appease James' doubts about Barkley, Menken invented absurdities. "He is the best man that ever breathed in God's World", she wrote. "I have known him intimately for *fourteen years*. He was my child ideal", she lied shamelessly. She wanted so much for the two men to be friends when they both returned to New York, leaving her, relievedly, to fulfil her destiny in Europe. Together they could, perhaps, protect her against the avenging husbands of the past, concerning whose imagined activities Menken was becoming quite paranoid. She urged James to keep an eye on poor old Newell, who was rapidly sinking into obscurity after his brief fame as the satirist of the Civil War. "Pray keep me posted about him," she requested James. "He means mischief." Her hectic imagination saw all her previous husbands fighting duels over her, or plotting to damage her great destiny. When Heenan turned up in London she went to extraordinary lengths to entertain him, even encouraging his vanity to believe that he was still the world-champion in her love-life; and she loaned him unspecified sums of money as well. She still had night-fears about the undying enmity of her first husband, the original Menken. Was he not still full of rancour and plotting against her? Projecting her own hostility, hatred and fears, upon all her previous husbands, she begged James, the one man in her life she had successfully converted into a protective "brother", to look out for her. "Be my guardian angel," she begged him. "I have no friend to confide in but you. The 'Prince' is my *heart's blood*. If you love me, as I believe you do, write me everything and keep your eyes open for my sake." The "Prince", of course, was the promoted Barkley, whose actual captaincy had always been a matter of some doubt in a period in which almost any Westerner or South-Westerner was, at least, a courtesy colonel.

Yet for all her anti-male paroxysms Menken would listen to no word against her current "Prince". She worked up sheer terrors over Newell and the rest, but Barkley and James were the best men in the world, and must be "brothers" to one another, regardless of the rather fundamental difference in their relationships with her. Meanwhile, Newell, who had never recovered from his tour with Menken, was trying to make a quiet living as a respectable literary journalist, fighting growing word-blindness and cramp, and drifting into the obscurity of his last dreaming years of life, still unable to forget Menken's desertion of him:

> Sinister e'en was the gleam she (the moon) threw
>   Over the carpet there at my feet,
> When, from my bosom, my own wife flew,
>   Out of the window into the street . . .
>
> Yes, it is said that my tears were few;
>   Said that I whistled and sang that week;
> Let them believe it if they think it true,
>   Little care I for the words they speak.

Even when he died years later in 1901, in miserable lonely circumstances, Newell was still wondering in his poetry and his unfinished autobiographical novel, what had hit him that night when he so coolly and critically watched *Mazeppa* open on Broadway. As for Heenan, in truth he was purchasable, as he always had been, with a joke and a drink; and Alexander Menken was lost deep in drink and the dry-goods business, flinching every time he saw his name appear in a theatrical context. One or two other men who, from time to time, captured a little press attention by claiming that they were early Menken husbands were broken, derelict ghost-ships of the past, compared with the Menken now in full sail, and destined, Ed James knew only too well, for the dubious haven of yet another marriage.

When Barkley returned to London in October 1865, the Menken had taken a fine house, 255 Brompton Road, furnished it in royal style, and was keeping court there day and night. Among her courtiers were numerous gentlemen who seemed to Barkley to be claiming liberties which were not entirely "sisterly", while his own claims upon Adah were reciprocated with a little less spontaneous passion than in the past. He was particularly jealous of Heenan, unable to understand why the Menken allowed the drunken giant liberties and gave him support and encouragement. She heavily romanticised her old affair with "Lord Carmel", as she now tended to call the former boxer, and Barkley began to suspect that perhaps an occasional replay of Anthony and Cleopatra was going on. He totally failed to recognise that Menken was merely trying to keep Heenan sweet, friendly and dumb before the press, and her great new friends. Barkley had the temerity to lose his gambler's coolness and show jealousy; he committed the heinous sin of distrusting the nobility of Menken's ever-faithful soul (though it was the antics of her vigorous body which truly disturbed him). They argued and fell out, and Heenan imagined, for a moment, that he could get back into Menken's life and fortune. But Menken had plenty of real and rich lords to choose from if she wanted to improve on her princely captain. Heenan never stood a chance, even when he tried to prove to Menken that he still loved her, by shipping his mistress, Sarah Stevens, back to California. But he at least convinced her that, "the dear boy is very kind, very fond of me. He would give his life to serve me." It provided Menken with a delicious vengeful pleasure, of which Barkley need not have been jealous:

> There is only one love to one life, *she wrote*. Carmel would die for me tomorrow. But it is too late. He has been the ruin of what might have been a splendid life. It was he who taught me to disbelieve in man; it was he who made me callous and unfeeling. I can never be what I once was to him, truthful, pure and good. He destroyed a beautiful and bountiful nature. He seeks to revive that which is dead. Now Ed, it is my turn to inflict suffering.

She remembered the times in New York, the loss of her baby, Heenan's desertion of her, and her symbolic suicide in New Jersey, and enjoyed her moment of revenge enormously.

I do not mean to hurt the only man I ever really loved, but I can not help it. It is too late. I do not tell him all of myself, for when he is with me the old dead power comes up, and I am silent and let him talk of his love and the reward he thinks he can bring me in his devotion and conscious faith. I know he is now true, but – too late. I can not believe again. He killed me – I died. There is no *resurgam*. I can not tear the bandage from my dead eyes even to say: "You crucified me." He knows it, but he hopes. Alas!

Having reduced Heenan to the lowest level of empty hope, Menken now felt like a satiated Bengal tigress. She paid him off, and by the end of the year he was out of England, returned as damaged goods to his waiting mistress, the ordinary little Miss Stevens. And that was to be his destiny, until a heart attack k.o.'d him in 1873 on the way to search, yet again, for a fortune in California.

Menken was keeping court, romancing, lying, and loving in Paris, when she heard that Captain Barkley was seriously ill in New York. She at once returned to London, instructed her English agent Pender to sell off her house, her carriage crested with the four aces which were her armorial insignia, her horses, and to find good homes for her dogs, with whom she had often been photographed, showing them in worshipping male positions, begging, as she raised her whip. She would return at once to the great love of her life in the city which had made her famous. She arrived there on 23 March, 1866, to find the old brownstone ablaze with welcoming lights, re-furbished and waiting for her, complete with a miraculously recovered, attractively pale Captain Barkley, who took her rapid return to be a clear acceptance of his endless proposals of marriage. But Menken wasn't ready for yet another production of that dangerous old show of hers. Though she allowed Barkley to be host at the lavish dinners and salons she held at Bleak House, as she amusingly dubbed her splendidly equipped brownstone, she expertly avoided committing herself to a contract or a date.

At Bleak House Menken entertained her New York friends and their wives and lovers, James, Gus Daly, Frank Queen, Colonel Browne, and Ada Clare, still one of the few women-friends she had ever made. The brownstone became the court of New York's Bohemia. Famous faces from politics and finance attended her dinners, and the whole town acknowledged that Adah Menken was America's first great international star. They were all very proud of her for it, and agents and managers called to see if they could make a profit on that pride. But Menken's price, $500 per performance, scared all of them away, except for George Wood who managed the Broadway Theatre. Menken signed a contract with him for twenty-four performances for a guaranteed $12,000. The production, naturally, would be *Mazeppa*, and the rumour was spread that just to make it worth what it was costing and to freshen up the appeal of the play, Menken would perform the notorious final sequence stark naked. It was all the additional publicity, along with her European reputation, that the short season needed to be a sell-out. Not to disappoint her public, Menken accompanied by ten grooms and the trainer of

An extract of a letter to Gus Daly, showing Menken's florid style of writing.

Black Bess, daily rode a white stallion around Central Park, to the applause of the crowds. The *Sunday Mercury* observed drily, that on these occasions Menken would, they presumed, continue to wear clothes.

The Broadway Theatre was sold out days ahead, with additional seating and standing room at premium prices. People even stood on the window sills, and Menken entered to enormous applause from one of the largest audiences ever to pack a theatre. She received thunderous rounds for virtually anything she did, each brilliant glance she threw the audience delighted, and she was awarded a standing ovation on the final curtain. The press agreed with the applause, except for one or two boring critics, who objected to her very personal style, delivery and pronunciation; especially the sour William Winter of the *Tribune*, who attacked her as, "a woman who would exhibit herself in public, in a condition closely bordering upon nudity", although he admitted that her "physical proportions were, in many respects, beautiful". But he found her elocution bad and concluded that she has not the "faintest idea of what acting is". Winter even hated the audience, describing the really rather distinguished throng as, "the coarsest and most brutal assembly that we have ever chanced to see at a theater on

Broadway. Every variety of dissolute life was represented in it. The purple nose, the scorbutic countenance, the glassy eye, the bull-head, the heavy lower jaw, the aspect of mingled lewdness and ferocity – all was there ... Old sports were abundant. The atmosphere fairly reeked with vulgarity." He concluded his somewhat slanted review by warning the decent to stay away: "the appearance of Miss Menken's *Mazeppa* in the Theater at Broadway is nothing less than a grievous discredit to the acted drama in this metropolis." But everyone knew that Winter was mentally disordered by Adah's "physical proportions", and his vilification of both her and the citizenry of New York did nothing to damage her business or improve his reputation. Neither could her old enemy Wilkes, commenting in his paper that, "she is best *on* the mare and the worst off that I have ever seen or expect to see", have the least effect upon her any more.

In spite of all the good notices and the support of the people of New York, Menken confessed herself "sad and depressed" by Winter's comments. "I am merely overwhelmed and grieved and discouraged. I know the article to be unjust and created through a petty personal spite." She was equally annoyed with the instant imitations which were staged to cash in on her business. Her old rivals, Mr. and Mrs. Barney Williams, tried to undermine her at the Winter Garden, and at the Mechanic's Hall on Broadway, a burlesque was staged of her show which was heavily funny and unrestrainedly vulgar.

Throughout the tensions of the New York season the affair with Barkley gathered momentum and, then, suddenly, on the night after her benefit performance at the Broadway, Menken collapsed, physically exhausted. She remained unconscious for two days, but after the ministrations of four physicians her vitality returned. Two weeks later she gave another special performance at the Broadway, "for the stage manager's benefit". This, her last professional appearance on a New York stage, was a typical act of generosity. It endeared her even more to the open-hearted New Yorkers, already mighty proud of the international star they had discovered.

Offers came from all over the country, but the only work Menken expressed herself interested in doing now was a serious play by a writer she respected, like Augustus Daly: "I - even me - pine for a Drama from you, or to secure your intellect and tact in my behalf" she wrote. Daly dramatised Charles Reade's new novel *Griffith Gaunt*, gaining permission from Reade through Menken's introduction, and thus started off a career which made him a dominant element in the American theatre for the next thirty years. But with extraordinary perversity, spurning all the offers open to her, Menken decided suddenly to go to Cincinnati in July, an awful time of the year to visit the city of Menkens where she could, at best, expect to find only more trouble. Instead she found ghosts. The Menken dry goods brothers had moved to Memphis, and her ex-husband, about whom she made extensive enquiries, had vanished as if he had been a figment of one of her fantasies. Once again she was playing Wood's Theatre, where Alexander had managed her in her great success, *The Jewess*; she was in the very same dressing-room in which she had first met the Anthony of her life, John Carmel Heenan, seven years before. Though it was a hot night the theatre was full and the city applauded her respectfully. The local paper reported that, "she wore a magnificent costume and appeared young, plump, and fresh, evincing no signs of either illness or dissipation", as if to disappoint all local rumours of the effects of her notorious life since she ceased being an honest Jewish wife in Cincinnati.

Menken had further successes in Nashville and in Louisville, but she felt lonely and bored, and cancelling her final engagements, returned by train to New York. She also felt rather sick, for the truth was that she was pregnant and had known it since her collapse at the end of May. All the activity of her tour had failed to dislodge Captain Barkley's love, and by now even the most carefully constructed costume could not conceal her condition. Though she had no inclination whatsoever for another marriage, it seemed she had no alternative.

Barkley was thoroughly satisfied with the situation. He agreed that they must marry immediately and proceeded with the arrangements. On Sunday, 19 August 1866, Adah Isaacs Menken married James Paul Barkley, in a ceremony performed

A rare picture of Menken pregnant.

by John Brice, president of the New York City Aldermen, in her exotic Bleak House. The marriage lasted three days. Apparently among the vows the Captain expected Mrs. Barkley to take was one reneging upon her long-planned Paris season. Menken was on the Cunard liner *Java* with her maid and her unborn child, leaving for Paris on the Wednesday following her marriage ceremony. According to Ed James, the parting scene with Barkley had been played out with some violence. Menken, "was so ill from an overdose of poison, whether to soothe her nerves or for self-destruction was never perfectly ascertained, we had to carry her from the tender to her stateroom ... The last we saw of this strange genius was when she could recognize nobody."

It would appear, then, that release from the Mrs. Barkley *persona* required the usual ritual symbolical act of suicide. The "poison" Menken took was, almost certainly, a heavy dose of laudanum which, in tincture, could be absorbed by Victorians to an extraordinary degree. The drug dissolved the latest marriage bonds, and released Adah Isaacs Menken from the back of her latest stallion (none too fiery any more), the dubious "Captain" Barkley, more, it now emerged, a professional gambler than a legitimate businessman. The romantic chancer was never to see Menken again, although he contributed, with gambler's generosity, $400 to the fund James raised in 1868 to provide a Menken monument. A year later he himself was dead, shot, rumour had it, in Denver in a gambling argument. Barkley had always lived dangerously; it was a great part of his appeal to Menken, but apart from losing that last game of cards in Denver, he never did anything in his life more dangerous than marry the newly released and, after a few days rest at sea, totally restored, Bengal Tigress, now some five months pregnant.

The Théâtre de la Gaîté, Paris.

Eleven

Enter La Menken – as Dada, the Queen of Paris

THE PARIS of Napoleon III, corrupt, ripe, sensation-hungry, extravagant, and totally theatrical in style, was ready for the Royal Menken when she arrived in September 1866, even if she, with her thoroughly noticeable pregnancy, was not quite ready for Paris. She had a contract for the New Year with the Théâtre de la Gaité, and meanwhile was content to keep as low a profile as her notoriety and shape would permit. She employed a skilled publicist, Susette Ellington, essentially to keep her presence out of the papers and concentrate the public's interest upon her arrival with a New Year which was to include, as a minor supporting feature to the Menken, the great Exposition. Meanwhile she entertained only her closest friends very privately, and fretted for an early and easy delivery of the love-child Barkley had imposed upon her career.

In November the child was born, an apparently quite healthy boy, a little earlier than expected (certainly according to her marriage lines), but then Menken was always somewhat vague about dates, other than theatrical ones. Within a few weeks she was playing one of them, an out-of-town try-out to polish up her talents and get her into form for Paris. She quickly visited the Liverpool Varieties Theatre for a fit-up of *The French Spy*, a safe piece for a safe date, which gave her some fast cash and confirmed her confidence that she had not lost one touch of the old magic, in spite of a year of that chronically bad marital luck which seemed to be the principal curse of her life.

Menken had, typically, cultivated the friendship of several key literary and opinion-forming writers in the course of her earlier Paris trips. Georges Sand, for her talent, her libertarian life-style, her assumption of men's clothes, her cigar-smoking, and her fearless opposition to male-imposed limits upon female behaviour, was to Menken an especially heroic figure. Sand liked Menken's style too, even if she was uncertain of her rather jejune and naïve American literary exercises. The two rebellious sisters met, talked, and smoked together, and when

Adah Isaacs Menken with her son, Louis Dudevant Victor Emmanuel Barkley.

Menken's baby was born, Georges Sand expressed herself happy to have the child dedicated to her, by way of becoming his godmother.

What could be more exciting and desirable from Menken's point of view? It was the living equivalent of having Charles Dickens accept the dedication of one's poetry, and she had no intention of missing such an opportunity. But she was a self-confessed and proud Jewess, maintaining that she was of Jewish birth, and not merely a conversion engineered by a Reform rabbi in an American provincial city. She knew very well that, according to classical Jewish law, a child whose mother is Jewish, is a Jew, regardless of the faith of its known or unknown father. For the old Jews who had discussed and determined with Talmudic subtlety these questions, recognised very well that it was an extraordinarily wise child who knows his own father, while mothers can never be doubted. Through the centuries of pogroms, Jewish women had been regularly raped by energetic christian peasants, moujiks, and cossacks, but nine months or so later, according to Jewish law, they had all been quietly delivered of Jewish sons and daughters; and so the long, painful, historical Exile of the Jewish People went on. Adah Menken, militant Jewess, Zionistic soldier of her People, student of their lore and law, knew very well then, that if *she* was born Jewish then her son was unchangeably a Jew. But, suddenly, a protean change of *persona* was about to take place. Adah, the Proud Prophetess of Israel, was about to drop that mask and put on a more modern one, that of La Menken, the modern Parisienne intellectual, whose son's godmother was an immortal French *littéraire* of aristocratic and Catholic origins. She discussed the problem with Susette Ellington, although she already knew that there could be no doubt as to the outcome. Ellington encouragingly pointed out that Barkley was of no known religion, and that Menken's marriage to him had been a thoroughly civic one. It would be absurd to become involved in the unpopular superstitious nonsense of Jewish rites, with their barbaric circumcisions and sinister prayers. Anti-semitism was endemic in French society, and though Menken might well get away with the exoticism of being a Jewish Creole, producing a properly processed Jewish son was not a good idea with the season about to get under way. Susette, Adah, and Georges all agreed: the Menken boy was baptised, in Ellington's account, "at the grand cathedral, with a prince for a godfather, and his godmother one of the first authoresses of Paris. The name given to this royal stranger is Louis Dudevant Victor Emmanuel Barkley!" Although there is no record of the birth in Paris, there he was, launched, the little fellow, a certified Christian, with half of the second Emperor's name, the family name of Sand, and a touch of Italian royalty for ballast.

If Menken was truly Jewish by birth and really knew it, and was as proud of the fact as she had, since her marriage to Alexander Menken, always protested herself to be, then the baptism of little Louis was a craven act for one who, whatever else she had been from time to time, had always remained proudly and insistently Jewish. But, on the other hand, as the wise old rabbis who had debated in Talmudic times the complex question of "who is a Jew" might have gently observed, surely, in this situation, the mother's behaviour demonstrated very clearly that she had the gravest doubts about her own Jewishness. She may, or may not, have had a Jewish father, but certainly the disapproving Creole mother who had rejected her as a girl, was no Jewess; and in truth, only that long dead lady could have commented authoritatively on the matter of Adah's obscure paternity. And what would she have known about Jews anyway, that Mrs. Theodore or Mrs. Campbell, soon to become, in the Menken's official Paris biography, "Lady" Campbell, wife of "Sir Campbell, *un gentleman du meilleur rang et un praticien du plus grand mérite*"?

It is at this point in Menken's life that one cannot avoid the sudden certain illumination that whatever her origins were, they were not Jewish; for surely no declared and militant Jewess, no defender of Rothschild and Shylock, could possibly have sacrificed her claim to Jewish continuity, her only son, for the sake of a little good local publicity. In any case, apart from a photograph of him with his brilliant mother nursing him on her lap while he looks straight to camera, there is no more reference in Menken history to little Louis, other than Frank Queen's observation that, "at the mature age of three months, he already understands and appreciates the theater". Apparently this premature wisdom proved fatal; the child died before the end of the summer of '67.

There were rumours stimulated by exclusive stories put out by Ellington, that Menken would appear in a play long-discussed with Gautier, and that Georges Sand had retired to her country house at Nohant to write a drama for her new American friend. The management of the Théâtre de la Gaité, was, in fact, somewhat embarrassed. For the truth was that, though they had Menken booked for a season, they had no vehicle for her. Why not *Mazeppa* in French? After all, it was Voltaire who had first drawn civilised attention to the fragment of Russian history, the romantic but hopeless rising of the Ukrainian Cossacks under their aged hetman Mazeppa (in treacherous alliance with Charles XII of Sweden), and their bloody defeat by Peter the Great at the Battle of Poltava in 1709, upon which Byron had based his inaccurate but heroic romantic poem of 1817. The Byronesque version had proved popular in France. Delacroix had painted a superbly dashing version of the naked ride, and Liszt had celebrated it in music. Even Pushkin's less romantic Shakespearean treatment of the material in his poem *Poltava* published in 1828, was known in French, the official language of all civilised Russians and Poles. Surely a French version of *Mazeppa*, the Romantic set-piece which Menken had made so refreshingly modern, was the best possible subject for her Paris season. Why the hesitation?

The truth, to be approached with some delicacy by Dumaine and La Roche, the managers of the Gaité, was that Mme. Menken's French, though, excellent and charming in the ordinary way of conversation, was distinctly Creole in its style, and unimproved by her American accent. The danger was that the dramatic lines and moments of *Mazeppa* played in French *à la Menken*, were likely to be treated by the snobbish Paris audience (always so aware of the stylishness of their own delivery of their great mother-tongue) as being more than somewhat comic. But how to put this to Mme. Menken? Someone, probably Ellington, eventually did, but not until a variety of excuses had been presented to her by the nervous management. They worried, they said, that her favoured pieces, *Mazeppa* and *The French Spy* would really lose much in translation. That while the Mazeppa ride, or its equivalent, was an absolute essential, surely for Paris, so knowing, so theatrically sophisticated, so determined upon being the originating centre of the cultural world, something else was necessary, something new. They put it to Mme. Menken that the best minds had studied the problems and the requirements of a unique artiste's talent, and had constructed especially for her, an entirely new epic spectacle, a melodrama full of action of a kind which only she among living actresses could essay, gun-duels, sword-fights, a ballet for her to lead, and for finale, a sensational, even more thrilling and dangerous ride *à la Mazeppa*. Even now, the famous boulevardier dramatists, Ferdinand Dugue and Anicet

The cast of The Pirates of Savannah, *with Menken at the centre.*

Bourgeois, were completing the epic. Titled *Les Pirates de la Savane*, it was a perfect Protean play for the world's greatest Protean actress mime, with barely a line for her to speak for most of the piece, through an astounding range of roles; for she was to play a mute!

Menken was no fool. Royal as her disposition was in London, and excellent as her French might seem to the English with their absurd accents, she knew that so far as *le tout Paris* was concerned, a girl born somewhere in the South West of the United States with a Creole here or there in her genealogy, was no French expert. Surprisingly quietly she accepted the suggestions of the management, and the efforts and inventions of the undistinguished but fashionable hacks they had employed, without argument. She even offered, Paris being Paris, to play without tights. The management was delighted. Menken's added touch was all their writers needed to make their work truly immortal. The show would, indeed, go on. And so would the publicity and all the normal premonitory signs of an imminent Menken opening.

Almost as soon as the two weeks' rehearsals began, a typically Menken-Ellington incident occurred. It made all the gossip columns. An aristocratic would-be lover who had failed to gain La Menken's attention in London, had followed her to Paris. Subjected to the intoxicatingly erotic atmosphere of Europe's premier city of love, this eager young milord (whose unlikely name was given out to be "Lord Albert Avon") had sent a pair of amazing diamond ear-rings, a priceless heirloom of the Avon family, with an impassioned note declaring his feelings for the star of the forthcoming spectacle *Les Pirates de la Savane*. Copies of La Menken's response were widely available for publication. "Your note was received", replied La Menken to milord. "I shall wear the diamond ear-rings, not for the donor's sake, but in hopes that their magnificence may create an impression upon the audience of the Théâtre de la Gaité. As for my accepting your Palace as a home, I can only say that my hotel is preferable. Go to your friends and tell them that Adah Isaacs Menken is an American woman, there is no French in her blood, and that all further attempts at *intrigue* are useless."

The demonstration is clearly a crude publicity squib; but it bears a little closer examination. Firstly, because it cues the audience into looking out for the thoroughly genuine jewels which La Menken was in the habit of wearing on stage – no paste for her. Secondly, it warns all would-be offerers of largesse in anticipation of liberties, that La Menken believed in the sound American principle that diamonds are an artiste's best friend, and should never be returned, no matter how affectionate or insulting the notes might be which contained them. She would always be her own woman, bestowing her intimacies where her fancy led. But, beyond all that, there is carefully established in the note a new *persona*, wearing the mask of a daughter of the Revolution, free of that taint of alien blood (even the best French vintage), "an American woman", no less; and, finally, who could dare after that, to criticise her accent in any of the infinite number of languages she could speak with ease? The occasion may have been false, but the letter reveals a true hurt. The Gaité management's criticism of Menken's accent and their complicated excuses for the great new word-less spectacle had not fooled the American woman, and she would not forget their insult. In fact, perhaps her offer to play without tights and show Paris a fairly large portion of her *derrière* was intended to be an intimate insult. The show's rehearsals went on, and throughout them La Menken wore her famous ear-rings, smiled on everyone, and spoke as little as possible. Reported the busy Ellington, "The actors did nothing but look at Miss Menken, and Mr. Dumaine forgot his lines in paying attention to the Emperor's Box", where Miss Menken was enthroned with champagne, pâté, and courtiers, between rehearsing her own silent but sensational scenes.

Always smiling, infinitely elegant, more beautiful than ever, accompanied by the famous, the elegant, and the lovely, but unusually silent and consequently rather mysterious, throughout the production period La Menken was seen at all fashionable venues and occasions, her name figuring in the papers every day in one context or another, often treated with profound respect, but sometimes not. While the Gaité anticipated modern marquée billing by having itself plastered with huge yellow and black posters consisting of the one word MENKEN, another word was coined by an unknown wit while contemplating a picture of Adah Menken on a horse. "Adah" sounds much like "Dada"; apart from being a French nursery name for a rocking-horse, "dada" is also a rude joke-word for sexual congress in the astride or what is sometimes described as "the Greek Position". The "Dada Menken" joke took on very rapidly with the Parisians, and endless anecdotes of Menken's actual and alleged rides followed in its train. Not terribly classy perhaps, but horribly show-business, and awfully good for the box-office. All seats were sold for that first night, and for weeks in advance. *Le tout Paris* saw the old year 1866 out a little early, on 29 December, at the first-night of Menken, the loveliest Dada of them all, in *Les Pirates de la Savane*, a spectacle of bare limbs, diamonds, danger, and other delights.

Menken received her usual treatment from the press following her Paris début. Some raved, some roared, some sneered, but no one ignored her, and the avalanche of newspapers deposited one solid nugget of pure gold in her treasury of appreciative riches, those testimonials to her star-quality for which a star is most avid. Théophile Gautier, one of the true immortals of French literature, wrote in *Le Moniteur Universal*:

> Miss A. Menken is, indeed, a very beautiful woman, her proportions elegant and *svelte* in their effect, who mimes with rare intelligence a mute protectoress of persecuted innocence.

No description could suit better La Menken's current *persona*, the perfection of "American womanhood", with its strong, silent Western freedom from all the old decadent taints which made Paris such a wonderful date. As for her Mazeppa ride, staged in *Les Pirates* with greater spectacle than ever, Menken felt that Gautier had perceived it truly for what it was, a moral emblem of the plight of Woman in a decaying male society. "Nothing is more frightening than this scene", he wrote. "If the animal's foot fails him, if a plank loosens, the Public would have the pleasure of seeing the total self-destruction of a superb beast and a charming woman, full of intelligence, *sang froid*, and courage." And, concluded the all-perceptive genius, who knew his fellow-citizens as well as any, "What greater attraction could one possibly imagine?" After that, what cartoons, what cries of

"Dada", what sneers could touch her? La Menken had the approval of the intelligent soul of French literature. She relaxed in the warmth of Gautier's words, securer as an artiste than she had felt for years.

The warmth induced by her reception, together with the old corrupting perfumes of Paris, inclined La Menken to thoughts of love from time to time. She was, so far as she was concerned, divorced from Barkley in all but detail, but she had as yet made no decision whom to choose from among the real-life "Lord Alfred Avons" who clustered around the stage-door and showered her with presents (which, as she had warned them all, bought them nothing and were never returned). Favourite among these admirers from the point of view of Lola Montez, an angle which Menken favoured and profoundly respected, was an actual king. He had been king since 1864 of a country not that much smaller than Bavaria; he was rich, royal and enamoured, and thus tended, in full dress uniform, complete with all the orders he had awarded himself for a life-time of dangerous encounters, to look extremely handsome, no matter how he might appear with his corsets off. King Charles of Württemberg, in Paris for a lengthy stay, with his entire Court ensconced in the Grand Hotel, made no pretence of his admiration and desire for La Menken. He was in his mature forties and had the popular image of being something of a freedom-fighter, having taken Austria's side against the hated sinister Prussians in the Seven Weeks War of 1866. Unfortunately the Austrians had lost, and the gallant gesture had cost Württemberg an indemnity of eight million gulden; but it gave Charles a romantic star to add to the cluster on his chest, and the Württembergers still seemed to have money for him to burn. Charles was reckoned a certain favourite in the Dada stakes.

Perhaps it was with her mind on this question, or the 346,000 francs (about $70,000 at that time), which the first eight nights of *Les Pirates* had grossed, or with her attention distracted by the elegants in the house that night, that Menken grew a little careless during the Mazeppa Ride. Suddenly the prophetic anticipations of the great Gautier were realised. The horse slipped soon after starting its run and fell heavily down on to the stage. But hop-la! Skilfully La Menken released the trick-strap which held her to the horse's back, and jumped clear, avoiding injury. Oh, how the house reacted! A great sigh of dismay, cries from nervous Frenchwomen, gasps and curses from the gentlemen, and then a wonderful great roar of thrilled approval for the perfect American goddess, as she leapt to her feet and graciously accepted their homage until the show was ready to go on again, galloping to its rapturous final curtain. Business would have improved, if it could, but tickets were already changing hands at unprecedented prices; now demand for seats became insatiable.

However accidental it was on that occasion, on 19 January the same type of accident happened again; but this time La Menken was unable to release herself in time. She fell with the horse, was knocked unconscious, and only avoided the great weight of the beast falling directly upon her by inches. This time the show did not go on. The shocked audience, proud and thrilled to have witnessed such a magnificent and tragic occasion, left the theatre relatively silently. Backstage it was discovered that Menken had two broken fingers on the left hand, her ear was torn, a wrist sprained, and her head and body badly bruised. She lay unconscious till the next morning. Two days later she insisted on returning to the Gaité, a triumph for her publicity and for the box-office. The season continued, an unprecedented success.

Weeks later Menken was under treatment for her wounds, and Susette Ellington reported to Frank Queen that Adah's fingers were still stiff and the ear "not yet well. I think I forgot to mention", she added, for ever the busy supplier of good paragraphs for gossip columns, "that the Emperor was prevailed upon to send his own surgeon to attend her, and had it not been for the skill and attention of M. Nelaton, she would have been disfigured by the loss of part of her ear and two fingers. Miss Menken trusted herself entirely to his care." It helped La Menken's reputation for courage and fortitude, and boosted the theatre's business, but this was not the first time that Adah had been seriously hurt. She had required medical attendance in London, and on other occasions there had been bruises from accidents and spills. Some of these accidents were planned parts of the act; but others, like this most recent occasion, planned or otherwise, had resulted in real injuries, both seen and unseen. The Emperor's Docteur Nelaton, though he did not have X-ray eyes, realised that Miss Menken might have sustained internal injuries. "He could not understand", reported Ellington, "how Miss Menken could play with such wounds, remarking that she had wonderful courage". And thinking, no doubt, that she also suffered from a wonderful folly.

The accident does not seem to have reduced public speculation regarding La Menken's love-life. Her courage, beauty, and talent were admired openly by Princes Jerome and Lucian, and the interest of King Charles of Württemberg encouraged that of the many titled, coronetted, and crowned visitors to Paris in the great year of La Menken and the Exposition. But the "affaire" with Charles got the most public exposure. The King was often seen riding with La Menken, and she was a familiar visitor to his Court, and he to hers. It seems most unlikely that, even with her newly aroused awareness of her purity as the perfection of American womanhood, Menken would have turned the King down as flatly as she did the apocryphal Lord Avon. She had no regular lover and no marriage that she would have considered serious at the time, and one does not lightly reject the advances of a monarch in reasonable repair.

The Württemberg affaire must have had enough reality to it for a most extraordinarily Lola Montez style of rumour to find credibility in cynical Paris. High society, remembering what Ludwig of Bavaria had done with Montez, talked incessantly of a secret "morganatic marriage" between La Menken and King Charles. When an American compatriot, the Texan Colonel Ochiltree, who, in Lone Star style, always shot straight from the shoulder, approached Menken and, with Western directness, asked her if there was any truth in the story, she asked for discretion and then whispered that she was, indeed, the new Montez.* Ochiltree swallowed the story whole, because from a Texan point of view, it was perfectly credible. When he returned to the States he dined out and drank often on the strength of his intimacy with Menken, and his tales grew taller, as they tend to do in the wide open spaces of the deep South West. It was he who was responsible for an unsubstantiated account of Menken's childhood and schooldays with him in the tiny town of Nacogdoches, Texas, where her family, said the colonel, kept a clothes-shop.

Ellington worked overtime building the Menken image. If the noted courtesan Cora Pearl, a crude whore interested in nothing but money, could catch Prince Jerome as a lover, then why should the American press not hear of the Emperor's interest in the Menken? He had sent his doctor to her; he had graciously received her. Why should he not be the favourite candidate for the newly vacated position of lover-in-chief? Ellington could hardly have got a placing for such a speculation in Paris, but the papers at home loved the idea of American womanhood moving in with the crowned heads of Europe. Princes had been featured in gossip stories out of London, and now the Emperor joined the court of La Belle Menken's royal lovers. But the truth was that though the theatrical Menken was the reason for the talentless Cora Pearl appearing in Offenbach's *Orpheus in Hades*, an opera bouffe which required her as Cupidon to do little beyond prance around with nothing much more than wings on, Menken had no ambition to equalise with Pearl in the field of courtesanship. She was earning plenty of money and why whore if one doesn't have to? Cora Pearl was pelted with rotten eggs and vegetables at her theatrical début, and Menken knew well that it is best to stick to one's speciality. She generously suggested that if Cora gave up the theatre, La Menken would agree not to take up prostitution, even with royal clients.

All the same, it would be pleasant to share such a time of great success with the right sort of lover. There she was, the Darling Dada of Paris, with her pictures

---

* Regarding marriage: Menken's fullest expression of her mature opinions on the institution are contained in a letter to Robert Reece, a young librettist who cultivated a romantic love for her.

They will be harmless to you, these ghosts of mine. They are sad, soft-footed things that wear my brain, and live on my heart, that is the fragment I have left to be called heart.

Apropos of that, I hear you are married. I am glad of that. I believe all good men should be married. Yet I don't believe in women being married. Somehow they all sink into nonentities after this epoch in their existence. That is the fault of female education. They are taught from their cradles to look upon marriage as the one event of their lives. That accomplished nothing remains. However, Byron might have been right after all: "Man's love is of his life a thing apart, it is a woman's whole existence." If this is true we do not wonder to find so many stupid wives . . . Good women are rarely clever, and clever women are rarely good . . .

Now a royal tigress waits in her lonely jungle the coming of the king of forests, brown gaiters not excluded.

decorating everything from shaving-mugs, to scarf-pins, and scarves, and everyone wearing hairstyles, hats, coats and trousers, all *à la Menken*, the uncrowned queen of Paris (whatever she might be to the King of Württemberg), and no great mind, superb talent, courageous soldier, elegant boulevardier, witty genius of an aristocratic poet with whom to share it all. For the greatest combination of all these manly qualities of a bygone age, still the most famous name in French literature, though old, overweight, terribly in debt from the excesses of building his fantasy palace Monte Cristo, and founding his own theatre, and now kept by his prissy son and creditors on a short rein, the great Republican musketeer Marquis de la Pailleterie, Alexandre Dumas Père, was beyond fulfilling the role for which his romantic eminence made him otherwise so perfect. Or was he? Certainly *L'Oncle Tom*, as the sneering midget poets of the day dared to call the old giant because of his negro mother, the old musketeer himself didn't think so at all. And Menken had frankly admitted that she had serious intentions toward him.

Dumas lost no time in expressing his reciprocated appreciation of La Menken. In his own not very successful paper, *Le Mousquetaire*, the day after her début, Dumas praised her beauty, and talent, and gave a full account of her history exactly as issued by the theatre's management and the clever Ellington. When early in the New Year, the theatre published a fourteen page *Notice Biographique sur Miss Adah Isaacs Menken, Artiste Americaine*, for sale "*à la Librairie Dramatique*" in the Rue de la Bourse, "*et chez tous les libraires*", it was said that the fine polish and style of the piece already spoke clearly of the friendship which had

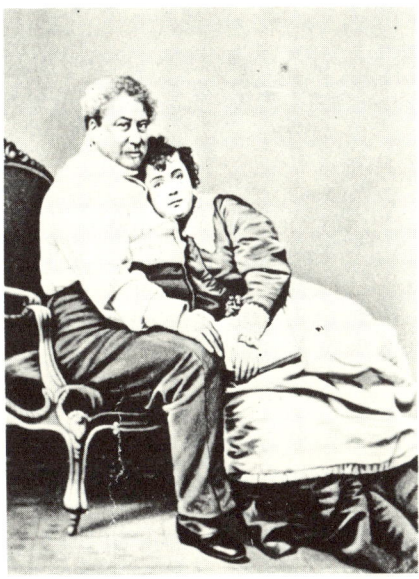

One of several scandalous photographs taken of Menken and Alexandre Dumas.

immediately occurred, *coup de foudre* style, between the Gargantuan D'Artagnan and Mazeppa. Certainly Dumas lost no time in calling on Menken, and, with unique and charming perverseness, she at once chose him for her companion. The great-bellied Père had enjoyed hundreds of women. Tied as his trim son and stiff daughter would have him be, to a small apartment at Boulevard Malesherbes 107, in spite of the limitations of age and relative poverty, he still did not restrict his admiration of women to merely ogling them in the theatre. Menken and Dumas talked poetry, novels, the romances and lies of their lives, and she confessed to him that she was, in fact, a quadroon. But Dumas wouldn't have minded if she wasn't. He had the full attention of the most beautiful and sought-after, the most notorious, the most famous, actress in Paris. He had the constant attendance and deep friendship of the first Great American International Star. A goddess who could not be bought and was therefore one he could afford, an incredible example of the new free female species, who paid for meals and left bank-notes around with the same kind of carelessly lavish *insouciance* which had enabled him to get through so many great fortunes. Suddenly it seemed in his not so terribly long life that he was young again. She adored, he was adorable, and his imagination and blood leapt like a fiery Tartar steed.

From the moment when first taken backstage to be introduced to the star by Gautier, that magical moment when the bare-limbed lovely Menken impulsively embraced him saluting his towering imagination and his magnificent talent, Dumas Père was transformed. Side by side with the petite Menken the giant D'Artagnan walked again, and Paris looked on amazed and envious. Who cared if Paris also laughed up its sleeve in its own especially cruel Gallic way? Who cared if a perverted and drug-addicted, fashionable but miserable poet, cruelly satirised the coupled Summer and Winter:

> L'Oncle Tom avec Miss Ada,
> C'est un spectacle dont on rêve.
> Quel photographe fou souda
> L'Oncle Tom avec Miss Ada?
> Ada peut rester à dada,
> Mais Tom chevauche-t-il sans trêve?
> L'Oncle Tom avec Miss Ada,
> C'est un spectacle dont on rêve!

At least if one is to be insulted in verse, it is flattering for it to be the work of Paul Verlaine. The Old Musketeer or La Menken could have wiped the sickly decadent out with a huge back-hand or a blow from a pretty parasol. But the truth was that neither of them cared. They both needed the dream of their love-affair. For her it was the ultimate answer to the snotty French with their anti-Creole, anti-semitic, *snobbisme*; and, in any case, Dumas was so much more fun than the idiotic King of Württemberg with his unsuccessful few weeks of heroic ignominious defeat by the Prussians. The Menken would show the world that to her, an old literary genius, a bankrupt Bohemian, was more than a stupid king or a vulgar bourgeois milliardaire. And she did.

Dumas was the guest of honour at her dinners, the great old lion, slightly mangy, of her salon, her companion on formal occasions, and on visits to galleries where he was better known than the most famous of the paintings. They gourmandised, and she paid with pleasure. Chefs excelled themselves producing incredible delicacies to delight the King of Romance and his last queen, lovelier than any other, he swore, with no rival ever to follow. How sad that all must pass and nothing remain, but such is the nature of life and love. Not entirely, thought Menken: not, anyway, since the advent of modern photography.

Menken was one of the first actresses in the history of the theatre to realise the importance of photography in star-making. Wherever she went she sought out the best local photographers and held long sessions with them, resulting in the circulation of hundreds of cartes de visite, photographic reproductions, roughly $2\frac{1}{2}$ inches by $3\frac{3}{4}$, sold or given away. She had first organised such photographic sessions in 1859, and since then conducted them in any city she was in where she could find a half-way good photographer. Several thousand photographs were made of her in the ten years of her career, and when she died she was the world's most photographed woman, the best-known female face and figure in the contemporary theatre. But in Paris she essayed two styles of photography which she had never before undertaken. She posed for a set of pictures, entirely nude except for a loin cloth, happily smiling as she adopted what she called her "Casanova" poses. Probably the photographer was Reitlinger, although the pictures were never signed or published, and only a few were given to very special intimates. The three originals pasted in a copy of the *Notice Biographique* in the Harvard Theatre Collection are the only known remaining original examples. One of them, however, escaped: it was picked up by a New Orleans photographer who retouched it to obscure a nipple, and published it. Lesser saw a copy and considered it a forgery, but it comes from the Paris set and is, undoubtedly, Menken. The other new-style photographic session was intended to memorialise something which was, to Menken, even more important than the beauty of her breasts; her intimacy with the Great Musketeer, the old half-negro Marquis de la Pailleterie himself, now in his mid-sixties, but still the only true Alexandre Dumas, the monumental Père of French romantic literature. Pierre Petit was chosen for this historic assignment, and in his studio a set of photographs were posed which were to travel the world, copied and re-copied, engraved, drawn, sketched, and published again and again. In them, an absolutely ravishing and clearly very happy Menken looks directly to camera, with Dumas's arm around her waist. But another set, shot a few days later, gained even more notoriety. They show a slightly déshabillé Dumas in shirtsleeves, the lovely Menken on his lap, her face upon his chest, her hand holding a book, as if she had been reading the old warrior his own amazing life-story. This second sensational set of pictures (imagine T. S. Eliot snapped with Tallullah Bankhead on his lap! Or Marilyn Monroe with, say, Arthur Miller!) was the work of another photographer, Liébert, who made a handsome fee out of the sale of many hundreds of copies; for Paris adored the pictures. They loved to think of their old hero capturing La Belle Menken. It made one feel proud to be a Frenchman.

A caricature taken from a photograph and widely circulated in Paris showing Dumas and Menken.

Menken and Dumas freely distributed copies of the pictures to their friends and admirers, signing them jointly. "My dearest love", wrote Dumas. "My dearest friend", replied Menken's huge proud signature, on their personal copies. Other signed and certified copies went to America and England, and wherever they travelled, they brought forth a chorus of amazed shock, admiration and cat-calls. The pictures were regarded as undeniable and incriminating public evidence of intimacy between the Father of French literature and the no-longer totally untainted daughter of the American Revolution, both of whom thus laughingly and shamelessly proclaimed their shocking personal and private relationship to the world. Others laughed too, and many admired the rash courage of the two great stars, for Dumas, the persistent Republican in Imperial Paris, had as many enemies as he had admirers, and Menken was always a target for moralists. *Le Figaro* sneered: "There are to be seen just now in the shop-windows a series of astonishing *cartes de visite* of Miss Menken and Alexandre Dumas, joined together in *poses plastiques*. Can M. Dumas be her father?" The answer, perhaps, to this satirical and contemptuously intended question was *Yes*; Père was the father Menken had never had, and always wanted. But it was the pre-Freud epoch, when the unconscious remained powerful because totally unrecognised. All Menken knew was that she was happy at having, at last, found herself a wonderful fatherly lover, and she didn't mind who knew it.

Whatever shock and consternation she and Dumas felt obliged to express in public over the affair of the photographs, the pictures could never have become current without their tacit consent, for neither of them was exactly naïve in the politics of publicity, and Dumas' failing newspaper needed attention as much as his failing sex-drive needed the flattery and adoration of the most desired woman in Paris. Both of them were unmoved by the endless rhymes and squibs and speculations about did they or didn't they actually do this, that or whatever. They agreed with Verlaine, the viciously brilliant not exactly normal poet, that "Uncle Tom and Miss Ada" were a dream realised, daughter-mistress and father-lover without any inhibitions about incest.

But unfortunately Père had a son. Alexandre Dumas Fils was not amused. He brought pressure of the most telling kind, financial, upon his indigent parent, resenting particularly bitterly the racist sneers, which had hung over Dumas throughout his life, and which were revived by accounts of the Menken's dark Jewish Creole blood. The columnists sniggered at Dumas' black mother, Marie Cessette Dumas, a lovely negress from San Domingo, and Fils demanded that Père protect the family honour which he had, with his typical boyish irresponsibility, dragged through the gutter. Thus pushed, old Dumas took Liébert to court on 27 April, seeking an injunction to prevent the sale of the offending photographs. Under cross-examination, however, Dumas agreed that he had given permission for the pictures to be issued and sold, and that he had been paid by Liébert for the rights. He was somewhat shamefaced over making the admission, for it brought once again to the public attention, the parlous state of his financial affairs. As for the rest he cared nothing. Inevitably the petition was denied. But the family insisted on pursuing the matter further, and, long after Menken had left Paris, they gained an injunction. But it was far too late. The photograph had entered theatrical history.

The court business was not good for Menken, and though she regarded the fuss as wholly absurd, litigation always made her paranoid. She felt she had to defend herself, and wrote a carefully worded letter to beloved Dumas Père, stating how badly she felt about his arrangement with Liébert, particularly as she had paid the opportunistic photographer off with five hundred francs! It was all "morally and financially" very disagreeable to her, and painful to their friendship. But they were together again within days, laughing, drinking, eating excessively, lying to one another, and admiring Liébert for paying off Dumas with Menken's money.

In May, La Menken gave the most distinguished dinner party of her Paris season, inviting everyone who was anyone. All accepted eagerly and when they arrived, found that the occupant of the seat of honour beside Menken was the indestructible old D'Artagnan of the boulevards, Miss Ada's "dearest friend", Alexandre Dumas the father. At that dinner he presented Menken with one of her greatest treasures, a photograph quaintly inscribed in bad English "To the Last Love of my Heart, to Miss Adah Menken, his faithful Alex Dumas". Dumas' prophecy proved to be true. Within two years the old musketeer was dead, but not before enjoying a revival of interest in his work, entirely prompted by "*L'Affaire Menken*". In 1868, five of his early plays were revived and running in Paris; for a short moment he was, once again, popular, admired and solvent. He had been the only Menken lover strong enough to survive and directly profit by the experience. Menken sent her young poet fan, Charles Warren Stoddard, a photograph of the old man. "Here is a treasure, the portrait and autograph of my friend Alexandre Dumas. Value it for his sake, as well as for the poor girl he honours with his love. O! how I wish you could know him! You could understand his great soul so well – the King of Romance, the Child of Gentleness and Love; take him to your heart forever!"

The Theatre am der Wien, where Menken suffered a dreadful experience – failure with the public.

Twelve

Enter Infelix Menken – in tales of old Vienna

Les Pirates, a melodramatic absurdity of a spectacle, in which the star spoke barely a line, broke Paris records by running for 150 house-full performances, a convincing demonstration that the star-system was, what it remains, an unbreakable show-business blessing and curse. By June of 1867, Menken was at the height of her powers, confidence, and value as a star, the first to have come out of America, and the creator of an entirely new style of entertainment and box-office business. Tights and legs were the easily imitated part of it, but they were only minor elements, the most easily copied and exploited. Little Lotta Crabtree, who had watched the Menken so closely in San Francisco, was now well on the way to becoming a Menken-style star herself. In New York the *Black Crook*, the first great musical spectacular, entirely developed from Menkenesque elements, with a full chorus in pink tights, was enjoying the longest run in theatre history. Menken had initiated what the stuffier critics would have liked to dismiss as "the naked drama". But they couldn't. The new free Protean mixed bag of female pulchritude, melodrama, music, dancing, bad jokes, circus acts, and anything else an enterprising showman could dream up, was the most rapidly evolving vital theatrical form of the nineteenth century, till now an endless doldrum of boring old melodramas, heavy comedies and poorly performed classics. The American musical had been born. Bastard it might be, and the Menken an appallingly careless mother, but she had borne it; it was lusty enough to survive its strange and confused origins, to grow up to become the American theatre's specific, irreplaceable, and inimitable contribution to the arts of modern urban entertainment.

Offers reached Menken from cities the world over. Melbourne begged for her, and might have been an interesting date *en route* to a return, by general and loud request, to San Francisco, where her luck had first hit real pay-load. But she was still bothered by the after-effects of her accident, and the long run, and the hectic social life, frenetic even by Menken standards, had tired her. A desire to conquer Europe theatrically as no one had done since Montez, and a Lolaesque inclination for the gilded courts of Europe, made the most attractive of the offers those which came from other European capitals, each with a long theatrical history and its contribution to make to her status as the First Great American International Star. And of the great cities of the Continent, next to Paris, came Vienna, the home of the waltz, the centre of a splendid Imperial Court, and, even if the loser of a recent ignominious war with the beastly Prussians, the heart of culture, still possessing a treasury of uncountable wealth. Now an offer from the Theatre am der Wien for a month's season, with virtually any guarantee La Menken might demand, arrived. Clearly the crooked finger of destiny was beckoning her to success in the splendid Austro-Hungarian capital; and how fortunate it was that they wanted the great new Paris success *Les Pirates*, for, in spite of her lessons long ago in Cincinnati, Menken's German was in as poor speaking-shape as her Latin, and far worse than her Creole-flavoured French. She accepted the Viennese offer, making for herself what seemed to be the best deal of her career. But destiny, like all good carnival magicians, is a trickster.

Noel Gerson, Menken's most imaginative biographer, in his *Queen of the Plaza*, insistently maintains that, when it came to the point, she never did play the Viennese date. After a rapturous welcome, and an innundation of social and other offers, Gerson reports a most astounding trick of fate, an encounter between the Menken and her past, that poorly-lit area between her teenage and her first touring dates *en route* to meeting and marrying Alexander Menken; an area in which no one had ever, till then, been able to perceive the movements and *persona* of our star very clearly. But Gerson, confidently drawing upon a holograph Menken *Diary* and other unpublished material in the theatrical library of his friend, an obsessional Menkeniana collector, Henry Ewing Hibbard of New York, was at last able to explain why Menken left Vienna so precipitately. Since the material is exclusive to Gerson's researches and book, one has no alternative but to quote it *in extenso*, for it has, since the publication of *Queen of the Plaza*, appeared in Menken history as often as her account to Lippard Barclay's actor friend of her capture by Indians.

As Gerson has it, Menken was in rehearsal and much enjoying the social life of Vienna, the perfect environment for iron butterflies, when "suddenly, Adah's past caught up with her. She returned to her hotel suite after rehearsal early one evening to find Baron Friedrich von Eberstadt waiting for her ... She greeted him civilly, but her *Diary* contains the icy declaration, 'I could have carved out his heart'." Who was the Baron, and why this murderous reaction to him? Gerson tells of Adah's first meeting with the degenerate Austro-Hungarian aristocrat earlier in his book. In 1852/3 in New Orleans, when Adah, an innocent seventeen, but brilliant, was working for fifty cents an hour as a governess to help keep her doubly or triply widowed mother, most recently a Mrs. Josephs, and not long since a Mrs. Campbell, and when married (or not) to Adah's father, perhaps, a

Mrs. Theodore, yellow fever hit New Orleans, a city often struck by epidemics. Mrs. Josephs was ill, and so was Adah's younger half-sister Annie, with whom she had danced as "The Theodore Sisters"; but, "Adah, who had developed into a remarkably robust young woman, was untouched". She continued giving lessons, and nursing, until there was no money left, all the schools were closed, and "the Josephs family faced starvation ... Then, suddenly, salvation appeared in the portly shape of Baron Friedrich von Eberstadt, an Austrian nobleman who was spending a year in the New World and whose daughter had been one of Adah's pupils." We are at once in that favourite country H. M. Newell charted, of readers of romances, not all of them women, which has proved irresistible since *Wuthering Heights*, *Jane Eyre* and *The Professor*, that wild romantic terrain dominated by the Brontësque hero-villain, the Man of Power, with his hard but hypnotic wordly eye fixed, immovable and fascinating, upon the tender tear-filled orbs of his little virgin governess-victim. A classic scene of nineteenth-century melodrama, and not a million miles from the realities of life in that or any other century. For when (until very recently, anyway) were pretty, clever young virgins not seduced, sooner or later, by worldly men of unbridled lust and no pity? If the heroines themselves truly hated it, of a certainty the readers loved it, and still do. And here Gerson had discovered in the writings of Menken's *Diary*, which, he maintained, she had kept intermittently throughout her life, a true Brontë situation. We must read on; such tales are irresistible; who is this Rochester with the Austrian accent?

> Von Eberstadt, a man fond of wine, women, and song in the best Viennese tradition, traced his aristocratic ancestry to the Holy Roman emperors. A staunch monarchist, he had, nevertheless, found it prudent to spend a year abroad after an embarrassing incident, allegedly involving a chamber-maid, that had shocked the austere young Emperor of Austria-Hungary, Franz Josef, and his conservative court.
> The Baron, whose funds appeared unlimited, had taken up residence in New Orleans with his wife, Selma, and their young daughter, considering it the only sophisticated city in the United States. When the yellow fever epidemic sent the Baroness and her child hurrying to New York, the Baron remained behind to dispose of their rented house and arrange for the shipping of their furniture and other belongings to the more salubrious atmosphere of Europe.

The inevitable happens. "One day in mid-October, 1853, the despairing Adah received a note asking her to call on the Baron the following morning. She speculates at length in her *Diary* on the work she hoped he would offer her, mind filled with dreams of the unattainable; perhaps she would be sent to New York as a governess for the Von Eberstadt child, and would accompany the family to Europe.

She dressed carefully for the occasion in her best gown, a black bombazine purchased for her stepfather's funeral. In order to make her appearance less sombre, she tied a scarlet sash around her waist and borrowed a frilly bonnet. She was dissatisfied with the effect, but could do nothing to improve it, and went off nervously to the interview. Her *Diary* for that night contains a single, hastily scribbled line: '*F. von E. loves me!*'"

And now, the Baron "an old hand", offers Adah "an all-expenses-paid vacation in Havana". She accepts happily, without any second thoughts as to his intentions, even perhaps, with a tacit acceptance of them. After all, seventeen-year-old part-Creole girls in New Orleans rarely were totally unaware of the sexual facts of life, one of the educational bi-products of witnessing the exploitations of slavery. The Baron provides money for the poor multiple-widowed mother and sick little sister, and something very much like a sexual deal (like yellow fever, fairly familiar in mid-century New Orleans) is struck. Adah sails with the Baron on the *Bianca* on 18 October; for Gerson, following Menken's *Diary*, is able to be very precise on such details.

In brilliant, exotic Havana, full of theatres and exciting social occasions, much more a capital city than New Orleans, Adah and the Baron take the best suite in the Hotel Obispo, and go shopping. The Baron introduces Adah to luxurious, flamboyant, shameless but exciting dresses; Adah naïvely notes in her *Diary*, "I have bought very little lingerie. It is so warm and close here that few ladies bother to wear it". The Baron encourages her boldness, and Adah loves it all, except, she confides to the *Diary* that "one flaw made the idyll less than perfect. The Baron's love-making disappointed Adah. She didn't know what to expect, what she was supposed to feel, but she realised that whatever it was, she did not experience it. Instinct, however, prompted her to conceal the truth, and she made a pretence of being a warm and enthusiastic mistress." Gerson is building up his intuitive assessment of Adah, his psychologically knowing perception that, while in love always with romantic Love, "Adah was frigid". That is why, he observes expertly, "Like so many women, throughout history and down to the present day, who took many lovers, it is likely that she was incapable of finding complete physical and emotional satisfaction and release in sex relations." It is a commonly accepted simplistic, somewhat macho fragment of post-Freudian sex-psychology, but one recognises exactly what Gerson is trying to establish. For Adah to grow up into the Menken, she needs a traumatic introduction to sex. And Gerson had found it in the *Diary's* revelations of the Von Eberstadt affaire.

Perhaps we may justifiably jump-cut to the inevitable master-scenes of this entirely familiar scenario. The Baron grows tired of his latest little conquest; the epidemic ends in New Orleans; the daughter and the Baroness Selma threaten to return from New York; and the "expenses-paid vacation" is over. In February 1854, the Baron catches Adah flirting with handsome young Ramon at the fashionable restaurant *Sevilla*. He uses it as an excuse to stage a terminal scene to the affair. The next morning "the management of the Obispo regretted to inform Señorita that the Señor Baron had paid the bill and departed with his luggage", for New York. He had left no cash; she had been too stupid and inexperienced to charm jewellery out of him, and he too knowing to have offered it. So there she was, alone in Havana, with only her lost innocence, her blossoming beauty, and her somewhat whorish wardrobe. What could she do, reader? It wasn't as if she had her innocence still to lose. She looked for work in the theatres of Havana, but her Spanish was not good enough to do anything more than order opulent dishes in a restaurant and make love. Adah, after a little weeping, and mature consideration, chose both. She put on her lowest cut dress, walked the streets, got herself picked up, and had the native common sense to make sure she was fed first. Gerson was fascinated to find that, "Her *Diary* for the next six months is a financial ledger devoid of all comments. It was strictly a record of income and expenses, and she scrupulously noted every transaction. When she knew the name of a client, she wrote such items as 'Capt. Gonzales, three dolars'. When her partner was someone she didn't know, she said, 'Stranger, three dolars . . .' She rose rapidly in her chosen half-world." High officials became her clients and her prices rose steeply with the improving market. "Her fees became increasingly high, and she now received anywhere from fifty to two hundred dolars from a man in return for her favours. Then, on 14 October 1855, Adah Bertha Theodore arrived in New Orleans, a wise professional prostitute at the ripe old age of twenty years."

The "lost" years of Menken's life have been at last (it seems) accounted for, and, here we are again, twenty years or so later, in a grand suite in a great hotel in Vienna, face to face with the villainous Austrian nobleman who had started Adah upon her career as a public entertainer and performer. No wonder she could have carved his heart out. Especially as "the Baron was older, greyer, and heavier, but was still the light-hearted playboy who had not hesitated to seduce a teen-aged girl, take her to Havana, and abandon her". How was Menken to have her revenge? Gerson's access to the *Diary* provided him with a dénouement in the grandest manner of romantic popular literature, a turn of which one feels certain the Menken would have been perfectly capable; "she concocted a scheme as diabolical as it was clever". Gerson deserves the honour of telling the thrilling climax of the story he put together from the Menken's *Diary*. After teasing the Baron for a while, Menken "informed him she would be willing to live with him again, discreetly, provided that he took her to the royal court and presented her to the Emperor. The Baron was shocked, and with good cause; Franz Josef was not in the habit of receiving foreign actresses of dubious reputation. But Adah insisted, waving aside the financial offers that meant nothing to her.

At last the Baron capitulated, and although he could promise no miracle, said he would do what he could. For the next six days Adah heard nothing. She rehearsed, went sightseeing, and dined with her new friends; she behaved as though all was normal. Only her *Diary* reveals her tension.

Von Eberstadt returned to inform her that he had accomplished the impossible through the help of a royal chamberlain who was indebted to him. The Emperor's next 'informal' reception was scheduled to be held at the Hofburg on the afternoon of 8 May, and an invitation would be sent to the American actress. The Baron made it clear that he intended to confine himself to a brief remark or two when he presented her to His Majesty, who would not appreciate details about the nature of the entertainment offered in *Mazeppa*. Luckily the court was inbred, interested only in its own doings, and as the play had not yet opened, it was unlikely that the gentlemen who combed undesirables from the list of guests would know either *Mazeppa* or its star.

Considering his mission completed, the Baron wanted his reward, but Adah firmly held him off. In the light of past experience, she told him, the bargain would not be concluded until she had curtsied before Franz Josef. Von Eberstadt grumbled, complaining that she was causing him all sorts of difficulty, including the need to send his wife off to their country estate. Adah remained unmoved.

No rehearsals were held on the great day. The Baron arrived at Adah's hotel in his court uniform, complete with the decorations and a plumed helmet. She greeted him in a floor-length cloak of embroidered, beaded silk and, following the custom of the Austrian court, wore a small veil.

Imperial troops stood to attention in the Hofburg courtyard, and household guards taken from a score of prominent regiments lined the corridors. Thousands of candles burned in magnificent crystal chandeliers, and Adah, making her way slowly toward the throne-room with Von Eberstadt, caught glimpses of rooms with damask-lined walls. The sumptuous elegance of the ancient palace of the Holy Roman Emperors was breath-taking.

Forty or fifty guests waiting to be presented to Franz Josef were milling in anterooms, and Adah's name was checked off several lists. The Baron was nervous, but she maintained a deceptive calm, which vanished when they were admitted to the throne-room. Still more troops were in place, swords drawn, and the guests were herded together behind velvet ropes at one side of the chamber. Dukes and archdukes entered and moved to the positions near the throne to which royal protocol assigned them.

Then the swords were raised in salute, and Franz Josef, imperturbable in side-whiskers and a white uniform, came into the hall. Men bowed low, ladies curtsied and he took his throne. The velvet ropes were removed and the presentations began. Members of the nobility came first, so Adah's wait was long. With nothing better to occupy her, she watched the Emperor, and saw that sometimes he nodded, and only occasionally did he design to speak. The routine of the 'informal' reception was dreary, and time dragged.

At last it was Adah's turn. Von Eberstadt led her forward, bowed, and spoke her name. She sank to the floor in a graceful curtsy, throwing aside her cloak. There was a moment of stunned, disbelieving silence, and no one moved. Adah Isaacs Menken, The Naked Lady, was wearing a snug-fitting gown of flesh-coloured jersey, remarkably similar to the Mazeppa costume she had made famous. From a distance of ten feet she looked nude.

A woman in the throng giggled hysterically, and several men coughed. Then Franz Josef stood, his face wooden, and, looking neither to the right nor the left, stalked from the chamber. The reception had come to an abrupt end.

Adah quietly gathered her cloak around her and walked to the courtyard, where carriages were waiting for the guests. The apoplectic Baron had stomped off, so the next scene of the drama was decidedly anticlimactic. One of the officers was forced to obtain a public carriage to take Adah back to her hotel.

Menken in her "floor length cloak", as worn in Vienna.

That evening Adah paid the inevitable penalty for her vulgar jest. A civilian official from the Ministry of the Interior and three uniformed officers were waiting at her hotel, and she was informed that she had been banished from the Empire. If she failed to leave Vienna within forty-eight hours and if she dared to pause anywhere within the imperial borders, she would be placed under arrest. The American legation, she was told, had been informed of the ruling ... Franz Josef had been made to suffer a personal affront, and the offender could not and would not be allowed to remain."

The Gerson account of Menken in Vienna is, without any argument at all, one of the most sensationally Menkenesque episodes in the star's career. His book, published in the United States by Funk and Wagnalls, under the *nom de plume* "Paul Lewis", and in London by Alvin Redman under yet another name, "Samuel Edwards", had itself an aura of mystery about it, similar to a Menken fantasy. But through the all-knowing Authors' Guild of America, the true identity of the mysterious "authors" of *Queen of the Plaza* was established. They were both pen-names of a long-time member of the Guild, Noel Gerson. He had written over two hundred books, and lived in Connecticut in the extraordinary house smothered with P's built by the founder of the Pond cosmetics firm, itself a rather Menkenesque manor.

I wrote to Mr. Gerson, expressing my appreciation and enjoyment of his treatment of Menken's life, and my puzzlement that the Harvard University Library, Cambridge, Massachusetts, where his bibliography stated that the *Diary* was part of "the Adah Isaacs Menken Collection", had brusquely denied all knowledge, not only of that priceless item, but of any such collection at all. I requested an introduction to his Menkenophil friend Henry Ewing Hibbard, and the privilege of studying his material. It was the beginning of a very affable and amusing correspondence with a life-long professional writer, now in his sixties, with the manuscripts of his long professional life securely entombed in the catacombs of Boston University's distinguished Mugar Collection, alongside such literary giants as Conrad, Whitman, and Leslie Charteris, creator of "The Saint". Mr. Gerson was still very active and, currently, commercially very successful with what he described as a sort of Western "Wheels" saga. He regretted the death, some time ago, of Hibbard, and had no knowledge of where his amazing collection might presently be lodged. He, too, had long been puzzled by the attitude of various Harvard librarians and archivists, who maintained this uncooperative attitude regarding the *Diary* and other papers concerning which, in the bibliography of his book he had written, "I am grateful for the privilege of having been allowed to study them there".

I wrote again to various Harvard libraries, continuing the quest for the Menken *Diary*, and received more curt disclaimers, and one down-right denial as to the presence of any Menken material at all in the collections. Again I picked up my correspondence with Gerson and, having by now collected together all the quotations in his book from the *Diary*, and feeling that the material did not totally match with Menken's styles in either her letters or any of her other writings, rashly addressed my senior colleague in the quest for Menken, as follows:

"I propose," I wrote, "in my own book, because she invented so much about herself, and so much was invented around her – and all of this, in a psychological way becomes, I consider, part of the legend of the lady – to deal with this legendary aspect of her personality, which made it possible for herself as a writer, and so many of the rest of us, to build material around her. So that it doesn't really matter to my purposes whether the *Diary* you quote from so extensively actually exists or not. I shall be referring to your book (with full acknowledgement of course), in my own and – as one old pro to another – let me give it to you straight. If you did, in fact, invent that *Diary*, I would simply consider it to be an achievement in fable-building which should be acknowledged for its creative force – and I am certain it would be so regarded by Mazeppa herself. So can I ask you quite directly – did you actually invent that *Diary* material? Or do you think 'Hibbard' invented it?" I did not add, "and did you also invent Hibbard", but there was no need to do so. Within a fortnight I received the following letter from Gerson:

> You have penetrated the iron wall, and all I can say is that it takes a pro to smell out a pro. After due consultation with the elusive Hibbard, I must confess to you that the A.I.M. *Diary*, which proved to be irresistible to write, is the product of my own imagination. So be it... Do what you will with the *Diary*. It is high time the hoax is exposed.

And there it was, like a lovely shattered Tiffany chandelier, one of the best Menken stories in the entire codex, around me in a thousand coloured little pieces of marvellous quotes: "He loves me! ... I think C.D. is frightened of women ... Capt. Gonzales, three dolars ... H.N. makes love divinely ..."; and the great peacock dome of the Von Eberstadt seduction and revenge, all blown away like irridescent bubbles. Menken, I felt, would have missed Gerson's inventions as much as I did.

When I visited the Harvard Theatre Collection, housed in the Pusey Memorial Library in Cambridge, to make a final check of what documents they did, in fact, possess, I found the curator Dr. Jean Newlin immensely helpful and apologetic for the negative responses of her former assistants. Indeed, she said, they did possess a great deal of Menken material; but she fervently hoped I was not expecting to find this *Diary* for which they had so often been embarrassingly requested throughout the past twenty years. They simply didn't have it, and as far as her researches went, they never had. I was able to relieve Dr. Newlin's anxiety that perhaps some incredibly precious manuscript had disappeared at some time from the collection, by telling her that the entire *Diary* was a hoax, an imaginative piece of fiction by an extremely professional writer, who had been unable to resist filling in Menken's missing years, and, being a compulsive story-teller, had paid off his invention with a tall tale set in Vienna.

That had been the weakest part of Gerson's account. Through it I had breached, fairly easily, his "iron wall". Checking the Vienna theatrical records, I found that Menken had actually appeared at the Theatre am der Wien in *Die Piraten der Savanna*. She had received an appalling response from the Viennese audiences, and scarifying notices: "a spectacular comedy of the primitive lowest type ... even the most pathetic parts generated dangerous laughter ... Miss Menken herself acts mute through the first four acts and dressed in such close-fitting costumes that even the most ardent theatre-goers had long faces ... By the time the Mazeppa ride came the public were too tired to applaud the bathing-dressed equestrienne." The Viennese, it seemed, were too serious for such French Dada nonsense. Press attacks and ridicule continued unabated with the anti-semitism of Vienna, so deeply entrenched, far worse than Paris.

Vienna, not so gay, after the defeat by the Prussians at Sadowa, simply was not Menken's city. She, who had invariably discovered in the warmth of her audiences' receptions, that she was of them and for them, could by no means she knew bring up the temperature of Vienna to blood-heat. An American reporter called on her backstage after one awful night's reception, to find the great Menken, "huddled in a corner of her dressing-room, like a bundle of rags, crying with rage and despair at her treatment by the Viennese". How she would have loved to have shown them her *derrière* with the Dada contempt which had won her the adoration of Paris! So happy she would have been if Gerson's adventure had actually taken place. So very sad she was, in fact, that while miserably playing out her contract in Vienna, she had heard of the sudden death of her little, carefully christianised proudly and resoundingly named son.

In the Archduke Charles Hotel Menken was spending her time quite alone, in a misery as utter and total as had been her joy in Paris. From there she wrote to Charles Warren Stoddard, the young San Francisco poet who was cultivating a long-distance idealistic love for her, a letter, one of two she addressed to him, the other from Paris. The letters, among the most revealing of her writings, were carefully edited by Stoddard when he eventually published them in 1905, in the *National Magazine*, nearly half a century after he had received them. Their publication, even in the edited form, radically affected memories and evaluations of Menken. Stoddard had edited the two letters into one continuous document, concealing the fact that he had never actually met Menken. He also cut any reference to his insistent pursuit of the autographs of Menken's famous friends, together with other minor re-writing to correct Menken's stylistic eccentricities. Stoddard also trimmed any of Menken's uninhibited references to friends and lovers which he thought might be denigratory to the high spiritual status to which he had elevated her. The original letters, published here for the first time, have the confused vitality and conflicting personality of the woman, even if Stoddard's goddess loses against his edited version.

Vienna, Austria
6th Mo. 24th D. '67

My poet –

I am so glad to know you.

Your letter came just today when kind and beautiful things were so much needed in my heart.

Your words of cheer and praise, and your thrilling poems fulfilled their mission. I am lifted out of my sad lonely self, and reach my heart up to the affinity of the true, which is always the beautiful.

I want to know more of you Mr. Stoddard. I want us to be friends – real friends.

I first knew you through my darling Ada – now I feel that I know *you*.

I am not in the condition to say to you all my impressions of your poems and letter. I have, today, fallen down into the bitterness of a sad, reflective and desolate mood. You know I am alone, and that I work, and without sympathy, and the unshrined ghosts of wasted hours and of lost loves always tugging at my heart.

But as the influence of your letter has done some good, we won't talk of that.

I enclose you a treasure. The portrait and autograph of my friend Alexandre Dumas. Value it for his sake as well as for the poor girl he honours with his love and friendship. It is the only autograph I can now part with. And to send you this is sending a bit of my heart out over the seas to you. True, I have hundreds of others but they are parts of the most charming and romantic letters to me – Even me! Oh, how I wish you could know him! You could understand his great soul so well. The King of Romance, and the child of gentleness and love. Take him in your heart forever. In a few weeks I will see him. Then a pleasant hour shall be made by reading, in my weak translations, what I like best in your poems. We always read and analyze our dearest friends. But Alexandre is too generous to be a critic.

Geo. Sand came to me. We have seen too much of each other to leave many writings. And have greatly abounded in telegrams. But I will get her charming name for you. She is a quiet little creature and getting – what a woman never should – a little old.

Victor Hugo is as you know exiled from Paris. He lives in Jersey. I have been invited to visit him with Dumas, but I live in the "tented habitation of war" and every hour of my life is a "scramble". I am sure to accomplish all the things I should not do, and leave undone those nice and clever things I should do.

I know Lamartine but never corresponded with him. I shall endeavor to open a discussion on politics with him immediately for your sake.

I am as fond of these grand autographs as you are. I am the happy owner of a large volume. I shall do my best to divide with you. I gave Ada two for you once, Charlie Sneade and Fechter. Did you care for them? They are my friends.

Ah! my camarade, Paris is, after all, the heart of the world! "Know Paris and die."

I beg you send me your book of soul poems. I will love them. Direct to care Theatre de la Gaite, Paris, France. That always reaches me. I will not remain here long. Vienna is detestable beyond expression.

Do write to me, and write from your inner life. Let me try to help you with my encouragement and the best feelings of my heart. Your future is to be glorious. Think of me, I am with you in spirit.

Heaven bless you.
Infelix –
MENKEN

9 rue de la Paix
Paris
Sept 21st '67

My Poet,

Your last letter is more charming than the first. I understand you better. But do, for my sake, try to write a little more distinct. I can not make out all your words. I love you too much to lose a letter of the most unimportant word. But for all, I understand the spirit beneath the words. If I had the fortune to know you in the flesh – just as you are – I should require no words to understand you. I already know your soul. It has met mine somewhere on the starry highway of thought.

You must often meet me, for I am always sad and lonely. Nothing but hard work saves me from *myself*. And you know I am a vagabond of fancy. No home – no plans – no ideas. I was born a dweller in tents – a reveller in the "tented habitation of war". Consequently, my dear Charles, my views of life and things are rather disreputable in the eyes of the "just". I am always in bad odor with people who do not know me, and startle all who do. Alas!

I am a fair classical scholar, not a bad linguist, can paint a respectable portrait of a good head and face, can write a little, and have made successes in sculpture. But for all these blind instincts for Art, I am still a vagabond, of no use to any one in the world, and never will be. People always find me out and then they find fault with God because I have gifts denied to them. I can not help that. The soul and body do not fit each other. They are always in a "scramble". I have long since ceased to contend with the world about myself. It bores me horribly.

Mutual subjectam, I must ask a favor of you. Please look up the *"Eras"* of the year I lived in California, and find a poem I wrote called *"Resurgam"*. It is nearly a column in length, printed on the first page of the paper. And another short poem of sixteen lines, the caption I forget, but the last word of the two verses is *"Beware!"* I think, or that may be the title. I forget all about it. Perhaps you can make out what I mean. I want those two articles immediately. Do your best for me, like my Charming Poet that you always are. You can depend on me, as one glad and ready to serve you in any way I can. I am getting my little attempts at verses ready for the press in both London and in Paris. And by my carelessness I am obliged to appeal to all my friends to help me collect the lost tribes of fancy. You will be glad to know that in the matter of this book, (to be called simply *Writings*), Dickens is my friend and adviser.

Cher Dumas is in the country, and working hard he writes me. I have been idle about getting autographs. I forget it always. I have many very fine ones in my book, but can not take them out, or I would divide with you. Today I will write to my good Geo. Sand for you. She lives far from Paris now.

I will leave you now to do unpleasant work. I am translating a German book into English. I hate it. Write often. I love your letters. Perhaps I shall not wait for you to reply to this before I write. Heaven bless you.

Your devoted
ADAH

The time had come for Menken to assume a new *persona*, for her to shed the carapace which she had borne from Paris, a bright shell, gone dead and heavy upon her in Vienna. The gay Dada Menken, La Belle of the Boulevards, was buried with her child – no one knows where, for like his birth, the little Barkley's death is not recorded. The poetess was about to be re-born in a melancholy low key, while an off-tempo waltz played on endlessly somewhere in the distance by a tired orchestra in a city grown "detestable beyond expression". Since first approaching Dickens two years before, with the offer of her writings for his critical comment, the Menken had been considering and planning collecting her poems together. Now the new face-mask was assumed. The principal objective now was the achievement of Menken's literary ambition in the best of company. London was the new venue, and the most promising of its younger poets the quarry to be pursued.

Charles Dickens, 1812-70, to whom Menken dedicated Infelicia.

Thirteen

Enter MENKEN ("no *A* and no *I*") – luxuriously printed, artistically designed, and dedicated to Dickens

CERTAINLY WHILE preparing *Infelicia* (as *Writings* became) Menken was ill. She had always insisted that she was psychic, throughout her life experiencing profound intuitions concerning her destiny. Through 1867 all her considerable willpower was concentrated upon collecting her poems together, with a view to publishing simultaneously in London, New York and Paris, a small, beautifully bound bid for immortality. It was to consist of 31 of the best of her poems (about half her total output), under the unhappy title she had for so long adopted as her own in both its genders. It was to be her first and only book, regardless of her frequent claims to have published an earlier volume called *Memories* under the pen-name of *Indigena*. The earlier "work" was a total fiction. Even the great bibliophile Dr. Rosenberg was never able to trace a copy of it and neither has any book dealer since. She wanted and was totally committed to fill this vacuum in her literary life. Her earlier dreams of authorship must be realised – it was now or never, she felt.

John Thomson, so handy about a literary household, offered to help her with his experience as secretary to Swinburne, though he had now graduated to writing dramatic criticisms for the *Weekly Dispatch*. According to George A. Sims, an enthusiastic theatre-writer, anecdotalist, and book-collector who obtained from Andrew Chatto (at that time an associate of the publisher, John Camden Hotten) the original manuscript, Thomson was madly in love with Menken. Sims naïvely quotes him as saying, "I worshipped the very ground she trod on"; not, perhaps, an unlikely posture for one of Thomson's inclinations. But it is doubtful that Menken would have needed Thomson's introduction. Hotten had spent some years in America before returning to London and establishing his famous bookshop and publishing house at 74 and 75, Piccadilly. His shop had become a London outpost for American writers with his publications of Artemus Ward, Menken's good friend, and her ex-husband's *Orpheus C. Kerr Papers* in 1865 and 1866. He had also had the courage and shrewdness to take over Swinburne's

Poems and Ballads in 1866, which had excited a prudish remonstrance on the count of indecency, causing their original publisher, Moxon, to withdraw. The courageous Hotten was the obvious publisher for an eminent American poetess, and Menken now sought him out.

Hotten's *Catalogue of Useful, Curious, and Interesting Books Published or Sold* by him from Piccadilly, "those Books offered at one-fourth of their published prices are as clear and as perfect as when sold at the full price", included Mrs. Beeton, and an amazing selection of the unusual; *The Earliest Known London Directory*, *The Army Lists of the Round Heads and Cavaliers*, *Cambridge Slang Phrases*, *Balzac's Droll Tales* illustrated by Doré; and the *Book of Common Prayer* illustrated by Holbein and Dürer. He also offered complete sets of *Fun*, the weekly rival to *Punch* which ran only from 1861 to 1865 and constantly sneered at and attacked Menken. He reprinted Joe Miller's *Jest Book*. To Menken the entertaining Hotten list and his hard-sell approach (he must have been the first of the great "remainder" bookdealers) seemed eminently suited to the commercial requirements of her own *magnum opus*. She submitted her poems to Hotten, somewhat regally. He, being a daring, but also a shrewd, publisher, agreed their quality, and accepted Menken's guarantee that a number of copies adequate to cover the costs of production would be certain to be sold. On that question Menken had no doubts, offering her personal assurance and, no doubt, some cash. An arrangement was concluded, and there immediately followed the normal irritable exchanges between publisher and author, with Menken, in her very first letter to Hotten, expressing anxiety and impatience. She was much concerned about the little headpiece and tailpiece engravings by A.C., Alfred Concannon, a specialist in frontispieces for sheet music, which were to decorate her book. She was more than somewhat worried about choosing a portrait of herself for a frontispiece, although she had, by now, more than a thousand photographs of herself by some of the best theatrical photographers in the world, from which to choose.

Dear Mr. Hotten, *she wrote from her royal suite in the Westminster Palace Hotel*, I am much pleased with the interview between yourself and Mrs. Ellington yesterday. Your ideas are all excellent, and I am confident that we will have a grand success. I will call at your office tomorrow about two o'clock, if you will be so kind as to be home to me. I am anxious to see the designs that are to be engraved; also I would be glad if I might look over the later proofs again, as I was very ill when they were corrected for me.

You know I never really liked the idea of my portrait being printed, but I am willing to submit to your judgment in all pertaining to our mutual interest. The proofs of the portrait you sent me are wonderfully well engraved. Believe me, dear sir, yours truly,

MENKEN

"There is no 'A' and no 'I' ", added the inimitable immortal, for she was presently signing her letters with a certain degree of royal delusion. The *diktat* is a clear indication that the *persona* now adopted was that uniquely literary historical phenomenon, MENKEN.

Now came a frenzied search for poems scattered throughout the periodicals and newspapers of America, and the editing and agonising over which to include, which to leave out, which to edit, what titles to change. Menken kept sending Hotten new material, ruining his estimates of the enterprise:

> Dear Mr. Hotten – I am glad we have found another copy of *Answer me*. I hope you will get it a good place in the book. It is a poem that I like and I believe you will. If you believe in my idea of omitting the *Karazah to Karl* you might put *Answer me* there. However, I am sure you will do the best you can for it. Can you get *Aspiration* in? Do try. When are we to see the final proofs? I am so anxious to get the book out. I fear you put others before me. In that case we shall certainly quarrel, and that would be vastly disagreeable to me. Do hurry those printers, and I shall like you better than I do now.
>
> When you have an idle day let me come and see more of your wonderful books.
>
> Yours faithfully,
> MENKEN

Already Menken's tone had grown threatening, for apparently Hotten, like all publishers, just wasn't moving fast enough. However, she had her way and *Answer me**, *Aspiration** and *Karazah to Karl* were all included in the collection. But Menken remained fractious, impatient to see herself between hard covers:

"Dear Mr. Hotten", she writes next. "How long to wait for the proofs? You do not forget? When am I to see you? When will you advertise the book?" The anxieties are not unfamiliar to any author, but the tone is unusual – that of an affronted queen. Graciously Menken continues; "Remember I ask these questions merely from curiosity. The affair is all decidedly yours." But she rode Hotten as hard as she did any of her horses or lovers. Finally Menken generously patted him approvingly on his sweating head. "I am satisfied with all you have done, except the portrait; I do not find it to be in character with the volume. It looks affected." So there were still to be problems, Hotten observed, wondering if in accepting this particular project he had shown his usual shrewd publisher's wisdom. Writers, as a rule, he could easily handle but MENKEN was like riding a nightmare.

The sad truth was that Menken's London portraits that year were coming out badly. In several of them she poses, looking ill-tempered, with whips, her round face showing a fullness she detested. Now the question of the portrait

---

* See poetry appendix.

frontispiece became all important to her. "Perhaps I am a little vain," Menken observed with unusual modesty and barely restrained tears, "all women are – but the picture is certainly not beautiful. I have portraits that I think beautiful, I dare say they are not like me, but I posed for them. Do tell me, mon ami, can we not possibly have another made?" It was that well-known female psychological and time problem immortalised in the unforgettable narcissistic query, "Mirror, mirror on the wall, who is the fairest of them all?" It seems that even Menkens aged, but this suddenness, this Dorian Gray-like extremity of the process, was too cruel.

Hotten really did not mind how many little drawings or frontispiece portraits were added or subtracted from Menken's book, provided she covered the costs. Finally it was agreed between them that the expenses of the re-engraving Menken demanded would be met by her. Yet, by the time the first proofs of the book were ready, she felt too sick and distracted to concentrate on them, and John Thomson undertook the proof correction. Soon, however, Menken was up again, warning Hotten that she would be calling soon to check on those damn little engravings again:

> If you will be so kind as to be at home to me. I am anxious to see the designs that are to be engraved; also I would be glad if I might look over the later proofs again, as I was very ill when they were corrected for me.

With justification she had no great faith in either Thomson's personal devotion or his proof-reading abilities.

Menken now added four lines to the front pages of the book, from that poem of Swinburne's which she, and many others, wrongly took to be his great personal tribute uniquely dedicated to her, *Dolores*. They were quoted without acknowledgement, perhaps because Menken had now found a more respectable literary name to front her book. Or perhaps she knew that, if approached for permission to quote, Swinburne would not be too helpful:

> Leaves pallid and sombre and ruddy,
> Dead fruits of the fugitive years;
> Some stained as with wine and made bloody,
> And some as with tears.

Menken was hopeful that the critics would observe in her collected poems, the great and powerful new American poetic influence, the modern force of Walt Whitman inspiring her own extremely free verses. But as Lesser perceptively observes of her sad quest for literary immortality:

> She lacked critical perspective to see that her poems expressed the very essence of the American spirit in their bold rhythms and lurid images (but)

that in their broad splashes of raw color and extravagant self-dramatizations they were completely alien to the trend toward decadence of contemporary English literature.

Of her poems Menken herself wrote, unaware of the unfashionable and vulnerable posture she was assuming:

> I have written these wild soul-poems in the stillness of midnight and when waking to the world the next day they were to me the deepest mystery ... They are strange and beautiful to me, for as I read them, I do not see in them a part of myself; they do not seem at all familiar to me. And yet I know that the soul that prompted every word and line is somewhere within me, but not to be called at my bidding – only to wait the inspiration of God. It is this soul that makes me religious, affectionate, and good in many things.

Infelix Menken, dubbed by her third (or so) husband, Robert Henry Newell, *Infelicissima* – the unhappiest – was now enshrined in a collection of thirty-one poems titled *Infelicia*. All that unhappiness would have been more than justified had she lived a week or two longer. But Menken died a week before *Infelicia* was published, escaping the worst critical savaging of her career. Most reviewers attacked her personal morals and character, dismissing the poetry as valueless, or attributing what qualities they might have to the good offices of others. The *Pall Mall Gazette*'s critic wrote, referring witheringly to those little engravings over which Menken had so agonised:

> Tears, so to speak, bedew every page. Each poem has a small headpiece, in which a young lady is depicted in those agonies of sorrow which tell directly upon the back hair. One, however, represents a toad fastened to a wall with a cable.

The kindest of her critics admitted that, "Menken is as bold in poetry as she was on stage," but even he considered that the poems had little literary merit. *The Boston Saturday Review*, however, thought the book "luxuriously printed, and artistically illustrated" and was modern enough to observe rather tartly the degenerate Whitman influence:

> The strongest, or apparently the strongest, are those in which the Whitman style of rhapsody is copied, and the language is thrown about wildly, with here and there a few happy combinations. People who have the English vocabulary to deal with, who never seem to pause to think, and who stick at nothing that will produce an effect, would be very unlucky if they always failed to "strike oil".

Other critics noted the influence of Ossian, the Old Testament and William Blake, and many were surprised that a woman who could engage in such "indecent displays" could also be a poet "who carried about with her a suffering heart". It was further well noted that Menken had a strong tendency to conscious and unconscious plagiarism. Her *Working and Waiting*, for example, was redolent of Hood's famous *Song of the Shirt*, and other literary echoes were loud and unmistakable.

William Rossetti, Dante's brother, including four of Menken's poems in his American Anthology on his senior's recommendation, acutely observed that they express, "a life deeply sensible of loss, self-baffled, and mixing the wail of humiliation with that of indignation". He also noted the not always benevolent influence of Poe, whom Menken had so greatly admired, rightly considering her Poesque moments to quite lack that poet's rigid disciplines. Menken's were "unformed rhapsodies, windy and nebulous; perhaps only half-intelligible to herself, and certainly more than half-unintelligible to the reader, yet with touches of genius which place them in a very different category from many so-called poems of more regular construction". It is a perceptive and not unfair evaluation, and about the best poor Infelix Menken was going to get from contemporary critics; though Dante Gabriel himself regarded the poems as "really remarkable". He advised his brother:

> Much the best piece in the book is one called (I think) *Answer me*; though I remember finding that some points of it were much better than others, and should have been inclined to print the good stanzas, which make a fine poem enough by themselves; but I don't know if such a plan would suit you. There is also a short rhymed poem which is remarkable, called I think *Ambitions*, or something of that sort (actually *Aspiration*), but it is defective of a line somewhere, accidental omission, I suppose. These two, I remember, are clearly the best. However, there are one or two others I had marked, but my copy seems nowhere. One of the most characteristic is that about "Angels, sweep the leaves from my door".

Hotten himself must have had severe doubts about the book, for it bore neither his name, nor his printer's upon its fore-pages, only the date 1868, and "London, Paris, New York". No doubt he thought it destined for remaindering "at one-fourth", or perhaps even feared a protesting article by the great and all-powerful Dickens. Yet *Infelicia* went through a dozen English and American editions, all pirated, of course, since the author was dead and had no literary inheritors. The last was published in 1902, and though it is difficult today to consider Menken's poems significant other than as projections of her extraordinary psychology and the postures imposed upon a woman of genius in her time, it must be admired that her book of poems was for forty years in print. Lesser considers that *Infelicia* did have some small influence on English and American literature and rather extravagantly asserts that: "the climactic soliloquy of Oscar Wilde's *Salome* clearly shows its dependence upon the Menken's *Judith*". He adds that the immaculate and ironic Wilde was once publicly accused of plagiarising Menken's passionate, impulsive lines, which sounds quite out of character for a poet who spent half the day putting a comma in, and the other half taking it out. Both Charles Warren Stoddard and George Sterling, writes Lesser, "freely acknowledged her influence upon their work, and Joaquin Miller credited her with having taught him all he knew about color, the strongest characteristic in his work", a comment of Miller's which we have observed could have been merely ironic. Lesser hopefully anticipated that, "future literary historians may also apportion to the Menken a fairer share of the credit now given to Walt Whitman for inspiring French literary schools and Amy Lowell's group of Imagist poets", and thus made himself Menken's most supportive critic. He expresses a generosity which few scholars have shared, towards the unhappy poetess who had the temerity to ride into the literary world naked on a wild steed. Concludes the Menkenophil Lesser, "it is as an Imagist as well as a pioneer in the use of free verse that the Menken must be considered. Never a slavish imitator of Whitman, she wrote with a dramatic intensity, a brilliance of imagery and a delicate femininity that sets her work distinctly apart from anything done by the bearded poet. Both poets drew upon the Bible as their model, but even the forms developed by the Menken are her own. Her rhythms, springing from the rise and fall of her emotions, have far less sweep than his, and her themes, likewise, are narrower in scope and vision." Perhaps suddenly feeling that his enthusiasm and compassion had taken advantage of his critical judgement, Lesser concluded: "There are, of course, barren stretches in the poems of *Infelicia*. Adah Isaacs Menken was not a careful poet. She wrote in haste and rarely had the patience afterward to edit her lines. Her first draft was usually her last; few of her manuscripts show the revisions that usually mark the work of other poets. Nevertheless, her strength lies in her skillful employment of free verse forms as well as in so-called poetic prose and in the passionate freedom of her imagery; her weakness, in the narrow confines of her vision."

Today Menken's vision hardly seems "narrowly confined". The true significance of her writing, indeed, would seem to lie not in its style or its influences, good or bad, but specifically in the writer's "vision" of her "true self" as Woman Released. Menken is, unarguably, one of the great women's rights protesters of the American nineteenth century. All her lives and writings project the same revolutionary sentiments: that a woman belongs to herself; that she has her own genius; that she has her own Eros; that her body is hers and hers alone; and that whatever postures she may adopt in attempted *coups* to take over a male-dominated world by out-playing or un-manning men, she is doomed to depression, and failure. No matter how brave, how gallant, how daring, how desperate, how cunning, how clever, she may be, if a woman has to adopt male-dictated postures, she will live outrageously and die miserably, mocked by many of the women she has attempted to free, and by the men to whom her entire life has been effectively subjected by the ruthless pursuit of independence and freedom from the dictates of their society. In this sense Menken, entirely uninterested as she was, quite rightly, in the details of male-dominated politics, is, nevertheless, a true revolutionary, a female libertarian, whose great illusion was that she could beat men at their own games and win, along with all the other glittering prizes, true and total freedom. Naturally she failed, but certainly she attacked many of the pillars of respectable literary society. Even the great Charles Dickens, by now a pillar quite rigid with respectability, was coaxed into allowing his imprimatur upon Menken's little book of poems. "TO CHARLES DICKENS", the volume is dedicated, on the page opposite the unacknowledged Swinburne quotation. And on the reverse of that page is a fawn-coloured block exactly reproducing a letter from England's greatest literary institution, apparently (if meanly) accepting the dedication.

Like so many Victorians, Charles Dickens showed enormous interest in "Fallen Women". In the middle-class mind (as often in fact), actresses had a very short distance to fall before becoming members of this deplorable but socially essential class. Dickens, always intensely interested in the theatre, was himself an eager producer and director of entertainments from conjuring shows to his own plays, giving, in the latter years of his life, much time and energy to personal performances of his works. His spectacularly successful tour of America in 1867 with the great strains and tensions it involved, was a major contributory factor to his death at the age of 56, three years later. He had then for some years been keeping an actress whom some might consider a somewhat fallen woman, a Miss Ellen Ternan, in a charming little house in Slough. According to some commentators (including one of his sons), Dickens had a child by her. At all events, theatrical and other fallen ladies exercised a strong fascination upon him. Between 1847 and 1855 Dickens persuaded Baroness Burdett-Coutts, the richest woman in England, to finance a home for fallen women who had somehow missed the theatre in their descent. The intention was to teach them home-making and useful crafts, and prepare them for export either to America or Australia, both of which desert continents were chronically short of women, fallen or otherwise, and were none too choosy.

Dickens planned the centre, designed pretty uniforms instead of the usual dull grey, and provided a pianoforte, and attractive though simple furnishings and decoration to encourage the inmates of his house. He composed an *Appeal to Fallen Women* which begins: "Do not think I write to you as if I felt very much above you ..." The house which was not a home he called "Urania Cottage", a most interesting Freudian choice of name, for Urania is one of the surnames of Aphrodite, "the Heavenly", no doubt equated by Dickens with the neglected spiritual potentials of his fallen friends. Unfortunately, Aphrodite Urania queened it over the fertility cults of the Eastern Mediterranean, presiding over the lower inclinations of sacred and other prostitutes, rather than their frustrated spirituality.

Urania Cottage failed inevitably, its salvaged occupants quickly growing bored with knitting, needlework, and even the readings and homilies of Mr. Dickens. A few were successfully exported, but most of them returned to that square mile of London's West End so rich in whores, theatres, and the Victorian gentlemen who patronised both so avidly.

But Dickens' interest in the theatre and theatricals persisted throughout his life, and with his own most secret production, Miss Ternan, tucked away first in Slough and later in "an establishment of her own in Peckham", he often took long walks in London at night at the end of his extraordinary working-day marathons. He tended to develop as a result of intense concentration, great heat in the head, causing his hair, rich and luxuriant in young manhood, to become frizzled and thatch-like in middle-age. Suffering one night in the autumn of 1864, from this "boiling head,"* Dickens "sallied forth from his office" in the direction of Waterloo Bridge. This was to result in his first contact with Menken. He wrote to Forster:

> At Astley's there has been much puffing at great cost of a certain Miss Adah Isaacs Menken, who is to be seen bound on the horse Mazeppa ascending the fearful precipices not as hitherto done by a dummy. Last night having a boiling head, I went out from here to cool myself on Waterloo Bridge, and I thought I would go to see this heroine. Applied at the box-door for a stall.
> "None left Sir."
> For a box-ticket.
> "Only standing-room sir."
> Then the man (busy counting great heaps of veritable checks) recognises me and says:
> "Mr. Smith will be very much annoyed when he hears you went away sir."
> "Never mind; I'll come again."
> "You never go behind I think Sir or –?"
> "No thank you. I never go behind."
> "Mr. Smith's box, Sir –"
> "No thank you. I'll come again."
> Now who do you think this lady is? If you don't already know, ask that question of the highest Irish mountains that look eternal, and they'll never tell you – Mrs. Heenan!

From this exchange ardent Dickensians, utterly devoted to the protection of what they consider to be their hero's "good name", vehemently insist that Dickens had virtually no contact with Menken; but then many of them also deny that he had anything but a fatherly relationship with Miss Ternan. In *The Dickensian* in 1917, B. W. Matz characteristically insisted that "history does not relate" whether or not Dickens and Menken became friends, yet *Infelicia* is clearly dedicated "To

---

* Page 271 of Volume 3 of the original edition of Forster's *Life* tells the story, deleted from later editions of the work.

Charles Dickens", and there on the back of the flyleaf, is that convincing miniature facsimile of a letter from him accepting the dedication. It reads thus:

The letter sent by Dickens, the authenticity of which is questionable.

The writing and signature are indisputably those of Dickens, although there is a slight discrepancy of angle and style in the writing between the first and second paragraphs. This is not surprising, for there is an earlier letter from Dickens to Menken, written on 10 July 1865 which politely acknowledges receipt of a note from her and continues:

> I also thank you for the verses enclosed in your note. Many such enclosures come to me, but few so pathetically written and fewer still so modestly sent.

It is the final letter from Dickens to Menken which is dated "Monday Twenty First October 1867" as is the one reproduced as a frontispiece to *Infelicia*. But the entire original letter reads as follows:

> Dear Miss Menken,
> I shall have great pleasure in accepting your Dedication, and I thank you for your portrait as a highly remarkable specimen of photography.

Visits and business so completely absorb my time at present that I am merely passing through my own house, and answer your note flying.

In haste

Faithfully yours,
Charles Dickens.

Dickens was in the midst of frenzied preparations for his long, immensely profitable, and totally exhausting American tour, a heroic marathon of readings and public appearances the strain of which was to contribute to his stroke and premature demise on 9 June 1870.

But the first paragraph of this letter does not make it clear whether Dickens is accepting a "Dedication" inscribed upon the "highly remarkable" portrait sent to him by Menken; or whether he is actually granting her request to dedicate her book to him.

It seems not beyond the bounds of the possible that during Dickens' absence, Menken and Hotten hit upon the ingenious idea of combining the first paragraph from the second letter with the second paragraph from the first letter, thus producing a perfect, if slightly forged, testimonial. Menken, so notoriously careless about official documents like marriage certificates, would have been unlikely to notice anything untoward in such a minor adaptation. Perhaps Hotten decided to leave his name off the book fearing Dickens might take some action over the matter when it came to his notice. But if Dickens ever did notice the mating of his two letters he made no comment. By the time he returned from America in April 1868, it would have been too late to do anything about the dubious dedication without producing the kind of scandalous rumour which, in these last few years of his life, Dickens hated and feared with almost pathological dread. His style in such situations was never very strong, and his nerves, made edgy by the middle-class public who worshipped him as their literary hero-god (but violently disapproved of his treatment of his wife), had been seriously shaken by his involvement in the Staplehurst train disaster in 1865. He had, on that dramatic occasion, been travelling with Miss Ternan and her mother, and though this compromising fact was generally ignored (or concealed), Dickens was in no mood or condition to bear speculations about whether the now dead Menken was fully licensed to dedicate her verses to his august but profoundly weary genius.

Menken's biographers have tended to make more of the implications of the "dedication" than its dubious circumstances will easily bear. The ever-imaginative Gerson gives an account of Menken bombarding Dickens with her poems, "expressing a humble hope that he would condescend to act as her literary advisor". Eventually, in Gerson's version, Dickens "sent her a short note, offering to meet her for lunch in the restaurant at Cataldi's Hotel on Dover Street whenever he could fit such a visit into his busy schedule". When the luncheon meeting finally took place, Menken's sensational dress and loud demeanour scared

Dickens; but it is an unlikely scene. He was also reported as being present on various occasions at Menken's salon, and the editor of the *Franco-American* includes his name among those present at a dinner Menken gave in Paris for Dumas Père: "on one side sat her old friend Charles Dickens, on the other sat the fiery Algernon Charles Swinburne. Also present were the opera star Hortense Schneider, and the Southern States General Breckinridge." Menken may well have used as an approach to Dickens, her good and close friend, the actor Charles Fechter. According to her account when Dickens eventually came to see her in *Mazeppa*, he was accompanied by their mutual friend, and did "go behind" to see her. But she was much more the handsome and philandering Fechter's style than she ever was Dicken's, for Little Nell was one part the Protean Menken could never have played; and it was Dicken's favourite female role, filled till the end of his life's play by Miss Ternan.

Menken frequently referred to her "friendship" with Dickens, always in the most elevated terms. He was for her, the acknowledged Master of the Literary Universe, and it was *his* cultural approval, above all others, that she wanted. We may well consider that, once obtained, it was a mean enough acknowledgement; but, the fact remains, that, by hook or by crook, Menken obtained it.

What emerges from the small amount of ambivalent material relating Dickens and Menken, may simply indicate the habitual graciousness of the Great Man, (as the ardent Dickensians consider it), and the opportunism of a lady who, we know, invariably got by one means or another what she wanted. Certainly though, it indicates Menken's extraordinary ability to manipulate literary men. Her technique, based upon a persistent bombardment of letters, manuscripts, and photographs, accompanied by extreme flattery, sincere admiration, and the worshipping expressions of a lovely face and body, concealing an eager and creative soul and mind, were an irresistible combination for literati, in many of whom there is more than a touch of Pygmalion. The "Dickens Dedication" exemplifies perfectly the Menken's skill in handling the difficult, quirky and vain literary sub-species of the male sex. We may reasonably deduce that if she could get what she wanted from the rigidly respectable Dickens who "never went back-stage", then she could certainly fulfill her requirements of lesser lions. Yet, of all the specimens of the breed that she was to attempt to tame, surely none could have presented more problems than her major London conquest, none less than the distinguished young alcoholic, homosexual, masochist and flagellant poet, Algernon Charles Swinburne.

The "infamous" photograph of Menken and Swinburne. It shows a declining Menken.

Fourteen

Enter Dolores Menken – as Dolorida with a whip

IN LONDON, in the 1860's, most intellectuals and all Bohemians believed that Algernon Charles Swinburne promised to be England's greatest poet since Shelley, and some dared say Shakespeare. Today many critics regard Swinburne's agonisingly cross-rhymed verses as being as purely Victorian as anti-macassars and the worst of Adah Menken's free verse. But the pre-Raphaelite group dominated by the prophetic and patriarchal Dante Gabriel Rossetti was convinced that Swinburne, still in his twenties, was a poetic genius and a literary comet of historic significance. But they were extremely worried about some of his habits. The fact that he frequently drank to excess and fell over, or that he nervously flapped his hands when excited like a penguin, were not unacceptable eccentricities in a society in which unusual tics and the consumption of several daily bottles of liquor of one sort or another, commonly occurred. Even Swinburne dancing naked around Rossetti's house in Cheyne Walk, Chelsea, where he was for some time an uncomfortable lodger, was not especially shocking to visitors. Dante Gabriel kept an extraordinary collection of animals including armadillos, hedgehogs, mice and dormice, a Canadian marmot, an ordinary marmot, a racoon, squirrels, wombats, wallabies, kangaroos, two owls (named Jessie and Bobbie), and peacocks. Swinburne was hardly out of place. Members or friends of the pre-Raphaelite Brotherhood might easily have taken him for a little red-headed faun, happy on laudanum or opium, common indulgences of mid-Victorian literati. In this group, quite as eccentric as the rest of Rossetti's zoo, were two gentlemen whose influence on Swinburne was profound; one Charles Augustus Howell, and the remarkable Richard Burton.

Swinburne was immediately taken with Howell, a sinister, vicious and dishonest, yet charming and witty conscientiously degenerate gentleman of dubious origins. He was half-Portuguese, his father being a drawing teacher in Lisbon. Howell lived there till at seventeen he was caught cheating at cards. He was sent to England under the guardianship of an unfortunate uncle, who, being Vicar of

Darlington, was thought qualified to cope with the moral lassitude Charles Augustus was revealing. In London he associated himself with the "revolution" (more, in fact, a rebellion of manners) of the pre-Raphaelites, and hung around Rossetti. Howell put it about that he was involved in political conspiracy, as a result, he said, he must leave London for a while. But in 1864 he was back, wearing a red ribbon which he said was a Portuguese order he had received in acknowledgement of his political virtue and bravery. Rossetti was not entirely taken in. He and his friends were constantly quoting someone's witty observation:

> The Portuguese person named Howell
> Who lays on his lies with a trowel.

But Howell, as Whistler wrote, offered "the greatest service to his friends ... he had the gift of intimacy. He introduced everybody to everybody. He entangled everybody with everybody, and it was easier to get involved with Howell than to get rid of him." Howell needed that "gift". Through it he was able to make a little money finding the blue and white china which Rossetti collected obsessively; and he sold paintings for his pre-Raphaelite friends on commission. He was also prepared to sell Rossetti drawings forged by clever Mrs. Howell. While looking after "the pulling" of Whistler's etchings as a kindness to the great artist, he helped himself to more than a few. Swinburne was a perfect subject for Howell's "gift of intimacy". The latter encouraged the poet in all his curious boyish habits, and later blackmailed him by threatening to sell his letters. Not surprisingly Howell died in a ditch in a Soho street, his throat cut and a gold sovereign clenched between his teeth, a fairly clear indication that some "intimate" had decided to finally pay him off for his dubious services.

Then there was the astounding Richard Burton, on leave from Fernando Po with his big nanny of an ambitious wife Isabel working hard to get him an important post somewhere. Burton was a sexual fantasist of unparalleled imagination and deliberate debauchery. In London he founded a secret group called the Cannibal Club, based upon a typical Burtonian joke. "Without Cannibalism how could the Zealander have preserved his fine physical development?" Swinburne was an immediate convert to the club, for though he had little interest in anthropology, he had always been excited by the thought of eating people. The club dinners, held at Bartolini's, were staged by Burton with full gothic anti-Christian trimmings, a mace in the form of a negro gnawing a thigh bone, and other gruesome cannibal touches. Burton's drinking capacity was far in excess of Swinburne's, but the little red-haired poet tried harder, and both of them were normally carried home in a state of total alcoholic collapse. At the Cannibal Club Swinburne met Thomas Bendyshe, the club's "chaplain", a self-confessed pagan

AS DOLORIDA WITH A WHIP 211

Sir Richard Burton, 1821–90, the eccentric explorer and scholar and fellow carouser of Swinburne.

who had translated the Indian classic *Mahabharata*. He also met there the notorious atheist Charles Bradlaugh, and wrote for him, and as a chant for the club's meetings a charming little anti-christian parody:

> Preserve us from our enemies
> Thou who art Lord of suns and skies
> Whose foot is human flesh in pies
>   And blood in bowls!
> Of thy sweet mercy damn their eyes
> And damn their souls!

Before the Burtons left England for the new consular post, which turned out to be, rather insultingly, a remote position in Brazil, Richard Burton had a farewell weekend with Swinburne and their conscientiously degenerate mutual friend, Lord Houghton, at his country house Fryston. By now even Houghton thought Burton could be exercising a corruptive effect on Swinburne's genius. The ardently Catholic Mrs. Burton, on the other hand, who never realised until her distinguished husband died, that he had all kinds of strange hobbies and activities of which she could not approve (she dealt with them by destroying large quantities of his manuscripts), was now convinced that Swinburne was exercising an evil influence upon her officially discriminated-against genius of a husband. When Houghton told Swinburne what Mrs. Burton felt about him, he replied pointedly, "How can she who believes in the excellence of Richard fail to disbelieve in the virtues of any other man?" But the stimulus Swinburne received from his friends added steam to his already over-heated poetic preoccupations. He wrote to Howell from the Swinburne family estate, Ashburnham Place,

> Infame Libertin ... I have added yet four more jets of boiling and gushing infamy to the perennial and poisonous fountain of *Dolores* ... Since writing the above I have added ten verses to *Dolores* – très-infâmes et très-bien tournés. "Oh! Monsieur, peut-on prendre du plaisir à de telles horreurs?"

Thus proving, apart from his poetic application, that *Dolores* pre-dates his relationship with Menken.

Yet, as Menken might have put it, the poet's destiny was preparing him well for his imminent meeting with the true Dolores, herself, Dolores De Ricardo Los Fiertes. But Swinburne still had a short time left for minor decadent activities around the Rossetti house. Yet even when the naked dancing was a *pas de deux* with the charming but thought-to-be somewhat sinister Simeon Solomon, Jewish post-pre-Raphaelite painter, self-confessed homosexual and dreadful drinker, Swinburne's performance was not considered by his friends to be particularly damaging to his poetic talents. After all, he was an Eton boy and such were the common games of many old Etonians. Even though the notorious Eton headmaster Dr. Keate had blessedly passed on in 1832, memories of him flogging eighty boys in a morning while admonishing the school, "Remember boys, you are to be pure in heart, or I will flog you until you are", remained a vital tradition. Keate's flogging block was an unforgettable fetish for many an old Etonian. So if Swinburne, in his late twenties, had developed the habit of visiting certain notorious "whipping ladies" in St. John's Wood, it was neither surprising nor unusual.

Swinburne's best modern biographer, Jean Overton Fuller, investigated the copy of the *Index Librorum Prohibitorum* of *Pisanus Fraxi* (the literary alias adopted by Henry Spencer Ashbee, a Victorian expert obsessed with curious erotica), and uncovered interesting evidence of the secret erotic practices of gentlemen who had, through the advantages of their educational background and superior social position, developed unusual tastes. Thus Ms. Fuller's insights into Swinburne's sexual inclinations and opportunities to satisfy them answer any English academics still naïve enough to follow Edmund Gosse in regarding the poet as being merely exotically highly-strung and imaginative. That industrious literary pundit delicately left out of his official life of Swinburne all such material. But Ms. Fuller exposed it.* She writes:

> I was able to obtain a check on Gosse's *Confidential Paper* by reference to the *Index Librorum Prohibitorum of Pisanus Fraxi*. There is in the British Museum *Private Case* a copy of the latter in which Fraxi has inserted handwritten leaves between the printed pages. Opposite p. xivi of the *Introduction* (Vol. 1), there is a bunch of such interleaved sheets, being a statement, dated 1875, from a Mr. Hankey, of 2 Rue Lafitte, Paris, for Mr. Ashbee (Pisanus Fraxi) concerning flagellation brothels recently or actually existing in London, for use in the work Fraxi was compiling. Because it contained a reference to an establishment still extant, Fraxi did not commit the matter to print but preserved it in this manner, in his private copy. According to Hankey, there was a Mrs. Colletti who ran a place first in Tansworth Court Gardens, afterwards in Portland Place and finally in Bedford Street (Russell Square), where she died; and there was a Mrs. Potter, who "ran a good business for a few years near Tottenham Court Road" until imprisoned. Hankey adds, "The birch at most of these places was provided by a Mrs. Potter living at Walworth." One may reflect that to keep all these places going there must have considerable numbers of men who shared Swinburne's perversion...
>
> "The only establishment I know of now is in Regent's Park," continues Hankey. At this one, he says, are two very young girls, who pretend to be schoolmasters and "whip fearfully severely". They would belabour clients across the knee, like children, which some clients liked, or in another position (the handwriting is poor, and I cannot read, though it is easy to guess the alternative posture). The premises can hardly have been "in" Regent's Park literally, and the reference is probably to the house in Circus Road, St. John's Wood (near Regent's Park), which was Swinburne's resort...
>
> ... It had been some time early in the summer of 1865 that Swinburne took chambers in 22a Dorset Street, and his letter to Lord Houghton containing the phrase, "old school habits return upon us unawares", written on a Tuesday in July, is the earliest of his preserved letters sent from that address. Swinburne was to keep these chambers for the next three years, so that the introduction to the house in St. John's Wood could have been at any time during this period.

---

* *Swinburne: A Critical Biography*. J. O. Fuller. Chatto & Windus, 1968.

In this period, then, Swinburne was obsessed with flagellation. Writing to his friend Lord Houghton, who shared Swinburne's tastes, but found his *Chastelard* "obscure", Swinburne commences his letter, "Please, Sir, don't hit very hard this time – I haven't been swished yet this half . . ." Throughout a long letter Swinburne maintains the fantasy of being a school-boy, an Etonian preparing for punishment; ". . . let down my breeches, pull up my shirt, and kneel down (for the hundredth time) on the flogging block . . ." The letter is signed, "Your affectionate though much-flogged pupil, Frank."

Swinburne wrote also to the half-Portuguese George Augustus Howell, Rossetti's odd friend whom he knew to be a petty thief, yet found amusing, a letter in which a postscript describes an arrangement between them to develop a flagellant literature.

It is thus clear that Swinburne was prepared to make literary deals to support his erotic habits. He wrote again to Lord Houghton in July, from the chambers at 22a Dorset Street:

> I may hope to be a good boy again, after such a "jolly good swishing" as Rodin alone can and dare administer. The Rugby purists (I am told) tax Eton generally with Maenadism during June and July, so perhaps some old school habits return upon us unawares – to be fitly expiated by old school punishment.

A tribute to the character-forming power of Eton education, perhaps. According to Ms. Fuller, Swinburne's access to these *jeux terribles* arose thus:

> One evening when Swinburne was visiting Saville Clarke at the latter's lodging house (he) took him down into the basement and introduced to him a boy, who, though only half-educated, read poetry. The boy's name was John Thomson, and later through Swinburne, Rossetti also met him. John Thomson had an interest, perhaps a share, in a house in St. John's Wood, where, in luxuriously furnished rooms, two fair-haired and rouged ladies whipped gentlemen who came to them for this service. A third, elder lady, very respectable in appearance, welcomed the guests and took their money. John Thomson introduced Swinburne to this house, and he became a regular client.

It seems likely that this same knowing little John Thomson also first introduced Swinburne to *Mazeppa* at Astley's. The subject's eroticism would assuredly be of interest to both young men, and the pushing young Thomson seems to have previously visited the theatre, and called back-stage on Menken. She was thrilled to meet someone who might justly describe himself as "social secretary" to the young genius whose work so excited her. So Menken enthused about Swinburne to Thomson, Thomson enthused about Menken to Swinburne, dreams were dreamt, and future possibilities established.

Both Rossetti and his famous Italian heroic friend Mazzini strangely passed over Swinburne's aberrations as mere youthful hangovers. Mazzini was encouraging Swinburne to work harder feeling that "he will not last more than one or two years unless he changes his habits". "I wish," wrote Mazzini, "very much, that he would, before vanishing, write something." His Italian intuition supported by the highly physical inspiration Rossetti always found in his own redheaded women, brought them both to the conclusion that what Swinburne needed was a real full-blooded lover in his life. "He might be transformed, but only by some man or woman," wrote Mazzini, "better a woman of course – who would like him very much and assert, at the same time, a moral superiority on him." They discussed various ladies who might be capable of exercising this influence. Mazzini even wrote to his revolutionary country-woman Emelia Venturi, appealing for help in the crusade to rescue the poetic grail secreted in Swinburne's soul. "I should like a certain degree of intercourse between you and him; it might do good, in your sense, to him." No doubt Mazzini's hope was for some sort of high-flown spiritual marriage between the souls of Venturi and Swinburne. But Rossetti and the astoundingly heterosexual Richard Burton with his wealth of Indian and Arabian erotica and endless exotic experiences, thought that a more practical female would be more likely to effect the conversion of Swinburne to that constant poetic output which, apparently, perverse heterosexual practices were considered to encourage. Or perhaps they were simply playing a joke on the often insufferable and obnoxious little genius, whose continuous boasting of endless *amours* may have seemed to call for such a jest. Mazeppa, they decided, was suitably androgynous to undertake the knightly task.

Swinburne having been taken to see *Mazeppa* at Astley's by the queer little working-class fellow, John Thomson, part pimp, part secretary, part male prostitute, the scene was set. Thomson, procurer for the whip-ladies in St. John's Wood, encourager of Swinburne's erotic inclinations in that direction, now offered the image of Menken, leather-strapped, prone, and apparently naked on the back of a wild stallion, a living fantasy certain to stimulate both young men. The suggestion made later by Edmund Gosse that Rossetti gave Menken ten pounds to seduce Swinburne is patently absurd. Menken could, at that time, have bought out Rossetti complete with zoo and china, and hardly noticed it. But an appeal to help regenerate Swinburne when the necessity for such a crusade was put to her, would have been irresistible. The sexual challenge of reclaiming a complex homosexual pervert, and saving England's greatest poet, synchronised with her own very practical requirement of the moment. She needed a talented versifier to polish her own poems, planned for simultaneous publication in London, Paris and New York. Swinburne would be perfect for the work, and was, as we have seen, not disinclined to make literary-erotic deals. She set out to save him at once.

"The work" began some time in the late autumn of 1867, with Menken arriving one night at Swinburne's chambers in Dorset Street, off Baker Street.

By all accounts, Menken was not expected, but perhaps she was hoped for. Swinburne had seen her show, met her, and experienced the full impact of her eyes, figure and admiration. Whatever they did that night can only, as with all love scenes, be surmised, guessed at, and fantasised about. But whatever it was it seems to have suited both of them well enough for the time being, for, according to John Thomson, Menken subsequently became "a frequent nocturnal visitor" to his miniature lyrical genius friend.

The chronically dirty-minded old Victorian literary men speculated endlessly about "the affair". Edmund Gosse reported that Swinburne told him that Menken's only fault as a lover was that she tended to wake up very early in the morning and recite her poems to him, "swinging her handsome legs on the edge of the bed until he thought they would turn to ice in the cold morning air . . . but the passion of her poetic rhapsody seemed to keep her warm". The scene certainly has an authentic comic element, and something of the feeling of the energetic Adah, whipping up the morning literary enthusiasm of the heavily alcoholic poet.

Rossetti, still talking about his amusing arrangement with Menken, said that she had reported to him that "she did not know how it was, but she had not been able to get him (Swinburne) up to the scratch, and could not make him understand that biting's no use". This report is not entirely convincing, for Menken certainly knew more than enough about the sexual eccentricities of the Victorian male to have got any of them "up to the scratch" one way or the other; and, in her Mazeppa *persona*, she knew more about leather bonds and pretty little whips than any of the professional highly rouged ladies of St. John's Wood. If a taste for these simple aberrations was the price the poet required to work on her verses, then her determination to make her poems as perfect as possible would, one feels, have inclined her to an arrangement which would have neither shocked her nor cost her very much effort. She was obsessed with her arrangements for publication with John Camden Hotten at the time, and editorial finalities and refinements were pressing. "Nocturnal visits" to Dorset Street would have been a small consideration for the critical contributions, casual, sleepy and post-alcoholic as they may have been, of England's greatest lyrical poet. But, in fact, the poet delivered little. According to Lesser, who made a detailed comparison of Menken's poems published before and after the encounter, Swinburne just touched up her grammar, capitalised a few words, and added one or two. What Menken did for Swinburne, we may only, like the Victorian literary gentry, surmise.

Swinburne called Menken "Dolores", which she told him was her true name. Though he had, in fact, written his poem of that title before their meeting, he was inclined to repolish and revise continually and his intimate experiences with Menken revived his interest in *Notre Dame de Sept Douleurs*. Some of the verses seem to bear reference to Menken's exotic background and supposed and boasted Jewish origin which was entirely accepted by Swinburne. There are also some fairly clear indications of their style of love-making in the following selection of stanzas from the fifty-five that constitute Swinburne's most memorable poem, *Dolores* (*Notre-Dame de Sept Douleurs*):

> Cold eyelids that hide like a jewel
>   Hard eyes that grow soft for an hour;
> The heavy white limbs, and the cruel
>   Red mouth like a venomous flower;
> When these are gone by with their glories,
>   What shall rest of thee then, what remain,
> O mystic and sombre Dolores,
>   Our Lady of Pain?
>
> O lips full of lust and of laughter,
>   Curled snakes that are fed from my breast,
> Bite hard, lest remembrance come after
>   And press with new lips where you pressed.
> For my heart too springs up at the pressure,
>   Mine eyelids too moisten and burn;
> Ah, feed me and fill me with pleasure,
>   Ere pain come in turn.
>
> Who gave thee thy wisdom? what stories
>   That stung thee, what visions that smote?
> Wert thou pure and a maiden, Dolores,
>   When desire took thee first by the throat?
> What bud was the shell of a blossom
>   That all men may smell to and pluck?
> What milk fed thee first at thy bosom?
>   What sins gave thee first suck?
>
> Could you hurt me, sweet lips, though I hurt you?
>   Men touch them, and change in a trice
> The lilies and languors of virtue
>   For the raptures and roses of vice;
> Those lie where thy foot on the floor is,
>   These crown and caress thee and chain,
> O splendid and sterile Dolores,
>   Our Lady of Pain.
>
> There are sins it may be to discover,
>   There are deeds it may be to delight.
> What new work wilt thou find for thy lover,
>   What new passions for daytime or night?
> What spells that they know not a word of
>   Whose lives are as leaves overblown?
> What tortures undreamt of, unheard of,
>   Unwritten, unknown?

Ah beautiful passionate body
    That never has ached with a heart!
On thy mouth though the kisses are bloody,
    Though they sting till it shudder and smart,
More kind than the love we adore is,
    They hurt not the heart or the brain,
O bitter and tender Dolores,
    Our Lady of Pain.

By the ravenous teeth that have smitten
    Through the kisses that blossom and bud,
By the lips intertwisted and bitten
    Till the foam has a savour of blood,
By the pulse as it rises and falters,
    By the hands as they slacken and strain,
I adjure thee, respond from thine altars,
    Our Lady of Pain.

Ah thy people, thy children, thy chosen,*
    Marked cross from the womb and perverse!
They have found out the secret to cozen
    The gods that constrain us and curse;
They alone, they are wise, and none other;
    Give me place, even me, in their train
O my sister, my spouse, and my mother,
    Our Lady of Pain.

When thy lips had such lovers to flatter,
    When the city lay red from thy rods,
And thine hands were as arrows to scatter
    The children of change and their gods;
When the blood of thy foemen made fervent
    A sand never moist from the main,
As one smote them, their lord and thy servant,
    Our Lady of Pain.

On sands by the storm never shaken,
    Nor wet from the washing of tides;
Nor by foam of the waves overtaken,
    Nor winds that the thunder bestrides;
But red from the print of thy paces,
    Made smooth for the world and its lords,
Ringed round with a flame of fair faces,
    And splendid with swords.

---

* Taken sometimes to be a stanza added, and celebratory of Menken's Jewish origins.

There the gladiator, pale for thy pleasure,*
    Drew bitter and perilous breath;
There torments laid hold on the treasure
    Of limbs too delicious for death;
When thy gardens were lit with live torches;
    When the world was a steed for thy rein;
When the nations lay prone in the porches.
    Our Lady of Pain.

They shall pass and their places be taken,
    The gods and the priests that are pure.
They shall pass, and shalt thou not be shaken?
    They shall perish, and shalt thou endure?
Death laughs, breathing close and relentless
    In the nostrils and eyelids of lust,
With a pinch in his fingers of scentless
    And delicate dust.

But the worm shall revive thee with kisses,
    Thou shalt change and transmute as a god,
As the rod to a serpent that hisses,
    As the serpent again to a rod.
Thy life shall not cease though thou doff it;
    Thou shalt live until evil be slain,
And good shall die first, said thy prophet,
    Our Lady of Pain.

The poem is almost a national anthem for flagellants, and certainly Menken believed that she, and her "affair" with the poet, were its inspirations. This conviction was supported by a lyric published in 1883 with the title "In the Album of Adah Menken". It is a charming and moving little poem of only two verses called *Dolorida*, and was written by Swinburne in his own typically crabbed hand in Menken's album, and attributed to him when it first appeared in public in the 1883 Christmas annual called *Walnuts and Wine*. Swinburne at once most vigorously disowned authorship, writing to the *Pall Mall Gazette* on 28 December, 1883, the following stuffy and pompous disclaimer:

    From the Pall Mall Gazette I derive the information that "Mr. A. C. Swinburne" contributes "Dolorida" to a "Christmas Annual" entitled "Walnuts and Wine". This announcement I presume to be a seasonable freak of jocose invention, and the contribution announced to be simply an example of Christmas burlesque; but, in case any too innocent reader should imagine it to be anything else, I may perhaps as well mention that the annual

---

* Said by some to be a reference to Heenan!

Dolorida, attributed to Swinburne, who denied its authorship on publication.

and the editor, the contributor and the contribution, are all alike unknown to your obedient servant.

But there is no doubt that *Dolorida* is by Swinburne, although it may not have been solely inspired by Menken; for it also appears in the poet's unfinished novel, *Lesbia Brandon*. In passing, one wonders why so many critics have commented upon the fragment so dismissively, for it surely shows a charm and restraint, as well as a degree of wit and feeling, normally quite lacking in Swinburne's hysterical and repetitive effluvia. Here it is:

> Combien de temps, dis, la belle,
> Dis, veux-tu m'être fidèle? –
> Pour une nuit, pour un jour,
>   Mon amour.
>
> L'Amour nous flatte et nous touche
> Du doigt, de l'œil, de la bouche,
> Pour un jour, pour une nuit,
>   Et s'enfuit.

George Moore, one of the literary gentlemen who observed "the affair" with amused speculation, translated the poem with suitable charm:

> How long canst thou be
> Faithful? she said to me
> For one night and a day,
>   Mistress, I may.
>
> Love flatters us with signs
> And kisses on mouth and eyes,
> For one day and a night
>   Before his flight.

Moore wrote later to Thomas J. Wise, the remarkable bibliophile collector, manuscript-dealer, publisher and, alas, it was later discovered, forger, a letter which appears to be in Moore's true hand. In it he writes, "Swinburne's relations with Ada (sic) are mysterious and need clearing up. Whatever they may have been she seems to have been *the only woman* in his life."

By now Swinburne had issued his shameful denial of the authorship of *Dolorida*, and any serious involvement with Menken, boys, whips, or anything else interesting. Moore shrewdly observed that Swinburne's "excuses for his denial of the verses are ingenious, but mine would have been simpler and perhaps nearer the truth – that he told a little lie at the instigation of Watts Dutton". Theodore Watts Dutton was Swinburne's self-elected literary nanny and protector during the latter years of the poet's life. He devoted much time and energy to keeping the little bearded quirky poet safe in his dark gothic house in Putney, alive, sober and well away from pretty little boys, for whom he tended nowadays to develop sudden extraordinary passions. Watts kept Swinburne respectable enough to occupy the high place on the Victorian Parnassus which the academic literary world had now unanimously awarded the middle-aged poet.

Yet Swinburne's correspondence excitingly, if sparsely, chronicles his affair with Menken. At the end of November, 1867, when he was in bed for several days with "influenza and bile" (often a medical description in Swinburne's case for the consequences of an extended drinking binge), his friend Purnell wrote to him: "Today I have had a letter from Dolores – such a letter; she fears you are ill; she is unable to think of anything but you; she wishes me to telegraph to her if you are in danger, and she will fly on the wings of the wind to nurse you. She has become a soft-throated serpent, strangling prayers on her white lips to kiss the poet, whose absence leaves her with ghosts and shadows. She concludes; 'Tell him – say out my despairing nature to him – take care of his precious life. Write at once; believe in me and my holy love for him. Let him write one word in your letter. He will, for he is so good.' What do you think of this? It is Cleopatra over again."

Soon after, Swinburne, perhaps under the influence of the same biliousness, fell from a hansom cab and cut his face on a kerb-stone. On 9 December he replied to Purnell: "If you see Dolores before I do, tell her with my love that I would not show myself sick and disfigured in her eyes. I was spilt last week out of a hansom, and my nose and forehead cut to rags – I was seedy for four days, and hideous."

Punch, with gentlemanly Fleet Street malice, enjoyed it all enormously. Shirley Brooks wrote facetiously that he had seen Menken and, "I am my own no longer, nor my wife's either ... I am Ada's (sic). Swinburne is the only rival I dread; he knew her first. But I shall sit on his corpse. He boasts – but he lies!" Burne-Jones is attributed with a series of cartoons which he sent to Swinburne celebrating "Ye Treue and Pitifulle Historie of ye Poet and ye Ancient Dame", but the only remaining drawing from the series was discovered by the forger Wise and may, perhaps, be held a touch suspect, although the joke-style of the drawing typifies the humorous manner of the literary group who both admired and laughed at Swinburne. Meanwhile the poet continued boasting to his friends about how heterosexual he was these days. To Lord Houghton, he wrote:

> I am glad you found (Lord) Milton enjoying even the immoral and illegitimate bonds of unholy matrimony, though I deplore the perversity which induces young men so far to forget themselves and nature. I also enjoy (*certainly*) not less the bonds of a somewhat riotous concubinage. I don't know many husbands who could exact or expect from a wife such indulgences as are hourly laid at my feet.

To his friend George Powell, Swinburne scribbled from the Arts Club:

> I am ashamed to have left your last note so long unanswered, but I have been so worried of late with influenza, love-making, rather unwholesome things such as business, money, &c., that I have "left undone all that I should have done". I must send you in a day or two a photograph of my present possessor – known to Britannia as Miss Menken and to me as Dolores (her real Christian name) – and myself taken together. We both came out very well. Of course it's private. I've done nothing for an age.

The photograph referred to (page 208) in which a suddenly tired, and over-weight, rapidly ageing and mortally sick Menken, seated, looks up at her demon poet-lover with an expression of pity, compassion, concern and fatigue, caused a scandal which made Swinburne very proud and happy. Menken maintained that Swinburne insisted upon the sitting for the photograph, to equalise the notoriety of the scandalous set of pictures which had been published extensively of herself with Dumas Père. But of the two, though Swinburne adored being notorious, it was Menken who had experience and training in the infant modern

American art of publicity. Certainly she got a great deal of it (together with a few toothmarks), out of the months of her association with Swinburne. She also got from him a gift beyond rubies; the inscription in her own copy of *Infelicia*, "Lo this is she that was the World's delight", something Menken had always aspired to be.

Swinburne's feelings (such as they were), for Menken, persisted for a short time after her death. He wrote to George Powell, again from the Arts Club, on 26 August 1868:

> I am sure you were sorry on my account to hear of the death of my poor, dear Menken. It was a great shock to me and a real grief. I was ill for some days. She was most lovable, as a friend, as well as a mistress.

A kindly little epitaph, but later he was far less generous when writing to Charles Augustus Howell:

> When poor old Menken was close on the end of her life's farce-tragedy, a Parisian journalist circulated the report that she was about to play Psyche to my Cupid in a new ballet or opera-bouffe. Complimentary to my appearance of youth at the time, if not to the discretion of my age.

Eventually "the affair" was blunted by the respectable literary establishment, although when Edmund Gosse was collecting material for his carefully restrained life of Swinburne, he received from a mutual old friend, Julian Field, the following note:

> I knew Swinburne intimately. He came down to Oxford many times when I was at Merton (1869–73), and how drunk he used to get; he told me all about Menken calling on him, and telling him bluntly she had come to sleep with him; and how in the morning, when she used to speak of poetry, he said to her, "My darling, a woman with such beautiful legs should not bother about poetry!" I daresay he told you the same tale. She was photographed with him.

Lafourcade, another Swinburne literary industrialist, smartly observed that at the time of "the affair", Swinburne was translating the substance of Baudelaire's sonnet *La Géante* into his own poetry and life:

> Hast thou found place at the great knees and feet
> Of some pale Titan-woman like a lover,
>   Such as thy vision here solicited,
>   Under the shadow of her fair vast head,
> The deep division of prodigious breasts,

> The solemn slope of mighty limbs asleep,
> The weight of awful tresses that still keep
> The savour and shade of old-world pine-forests
> Where the wet hill-winds weep?

Menken was, actually, not very tall or large-breasted, but then Swinburne was minute. Certainly the verse expresses what the little poet may well have felt in the presence of his symbolically enormous Earth-Mother "mistress". But Baudelaire's original has much greater power than Swinburne's use of it in *Ave Atque Vale*. The French poet wrote:

> J'eusse aimé vivre auprès d'une jeune géante,
> Comme aux pieds d'une reine un chat voluptueux.
> J'eusse aimé voir son corps fleurir avec son âme
> Et grandir librement dans ses terrible jeux.

"Terrible games" would certainly seem an appropriately evocative if over-theatrical description of the transactions which had occurred between England's great sado-masochistic lyrical poet and the remarkable American equestrienne. They must have thoroughly discouraged the idealistic Mazzini. When the photograph of Swinburne and Menken appeared all over town, together with the rumours that the poet was drunkenly boasting he was about to appear on stage with his *inamorata*, the Italian patriot wrote irritably; "I did not ask Swinburne about the stage or the photograph. I really could not play the part of spiritual father to him." It was a sound conclusion in which Swinburne's actual father, the Admiral, and his mother Lady Jane (an Ashburnham of the bluest blood), heartily concurred when someone thoughtfully sent them a copy of the infamous photograph.

It is sometimes argued that Swinburne merely used Menken to counteract the growing scandals of his homosexual relationships, but the silly photograph for which he had been vain enough to sit, scared him as much as it thrilled. He wrote to Powell:

> There has been a damned row about it. Paper after paper has flung pellets of dirt at me, assuming or asserting the falsehood that its publication and sale all over London were things authorised, or permitted, or even forseen by the sitters: whereas, of course, it was a private affair, to be known (or shewn) to friends only.

By the end of May, Menken had returned to France, the charade was over, and Swinburne was back to his normal comic performance as England's most promising poet with an unfortunate tendency to what were euphemistically described as "fainting fits" brought on by excessive drinking, and his other odd habits. He wrote to his friend John Nichol, his face covered with sticking plaster:

I am none the worse for a fainting fit brought on by the damnable unventilated air of the Museum ... I went early to the Brit. Mus. to look up certain references – met a man I know, about to leave – and agreed to wait till he could return at 1 or 1.30, when we were to go and lunch together – began to feel giddy and faint in an hour or so (no wonder you would say, if you had breathed the atmosphere that day) but thought I would hold out and keep my promise, and consequently after some twenty minutes' struggle fainted right out, and in falling, cut my forehead slightly.

In that same Brit. Mus., if one passes through a complex ritual, one may be conducted (as was Ms. Fuller), "to a special seat marked *Reserved for Special Books*, and there study, under the vigilant eye of the Custodian, books from the *Private Case*, a collection not generally available to the public". One of those books is a pseudonymous work by Swinburne published in a limited edition of 250 copies in 1887. It is called *The Whippingham Papers* and consists of a collection of stories, articles, and poems over various schoolboy-style punny names, all concerned with flagellation. Menken's poet-lover is also memorialised in the Museum's Manuscripts Department, in the section classified *Reserved from Public Use*. In a bundle of papers there is so reserved a work written on blue and white foolscap pages, a poem in twelve eclogues entitled *The Flogging Block. An Heroic Poem by Rufus Rodworthy, Esq. With Annotations by Barebum Birchingham, Esq. London 1777*. The eclogues have titles like "Algernon's Flogging" and seem to have been written (according to the watermarks on the paper), in Swinburne's Putney period, presumably a guilty secret kept from his very straight custodian, Watts Dutton. It is hardly a shocking work of pornography to any contemporary habitual paperback reader, but it conclusively demonstrates the life-long pre-occupations of Menken's "lover". The verse is unrelievedly schoolboy in tone. Observes Wilfred, one of Algernon's party:

> What a great fleshy bottom – both fleshy and brawny.
> As plump as two peaches, not skinny and tawny.

Chorus responds:

> Algernon's bottom and Birkenshaw's rod,
> A'n't they a couple of lovers, by God!

Algernon comforts a younger boy, Charlie, as he tremulously approaches his first flogging:

Charlie: I know I shall cry
           at each cut of the birch.

Algernon (smiling):
>Well my boy, so do I
>Quite as often as not. I don't see why
>one shouldn't
>Sing out, if it hurts – if one likes:
>but one wouldn't
>Sing out if it didn't. And sometimes to tell
>The truth, when the master was flogging me well,
>I've howled at the very first cut, & implored
>Him to spare me, & bellowed, & wriggled, & roared,
>And cried till the tears ran all over my face –
>Couldn't help it – can't help it – & where's the
>disgrace?

Ms. Fuller, very reasonably, concludes that the poet's experience of flogging at Eton "was one from which he never recovered. He was at least forty-four when

Striking Parisian cartoons like this one announced Menken's return. Ironically, she lay dying as they appeared.

he wrote these lines ... still psychologically domiciled in the flogging room ... the experience, with its pain, its humiliations, its terrors and its ecstasies had dominated his entire existence, to the extent of making him incapable of a passionate experience in which it played no part."

Meanwhile, as Swinburne, yet to write the schoolboy aberrations in comic verse now interred in its sacrosanct secret archives, had his "fainting fit" in the Brit. Mus., Menken, in Paris, prepared for a production in which she was never to appear, for she was about to take a fall from which, unlike her comic and sad little English poet lover, she would never recover. According to Edmund Gosse, she sent her final selection of poems from Paris for the great poet to look over, and Swinburne reported that, "not only had he done so, but thought he had improved some of the lines considerably". The changes were little enough but Menken had produced a convincing atmosphere of high poetic class around the project which she now felt to be the most important of her life. Throughout 1867, she was constantly pre-occupied with the necessity and urgency for her book to be perfectly designed and published. Perhaps, with her vitality fading, she had for the first time some intimations of mortality. Certainly she was not looking her best, her depressions grew increasingly frequent, and her desperation with the "soul-selling" aspects of a successful theatrical life and the general wear and tear of being Mazeppa, were making her moody, temperamental and demanding. She may even have been in some considerable physical pain throughout this period. Some years later, a Dr. Martin of Guys Hospital, gave an interview to the press which could well account for Menken's physical and psychological state at this time.

Dr. Martin describes visiting Astley's some four months before Menken's death in Paris:

> With another doctor, my immediate superior, we went to see *Mazeppa* one night. The big thrill came when the wild steed galloped into view, through scenery representing the mountains of Tartary, appearing and disappearing in the distance, until through clever staging, the horse and the living form bound on his back appeared small in perspective.
>
> Suddenly the house re-echoed to a woman's scream. The curtain was rung down. The manager came forward. He stated that Miss Menken had sustained a slight injury, and requested that, if there was a doctor in the audience, he would go back stage to her.
>
> We were in the front row, and immediately responded to the call. Miss Menken was lying in the Green Room. "I'm not much hurt," she said smiling. "When turning a corner the horse went too close to one of the flats, and grazed me." The wound was not serious, though painful. We dressed it.

Dr. Martin says he later went to Paris to attend Menken but arrived several hours too late. He observed that all the newspapers gave the cause of her death as consumption, but that was not the case. "She died from a complication of diseases, brought on in the first place by the shock sustained in the accident at Astley's. A cancer growth formed. Her case was incurable." But then everything about Menken was.

A memorial publication showing the many faces of Menken.

Fifteen

Exit Menken, Adele Isaac Barkley – and a curtain call with a bouquet of artificial gardenias

In order to get back to London, the Mecca of poetry, the only possible environment for her final poetess *persona*, Menken had entirely neglected experience and her reputation, so bitterly and successfully fought for and won, of being the world's most expensive artiste. Valuable serious offers were coming in from all over the world, regardless of her virtually unnoticed fiasco in Vienna. But Menken herself felt that failure deeply. The need to pursue her poetic career, so dependent she felt, upon the good offices and support of the literary lions of London, was now paramount in her thoughts and feelings. The theatre seemed suddenly the lowest of the worlds which she aspired to conquer. She had drunk deep of that cup, and seen the spider.

Menken's letters to Stoddard from Vienna and Paris are fascinating, for they contain her evaluation of herself at that moment when the theatre had become nothing but pain, physical pain too, and bitter shadow fruit. "I know your soul!", she wrote to the distant poet for whom she knew her idealised portrait was still unimpaired. "It has met mine somewhere in the starry highway of thought. You must often meet me, for I am a vagabond of fancy without name or aim …" Surely the most accurate description the Menken or any of her publicists or biographers had ever applied to her …" *a vagabond of fancy without name or aim. I was born a dweller in tents, a reveller in the 'tented habitations of war'; consequently, dear poet, my view of life and things are disreputable in the eyes of the 'just'. I am always in bad odor with people who don't know me, and startle those who do. Alas!"* Poeticised as it is, there are valuable fragments of biographical information in her words, with their strong images of the army, an early travelling "tented" life, and the gypsy background of a nomadic carnival and circus player. Menken very rarely gave away such clues to her early years, but in the letter to Stoddard she reveals more than she intended. There we see her, for a moment, the little equestrienne performer hurling herself around the grubby ring in some desolate small provincial town of the South West, treated as a whore with an amusing and daring tom-boy's contempt for danger and an unusual power over horses and, by implication, over men too. There she was again, in the warfare of a travelling entertainer's life, the receptor of the projections of the crude and simple audiences for whom she performed for pennies. And from that lowest rung of the theatrical hell, she had clawed her way up to the greatest heights of the profession, conquering New York, London, and Paris. "Ah! my comrade," she exclaimed to Stoddard. "Paris is, after all, the heart of the world. Know Paris and die". There it was, the shadow history of her entire career behind the sighing affectational style of a typically Bohemian oration, from poetess to poet, a starry soul yearning for oblivion. But we have observed before that these symbolical death-scenes played out by the Menken were always quickly followed by action, the assumption of a new mask, another identity, and an extraordinary burst of manic energy.

Since London was now her aim, she was uninterested in $500 per show offers from wherever they came. If the fickle London theatres, now all committed to new attractions, could offer Menken no significant deal, then she was prepared to pay to get back there. She would accept whatever was offered. Thus the London theatrical public was amazed by an announcement that Astley's would be unexpectedly adding to their seasonal pantomime *Little Jack Horner*, an unprecedented bonus in the form of a return visit by the world's most highly paid star, Adah Isaacs Menken, in her proven success *The French Spy*. It was fine for Astley's but, said her London friends, a dreadful mistake for Menken, most detrimental to her image and status. But she cared nothing for that old mask. For the moment all that concerned her was getting back to London at any price.

In the event, two weeks of sharing applause with *Little Jack Horner* was as much as Menken could take. It was announced that the short appearance was a "farewell engagement previous to the Menken's embarkation for California". In the interim the Menken would be concentrating upon her many other interests, especially the preparation of her collected poems, in which she had the active support of Algernon Charles Swinburne, as great and notorious in poetry as she was in the theatre. But it should be recollected that Miss Menken wasn't simply an actress. As she had described herself to Stoddard, she was "a fair classical scholar, not a bad linguist, can paint a respectable portrait of a good head and face, can write a little and have made successes in sculpture". Why should such an all-round artist limit her activities to the always degenerative theatre? So, living on the proceeds of her Paris and Vienna earnings, supplemented by the sale from time to time of the jewellery which she had never sought with avidity but had, very sensibly, held on to whenever it came her way, she set herself up again in the same suite in her old London Palace, the Westminster Hotel, nursing herself back to health while pulling the strings of her literary *persona*.

For the first time in her life Menken's apparently unbounded vitality was lagging. She avoided exercise, ate too much, a bad tendency which had reasserted itself in the misery and loneliness of that detestable Vienna where, one had to admit, the cuisine was excellent. She had put on weight. Portraits of her taken in Vienna show her very much too full in the face and figure, and wearing, presumably as a prophylactic against the virulent anti-semitism of that city, a prop pearl crucifix.

A tired and overweight Menken.

It had no doubt shocked Menken profoundly to discover that the racist prejudices against which she had written with such animation in America, were, in Europe, an actual malice, certain to be encountered by one who had so publicly committed herself to being a Jewess. The experience must have been traumatic, for Menken came from a society in which there were only three kinds of people

– black and white, and some red ones still left somewhere up in the hills. To be on the wrong end of racist hatred, discrimination, and prejudice, was an integral part, and a repellent one, of her European experience. In the South West of America, because of the shortage of Jewish women, Jews had often married out, so much so that Reform Judaism became a necessary adaptation, a means of survival not unlike the classic solution of European rabbis to the problem of ensuring that the children resulting from pogrom rapes were Jewish. The discovery of the negative aspects of the Jewish identity in Europe must have been profoundly disturbing and confusing to Adah.

Menken looked older after Vienna, and that, too, reduced her self-confidence and energy. Her incessant smoking had given her a chronic cough, her complexion was sallow, and her temper edgy and uncertain; she was subject to bursts of self-pity and grandiloquence, a lovely queen who had degenerated in exile. But now, in royally decisive style back in London, Menken decided to change her luck once again. As if playing faro, she threw a large part of her funds on to the table, and took a lease on the Sadler's Wells Theatre Royal. There, acting as her own management, and "directrice", she announced her intention to mount *Mazeppa* as it had never been staged before. The decision revivified her. She got back into shape and training with that amazing speed which artistes often reveal, a kind of magical transformational power of their wills. On 11 May, the new production opened.

At first, it seemed that Menken still possessed her magical power over the London audiences, and for several nights business was good, almost to capacity. But she was exhausted by the effort of putting together and personally rehearsing a company which was not of the best. Her funds were rapidly running out, and the business quickly dropped off. London was tired of *Mazeppa;* many were now asking how it could ever have been regarded as such an amazing spectacle, played, as it was, by an artiste so lacking in vitality and that essential power of the star to communicate joy and fear to the jaundiced seat-buyers. Her friends realised that the brilliant comet of her professional life was reaching the end of its incredible but short course, and so did she. After a month of struggle with the show, the horses, and the public, Menken declared her position simply and finally. "I'm shot!", she admitted, and closed the show.

And now Menken truly felt tired, and at the point of death. She made a will, witnessed by her friend Susette Ellington, whom she instructed, very specifically, to ensure that she was buried according to the Jewish faith. A plain coffin, a simple funeral service, and the plainest marker with her name were all she requested; and an epitaph which expressed completely the great problem of her life, her constant uncertainty of identity, the sadness of a "vagabond without name". It should be two words hopefully addressed to a Higher Power, some sort of loving Père somewhere in the Universe, who, being all-knowing, would have the answer to that Ultimate Question which Menken had never been able to solve – *who was she*? The two words, taken from Swinburne's poem *Ilicet* were, "Thou Knowest". It was the closest the Menken had ever approached to the edge of an actual grave, much closer than the "suicide" in New Jersey, more real a sense of mortality than when she took the overdose and ran away from Barkley and marriage.

But now, a little late on cue, came the cliff-hanger rescue. Louis Dumaine offered Menken a return to Paris,* Dada, and Dumas, the re-birth of La Belle Menken. He and La Roche had leased the Théâtre du Chatelet and wanted her to star in a new melodrama by a real dramatist, Henri Rochfort's *Theodorus, Roi d'Abyssinie*. It was unbelievable. There, at the very edge of the pit, there were the outstretched supporting arms of her Heavenly Father. If she had ever prayed for a sign, how could she have been offered one of greater significance and better auspices – for was not *Theodorus* her true name, and the role of a dramatic actress the true nature of the unknown woman who had made herself into the Menken? Now there would be an alchemical fusion of Bertha Theodore and all the rest of her dying and dead personalities, into a new and wonderful creation, "Mlle. Adah Isaacs Menken, the Great French Actress". She accepted the offer of a new life gratefully from her Paris friends. First, she would take a little vacation at Le Havre, to get into condition for this attempt upon a higher peak than she had ever yet essayed. Then she would come to Paris and fulfil her destiny. She would become a great actress, her only totally true self would finally be realised.

Menken spent the month of June–July resting and recuperating in fashionable Le Havre. The papers noted that she swam vigorously, and published a cartoon of her among the famous authors, observed in a revealing bathing costume by a giant Dumas and a miniature Swinburne.† She rode, she ate well but with unusual restraint, drank very little, regained her figure, and felt better than she had since the Paris accident. Even though the city would be hot and rehearsals no great pleasure, she looked forward to studying the great new role written for her by the talented Henri Rochfort. Dumaine and La Roche welcomed her with respect and delight. Truly, she looked like a star; but they seemed somewhat uncomfortable and, from time to time, glanced at one another nervously, as if each hoped that the other would spoil the moment with bad news. Finally, it had to come out. The Rochfort play was not ready; it was simply not yet fit for production; the author was still struggling with the words. Menken stared at the producers, her great eyes full of – what? They expected her to produce a scene of temperament and fury, for all knew her capacity in that regard. Would she suspect that, perhaps, the play *was* actually ready, and that all of them had decided that Menken simply could not cope with it? Were they about to lose

---

* She replied to him royally, on tour in Birmingham at "Hen and Chickens Hotel", stating (untruthfully) that her terms were normally "one clear half of the receipts for each night", but for him and Paris, she might accept a little less.

† See cartoon pp. 138–9.

the star, and the season? But Menken was sphinx-like in her silence. While Dumaine explained, nervously, the problem was that the theatre must open on the agreed date; that there was no alternative but to hold over the Rochfort production till later; but, in the meantime, why not, he put it to her, why not give Paris what she had never tired of getting from America's First Great International Star, who was, above all others, an astounding and deeply moving mime; why not, he concluded, present again, for all those thousands of Parisians for whom it was already a myth of the theatre, her amazing spectacle – *Les Pirates de La Savane*?

Remembering the reception she had received in *Die Piraten* in Vienna, seeing her chance to be a serious actress disappear, asking herself what destiny meant by these rapidly changing signs and portents, Menken nevertheless amazed the producers by offering neither argument nor resistance. She accepted, without one word of abuse, one scream of betrayal, one tear of sadness. She agreed to begin rehearsals at once. If she thought that the Rochfort had been cunning bait to draw her back to the theatre of spectacle which she now so deeply loathed, she never said so. Quietly she determined to accept what could not be avoided, and concentrate upon supervising her now even more precious and essential project, the collecting of her poems and the publishing of *Infelicia*. Only thus could she conquer her seemingly inescapable fate to remain forever a contemptible "flesh artist".

The weather was unusually hot, and the theatre unbearable. At the very first rehearsals it was noted, worriedly, by the managers and the rest of the company, that La Menken was not herself. She was listless, silent, lacking in spirit and humour, and seemed often to be in actual discomfort, perhaps even in pain. Ellington knew that Menken had never totally recovered from the accident in her first Paris season. She also knew that Vienna, the macabre affair with the repellent little Swinburne, heavy financial losses in London, and Adah's growing sense that her time was running out, had all worked upon her to produce a mood of profound melancholy, not at all the temperament Adah would need to carry her through the enormous physical demands of another Protean performance. If only she had been able to go on with the relatively physically undemanding project of a dramatic vehicle, she might well have been able to survive, once again, a major crisis in her life. But Menken, in her early thirties (whatever Ellington's press releases said to the contrary), had been abusing and punishing her body for twenty years. She was old in her profession, too old to revive the gay, energetic Dada of *Les Pirates*. Ellington suspected, too, that the pain Menken now suffered from constantly in her left side, was something worse than she would admit.

At the end of the first week's rehearsals, Menken left her box wearily, to make her way down to the stage. She entered and, without uttering a word, collapsed. This time it was no mime performance. She was seriously ill, and all could see it. Rehearsals, it was announced, would continue without her for a few days. All knew, said the producers, worried but hopeful, Mlle. Menken's amazing powers of recuperation.

In an inexpensive, small, and obscure hotel in the Rue Caumartin, Menken rested in her tiny suite, inviting only her best friends to call on her. She talked over with Susette publicity plans for the show, and tried to convince her doctors that the abscess in her side was hurting less and less. She was sure, she said, that it was healing. A journalist friend, Adrien Marx, described his visit to the Rue Caumartin, the first time he had seen "La Belle Americaine" for a year. Then she had been brilliant, beautiful, and successful beyond dreams, in an elegant dressing-room at the Gaité, crowded with the famous, the wealthy, and the fashionable. Now he saw a sick woman, suddenly aged, a magical princess upon whom some maleficent spell had fallen, propped up in bed, smiling, but very sad. He was shocked by her appearance and she saw it. "My poor dear boy," she said, "I feel I am very ill." Marx made the usual denials and noises of encouragement. She took his hand. "I have received my death-wound," she said quietly. "I am lost to art and to life". Very moved, Marx turned away. The Menken pressed his hand harder. "Never mind," she consoled him and herself. "I have lived more than a woman of a hundred years of age; it is only justice I should go to where they carry the old." Marx assured her that her indestructible vitality would soon return and bear her back to success. She thanked him for his confidence, and smiled wryly, the old Menken for a moment, manipulating the nearest writer. "You have never written an article about me," she rebuked him. "Make haste, for if I die you will lose your most admiring reader." Marx assured her that she would read all her marvellous notices for the revival of *Les Pirates*. At this Menken wept bitterly. "They will find someone else," she sobbed. "They always do."

A week later, Menken tried to make sure that didn't happen. Still very ill, she insisted on attending rehearsals, and got through a whole exhausting day of work. The next morning she was on time, and the business continued. But suddenly, Menken's face and body were contorted with pain. She fainted, collapsing on the boards. The company watched in shocked awe, for it was positively her last appearance on any stage, and suddenly, they all knew it. In spite of the sultry heat, they felt chilled by the presence of a dreadful power cruel enough to bring down for no understandable reason, even the greatest of the puppet "immortals" of the theatre.

Susette and Dumaine brought the barely conscious Menken back to the hotel. Several doctors were called in to see if some medical magic might restore her. The doctors argued over their diagnoses, while Menken grew rapidly worse. Some attributed the cause to tuberculosis, the *sine qua non* of all great nineteenth-century actresses' death-scenes. Others supported the theory that the abscess was part of a cancerous growth. Or it might have been a ruptured appendix, with peritonitis having set in. The posthumous conclusion of the medical opinions consulted by the press were that it was one or the other, and possibly all of them. But no post-mortem was held, perhaps because the dying Menken, at the last intensely Jewish again in her beliefs, insisted that the orthodox Jewish embargo on post-mortem be observed. In any case, no one bothered to pursue the matter. The Menken was dead; what more was there to be said? Quite a lot, it seemed, by a surprising range of people. Newspapers all over the world ran stories summarising one or other of the many accounts of her lives, legends and loves. Menken mythology was revived, renewed, and quickly forgotten, like all dreams.

One of the most unexpected characters to suddenly re-emerge in the final scenes of the tableau, "The Last Days of Menken", was that untalented dramatist, *soi-disant* great lover, and protector of the public morality, the first and most vicious of Menken's London critics, H. B. Farnie of *The Orchestra*. According to Farnie, he had become a close friend, and was with the Menken constantly in her last days. He made sure that he obtained the maximum credit and publicity for so being, by writing his own account of the tragic climax, and his moving part in it, to the newspapers. The New York *Clipper* tearfully published the Farnie account in full:

THE LATE MISS MENKEN

The following, which was furnished us by a gentleman who was with Miss Menken during the period of illness preceding her death, is the first and only direct information we have received concerning the last hours, death and funeral of the poet-actress. We commend it to the perusal of our readers:

TO THE EDITOR OF THE CLIPPER – Sir, – After reading several notices of the late Miss Menken's last illness and death, more distinguished for uncharitable surmise than correct information, I cannot refrain from asking you to allow me a little space in your paper, on the same subject. A feeling of camaraderie alone – putting common charity out of the question – impels me to this course. I was engaged by the administration of the Chatelet to write a drama for Miss Menken, in June last, the date of her arrival in Paris; and from that time until her death, in August, I had frequent opportunities of seeing her. She had only attended two rehearsals of the "Pirates de la Savane," in which she was to open at the Chatelet in the beginning of July, when she was prostrated by the painful illness which eventually killed her. The medical men at Paris were puzzled at first with the symptoms; and Miss Menken herself believed that it was inflammatory rheumatism. Later on, it was discovered to be caused by an abscess under her left side. This abscess was supposed by her medical attendants to have been of at least three or four years' growth, and from the moment of discovery they gave up all hope of saving her life. I can bear witness to the exquisite suffering she endured for these three months, and to the resignation and patience she invariably showed. Food she scarcely ever tasted; and she drank nothing but iced water.

Once, and only once, she rose from her bed in the Rue Caumartin, and that was to try the effect of change of air at a pretty little village up the Seine at Bougival, a few miles from Paris. Accompanied by her maid, myself and another friend, she managed to make the little journey; but the effort was too much for her enfeebled frame, and immediately on arrival she went to bed very ill, and there continued till her return to Paris two days afterwards. This melancholy excursion has, I perceive, been described as "an orgie," " a scene of unbridled dissipation" – Menken a Bacchante and her friends Rochesters with a dash of Silenus. How different the fact was, let the kindly patronne of the Hotel des deux Ponts at Bougival testify!

Miss Menken died in the possession of the Jewish faith, and was attended by ministers of that religion. With her past private life neither I nor any writer in public print, has aught to do; but this I may say, without violating the sanctity of the character of death, that however stormy that life may have been, the end was peaceful and serene. "So may she rest, her faults lie gently on her."

I am sure, sir, that you will allow me, in conclusion, to protest against the ghastly pleasantries which are bandied over that poor, dear woman by certain portions of the press. Surely the noble maxim, "Of the dead naught but good," is lesson enough to guide us still in such matters. Tennyson has said –

"We cannot be kind to each other here for an hour",

and the accounts of Menken's death have only served in several instances to point the bitter truth.

She was a woman of an excellent heart – careless and prodigal, it is true, but ever unselfishly. As Alexandre Dumas said to me at Havre, when I told him of Menken's death,

"Poor girl, why was she not her own friend?"

Very truly yours,   HENRY B. FARNIE.

P.S. – One point, I find, I have omitted – the paucity of mourners at her death. There were nearly a hundred present at Père la Chaise, and there would have been three times that number had time permitted; but the French law compels interment within 48 hours, and it was exceedingly difficult for her kind friends who helped in the arrangements, to get at the addresses of friends and acquaintances."

The Farnie letter has often served as the authoritative basis for accounts of Menken's last days; but it contains so many false notes (not the least being its authorship) that one finds it difficult to accept totally; though, no doubt, Farnie was around Paris at the time, and, Paul Pry of the theatre that he was, got in on the act as much as he could. But the character of the Menken was not strong on christian forgiveness, whatever religion she was protesting at any time. It is difficult to see her suddenly accepting tiny sips of iced water from the hands of the suddenly tender Farnie, and taking little rural outings with him. And note too, how the self-made Silenus goes to the trouble of denying rumours which did not exist until he denied them, that this sad dying creature was engaged in "unbridled dissipation" in *his* company; for all knew what a great lover was H. B. Farnie and he must, in all conscience, protect the dead Menken's reputation from the shadow of his own satyr-image. The Farnie letter is a singularly repellent piece of English Victorian hypocrisy and cant; certainly it seems most unlikely that Menken, the Chatelet management or Henri Rochfort would have required the services of one whose writing talent was generally recognised to be tenth-rate.

Yet the Farnie letter is a fascinating document of what stars do to fans; for Farnie was, fundamentally, not much more than one of Nature's fans. Once an artiste was recognised as a star, then there he was to offer iced water, arrange little picnics and clean up after the pet dogs. He epitomises and anticipates that sub-species of journalist who fly around like carrion-crows whenever the elephants have passed, pecking out a fair living from the ordures left behind. Adrien Marx also wrote up Menken's last days, but with some real feeling. Farnie apparently sent him a telegram announcing, as if it were a first night not to be missed, "Come quick the Menken is dying". Marx hurried to Bougival to find Menken delirious and crying for brandy to kill the pain. He assisted the following day with the arrangements to bring her back to Paris. He never saw her again.

Several others, more acceptable than Farnie, visited Menken in those last few days in the Rue Caumartin. Susette Ellington was with her throughout; most of the visitors were writers. Throughout those days and nights of pain and delirium, in her clearer moments, Menken was obsessed with literary matters. *Infelicia* was finally about to be published, and she loved to touch her copy of the little book with the now ironic Swinburne inscription on it.

Thomas Buchanan Read, an author she much admired, visited her and added to her Album the well-intended but comfortless lines:

> To the Menken in her illness.
> We nightly die ourselves to sleep, –
> Then wherefore fear we death? –
> 'Tis but a slumber still more deep,
> And undisturbed by breath.

But Read was a true friend, and knew exactly the sort of comfort Menken now needed. He brought the patriarchal, white-bearded poet, Henry Wadsworth Longfellow, to salute her, one great American artist to another. It was the famous poet's one day in Paris *en route* to Italy, and he spent a good part of it with Menken, composing a poem for her in the Album, that precious collection of testimonials to her worth as an artist, a true artist, not just a "flesh" one. *Infelicia*, her Hebrew Bible, and the Album were now the only possessions upon which she placed any value. It was a vapid enough little lyric Longfellow added to her collection; but the sentiment doubtless brought tears to Menken's eyes in her weakened emotional condition:

> The brook is voluble with song
>   As it murmurs down the mountain;
> And strange soft airs the winds prolong,
>   Replying to the fountain;
> And the jubilant birds from each leafy spray
> Sing till they sing their lines away.
>
> What is the song of brook and breeze?
>   And that sets the fountain flowing?
> And that the birds sing out of trees
>   Whenever the South wind is blowing?
> Oh jubilant heart, the answer is plain,
> 'Tis Love, fond Love that awakens the strain!

Longfellow was to be the last poet collected by Menken. Swinburne was busy disowning her in London; Dumas was deeply involved in the productions arising out of the recreated interest in his work following the publicity of his *affaire* with Menken. He may or may not have given Farnie that dreary little quote: "Poor girl, why was she not her own friend?", but certainly, she had been *his* friend. It was said that Dumas, her Père and last lover, had no time to call upon "the poor girl" in her last days. No doubt there is a gallic expression which, translated roughly, means "that's show business".

The Album* containing her treasured testimonials, including those from Swinburne and Dumas, Menken left to Hotten, hoping presumably, that he who had published everything else, would immortalise them in print some day. There seems no other reason why she should have left so precious a record of her literary status to a publisher. But perhaps she had not noticed that Hotten had removed his distinguished name (and even that of his printer), from their edition of *Infelicia*.

Menken's Hebrew Bible she left to her "brother" Ed James, who certainly must have loved her, for he never complained of the gift, was in a bad way financially, and could have done with something a little more negotiable for a non-conformist journalist. Anyway, apart from some ordinary clothes, there was no money, jewellery, furs or expensive costumes left. The last weeks of illness had consumed the Menken and her estate completely. Although in the past few years she had earned many hundreds of thousands of dollars, she had kept no accounts, and had saved nothing. She left, apart from the Album and her Bible,

---

* The Album is now in the Brown University library, at Provincetown, Massachusetts.

only her writings, thousands of *cartes de visite*, posters, programs, and good and bad notices, the litter of a true star.

It was said that she died "at peace", a rabbi being present to conduct her whispering through the necessary prayers. *Kaddish*, the Hebrew prayer for the dead, that most moving of total submissions to the inexorable and unknowable Will of the Almighty, was made for her by unknown members of the Jewish Burial Society of Paris. She was to be carried, as she put it, where the old people go, the old Jewish people who are strangers, and are buried by the gates. The official document was issued permitting "l'inhumation" on *10 Aôut 1868*, in the first division east, third line south, of the Jewish section of the Cimetière Parisien, the Père La Chaise.

Menken's famous invocation, *Thou Knowest*, was addressed in vain to the

The burial certificate.

Direction des Affaires Municipales et du Contentieux, the section of the immense Paris bureaucracy responsible for issuing certificates permitting burial. Her certificate is issued in the name of "Menken Adèle Isaac Barclay". Not even the great Paris bureaucracy, such a stickler for accuracy, was able to decide who she was.

That burial ceremony, simple, and brief, in a grave marked only with a wooden shield, was attended by one of the smallest audiences the Menken had ever drawn, no more than a hundred mourners. But her curtain call, and it was, given the nature of the Menken, inevitable that she should rise again for a final adieu, was witnessed by even fewer; only four mourners were present. Ed James filed the macabre Poesque account to the New York *Clipper*, and reprinted it in the sad 24-page pamphlet he wrote and published twenty years later.

In 1869 James, who had been unable to get to Paris during the Menken's illness and death, and had brooded on it, was losing his sight through "an incurable affection of the eyes, contracted while going to the funeral of Harry Lazarus, who was murdered in New York by Barney Friery". Now he had come over to seek, somewhere in Europe, a specialist who might perhaps be able to save his eye-sight. His story continues, thus, the strangest, simplest, straightest, and most moving press release he ever wrote for his lovely "sister":

> It occurred to us that the trip might be made commemorative by placing a monument over the remains of Adah Isaacs Menken, who died a few months previous. To this end many Americans, English and French professional acquaintances were sought out and an effort made to get up a benefit. Failing to raise the money this way, a private subscription was started, but the great heart had passed away, and neither Dumas, nor Swinburne, nor any of the thousands of leeches who drank her champagne in life and reveled in her society and manifold charms know her in death, and we had to give it up as far as the theatrical or literary fraternity of London or Paris were concerned, although she had been the greatest female American star who had ever appeared in either of those cities. We determined, therefore, to make the attempt alone, which was carried out in spite of all obstacles and criticisms, receiving but one loan from any source whatever towards the two thousand francs, and that from, perhaps, the last person we ought to have expected it, viz: Captain James Barkley (sic), of California, Adah's last husband, and who has since joined her in the spirit land.
>
> It was with the greatest secrecy and difficulty we managed to carry out our plans, as it is strictly against the Jewish customs ever to remove the dead when once buried; but by means not necessary to tell everybody, we finally accomplished our object in Paris a little over eight months after her death. We might here mention that certain forms had to be complied with, and in order to accomplish the work it was necessary to make application as the brother of the dead actress; and here, strange as it may appear, the relation she assumed towards us in life now had to be used or the mission failed.
>
> The day set apart for the exhumation, April 21, 1869, began with a

heavy rain storm, but at ten o'clock it gradually cleared up, and at eleven the sun shone out in a blaze of glory, the sky became cloudless, and the air was as pure and fresh as could be desired.

Accompanied by a professional lady friend of Menken's we went to the maison of M. Latour, the sculptor, 16 Rue la Roquette, Paris, and from thence to the Cemeterie Père la Chaise. At the gates of the Jewish burying ground (where strangers only are interred) the hearse was waiting, and proceeded to the grave, which had been already opened. While the workmen were engaged in raising the coffin, a simple pine box with four handles, a coincidence occurred worthy of mentioning. With the exception of the gendarme and necessary workmen, only Adah's lady acquaintance, the sculptor, interpreter and the writer were present, but just as the coffin was about to be placed on the bier to be carried to the hearse a lady and gentleman with one of the guides entered the enclosure, having come from Rouen the night previous especially to see poor Adah's grave. The party turned out to be Americans, Mr. J. B. Miller, of Philadelphia, and his sister, both great admirers of the deceased as a poetess, and for her mental abilities. They presented us with a bouquet of artificial camelias and violets to place on the new grave.

At 12:15 p.m. of the same day we started from the old cemetery and reached the Cemetery Mont Parnasse [sic] at 1:05 p.m. Everything had been managed so as to avoid display, and with the exception of M. Latour, Mr. John Leighton (our interpreter), who went in the same carriage with us, no one in Paris, beside the officials, knew anything whatever about the movement.

On entering the Israelite part of the cemetery the Menken monument was the first to meet the eye. At 1:10 the coffin was lowered into the vault, and previous to being covered four immortelles, wreaths of black and white beads, were placed upon it. It was then covered by a large square of granite, resting on ledges at each side of the vault, which were cemented together, and also at the ends and sides, thus forever closing in the remains of the once far-famed "Menken!" Two little mementoes in glass cases (a pansy and forget-me-not) were placed over the head of the coffin on the granite. The tomb was then closed. Every little token of remembrance found in the grave at Père la Chaise was sacredly transferred to the one at Mont Parnasse, and arranged about the monument and railings. There were in all twenty different tributes of affectionate remembrance. The inscription in front of the monument which stands eight feet high, reads thus:

ADAH ISAACS MENKEN
Born in Louisiana, United States of America
Died in Paris, August 10, 1868

On the south side of the tomb facing the cemetery are the words, "Thou Knowest".

That monument with its unanswered query has long since disappeared.

Postscript

IT IS, perhaps, somewhat foolhardy to undertake the writing of a biography of a woman whose identity for the first half of her life is, in terms of verifiable facts, virtually unknown. Yet that very anonymity, determinedly protected by multi-coloured clouds of fantasies (not to say downright lies), the inventions partly of our subject, and later of those who eagerly projected their own dream requirements upon her, is in itself a significant quality of stars. Many performers both suffer from, and enjoy, the psychological pressures and practical advantages of a fluid identity. The pursuit of a public image, in whatever masks may assist to that end, is an essential ingredient of the fuel that drives such artists. They take their terrible uncertainty and use the energy it generates to propel themselves forwards and upwards at super-normal pace, reflecting on the audience as much brightness as it focusses upon them. If they move fast enough and shine brilliantly enough we call them *Stars*, and then their identity problems are of no consequence to us, for their function is to play out our fantasies while stitching together their own. Neither we nor they have any profit to draw from knowing the petty details of a life which makes us so tediously real, and the apparent absence of which makes them so brightly huge.

Maybe, then, in undertaking to quest after the "real" Adah Isaacs Menken, one is immediately cancelling out the only Adah Isaacs Menken. For the Menkens are never "real" in that sense; they are mythical. Now, if you are to invent yourself, and manipulate and stimulate, seduce, cajole and bribe others into accepting your myth, it is a distinct advantage to start off by not knowing who you are. You are then free to become Someone, Anyone, to assume a mask, take up a *persona*, or a dozen masks, a dozen *personae*; if you can do it successfully in front of enough people for long enough, then you will become, as they say, a living legend, a myth, a star. You need not have an excess of any particular talent to undertake this odyssey. If you are very beautiful, then that is enormously helpful, and a true talent in itself; but you need not be a very highly creative person. That could make you too demanding of yourself; your perfectionism might undermine your success. You need not be too brilliantly clever either, or over-educated, for then you might o'erleap your public. In any case "genius" in stars is what the spokesmen of the public call the finished dazzling product, if it is reasonably intelligent as well as beautiful, and can talk with relative coherence and ease on fashionable questions.

It will help to be subject to moods of great self-doubt, sudden total loss of identity, profound melancholy, combined always with insatiable greed for love. The public is always romantic and associates such states with the exceptional individual, the artist, the Bohemian, the star, the genius. It also expects and considers it morally just that, in order to pay for the riches and acclaim heaped upon them, our minor gods and goddesses should suffer from dreadful uncertainties, madnesses, and tragic losses, in all those areas of life through which we, the simpler, poorer, and unbrilliant members of their public normally pass with merely ordinary pain and despair. Great people, with great destinies, and great successes protect us from great tragedies. We enjoy equally watching them in ecstasy or agony, entertaining us. We are voyeurs and our mirrors are the media. These in the nineteenth century were only printed words and theatres of one sort or another. The woman who was Menken used them to create herself.

Adah Isaacs Menken didn't know who she was, and no one has ever found out. Why should it matter, anyway? A sensational actress of a century ago, a comet with a brief brilliant path and a fast disappearance, why should anyone care about the true identity of such a forgotten wonderwoman? Yet I have found her tracks, faded but still quite distinct, in all my journeys through the deserts and jungles of theatre and film. Making herself into America's First Great International Star, Menken invented many of the techniques of the modern star-making business. She did it with some talent, much personal courage, immense beauty in the style of her time, total brazenness, incredible ambition-drive, great intelligence, and the driving force which comes from the need for, and pursuit of, an identity.

Do all artists experience doubts about who they really are? Does the soaring imagination, the unbridled fantasy, lift the theatrically creative off and away from the ability to recognise and accept what is ordinarily regarded as "reality"? Is the rebellion of the old-fashioned "Bohemian romantic" merely a pose of creative personalities? Or is it a true heroism, mad enough to confront a world that has never been, and never will be, very safe for artists or pretty little girls without names? Questing for Menken has been for me an exploration of the nature of the actor-artist-showman-woman. It has had the lovely quality of being both brave and comic, a magical style sadly missing in the lives of those who are not excited by comets, however brief their progress. Of course, I haven't found out who she was.

Wolf Mankowitz
Ahakista, Co. Cork

APPENDIX

A Selection of the Poems of A. I. Menken

My Heritage

"My heritage!" It is to live within
        The marts of Pleasure and of Gain, yet be
No willing worshiper at either shrine;
To think, and speak, and act, not for my pleasure,
But others'. The veriest slave of time
And circumstances. Fortune's toy!
To hear of fraud, injustice, and oppression,
And feel who is the unshielded victim.
        Cold friends and causeless foes!
        Proud thoughts that rise to fall.
Bright stars that set in seas of blood;
Affections, which are passions, lava-like
Destroying what they rest upon. Love's
Fond and fervid tide preparing icebergs
That fragile bark, this loving human heart.
        O'ermastering Pride!
        Ruler of the Soul!
Life, with all its changes, cannot bow ye.
        Soul-subduing Poverty!
That lays his iron, cold grasp upon the high
Free spirit: strength, sorrow-born, that bends
But breaks not in his clasp—all, all
These are "my heritage!"
And mine to know a reckless human love, all passion and intensity, and see a mist
come o'er the scene, a dimness steal o'er the soul!
    Mine to dream of joy and wake to wretchedness!
    Mine to stand on the brink of life

One little moment where the fresh'ning breeze
Steals o'er the languid lip and brow, telling
Of forest leaf, and ocean wave, and happy
Homes, and cheerful toil; and bringing gently
To this wearied heart its long-forgotten
Dreams of gladness.
  But turning the fevered cheek to meet the soft kiss of the winds, my eyes look to the sky, where I send up my soul in thanks. The sky is clouded – no stars – no music – the heavens are hushed.
  My poor soul comes back to me, weary and disappointed.
  The very breath of heaven, that comes to all, comes not to me.
  Bound in iron gyves of unremitting toil, my vital air is wretchedness – what need I any other?
  "My heritage!" The shrouded eye, the trampled leaf, wind-driven and soiled with dust – these tell the tale.
    Mine to watch
  The glorious light of intellect
  Burn dimly, and expire; and mark the soul,
  Though born in Heaven, pause in its high career,
  Wave in its course, and fall to grovel in
  The darkness of earth's contamination, till
  Even Death shall scorn to give a thing
  So low his welcome greeting!
  Who would be that pale,
  Blue mist, that hangs so low in air, like Hope
  That has abandoned earth, yet reacheth
  Not the stars in their proud homes?
  A dying eagle, striving to reach the sun?
  A little child talking to the gay clouds as they flaunt past in their purple and crimson robes?
  A timid little flower singing to the grand old trees?
  Foolish waves, leaping up and trying to kiss the moon?
  A little bird mocking the stars?
  Yet this is what men call Genius.

Judith

"Repent, or I will come unto thee quickly, and will fight thee with the sword of my mouth."
– REVELATION ii. 16.

I.

ASHKELON is not cut off with the remnant of a valley.
  Baldness dwells not upon Gaza.
  The field of the valley is mine, and it is clothed in verdure.

The steepness of Baal-perazim is mine;
And the Philistines spread themselves in the valley of Rephaim.
They shall yet be delivered into my hands.
For the God of Battles has gone before me!
The sword of the mouth shall smite them to dust.
I have slept in the darkness –
But the seventh angel woke me, and giving me a sword of flame, points to the blood-ribbed cloud, that lifts his reeking head above the mountain.
Thus am I the prophet.
I see the dawn that heralds to my waiting soul the advent of power.
  Power that will unseal the thunders!
  Power that will give voice to graves!
    Graves of the living;
    Graves of the dying;
    Graves of the sinning;
    Graves of the loving;
    Graves of despairing;
And oh! graves of the deserted!
These shall speak, each as their voices shall be loosed.
And the day is dawning.

II.

Stand back, ye Philistines!
Practise what ye preach to me;
I heed ye not, for I know ye all.
Ye are living burning lies, and profanation to the garments which with stately steps ye sweep your marble palaces.
Your palaces of Sin, around which the damning evidence of guilt hangs like a reeking vapor.
Stand back!
I would pass up the golden road of the world.
A place in the ranks awaits me.
I know that ye are hedged on the borders of my path,
Lie and tremble, for ye well know that I hold with iron grasp the battle axe.
Creep back to your dark tents in the valley.
Slouch back to your haunts of crime.
Ye do not know me, neither do ye see me.
But the sword of the mouth is unsealed, and ye coil yourselves in slime and bitterness at my feet.
I mix your jeweled heads, and your gleaming eyes, and your hissing tongues with the dust.
My garments shall bear no mark of ye.
When I shall return this sword to the angel, your foul blood will not stain its edge.
It will glimmer with the light of truth, and the strong arm shall rest.

III.

Stand back!
I am no Magdalene waiting to kiss the hem of your garment.
It is mid-day.
See ye not what is written on my forehead?
I am Judith!
I wait for the head of my Holofernes!
Ere the last tremble of the conscious death-agony shall have shuddered, I will show it to ye with the long black hair clinging to the glazed eyes, and the great mouth opened in search of voice, and the strong throat all hot and reeking with blood, that will thrill me with wild unspeakable joy as it courses down my bare body and dabbles my cold feet!
My sensuous soul will quake with the burden of so much bliss.
Oh, what wild passionate kisses will I draw up from that bleeding mouth!
I will strangle this pallid throat of mine on the sweet blood!
I will revel in my passion.
At midnight I will feast on it in the darkness.
For it was that which thrilled its crimson tides of reckless passion through the blue veins of my life, and made them leap up in the wild sweetness of Love and agony of Revenge!
I am starving for this feast.
Oh forget not that I am Judith!
And I know where sleeps Holofernes.

One Year Ago

In feeling I was but a child,
    When first we met – one year ago,
As free and guileless as the bird,
    That roams the dreary woodland through.

My heart was all a pleasant world
    Of sunbeams dewed with April tears:
Life's brightest page was turned to me,
    And naught I read of doubts or fears.

We met – we loved – one year ago,
    Beneath the stars of summer skies;
Alas! I knew not then, as now,
    The darkness of life's mysteries.

You took my hand – one year ago,
    Beneath the azure dome above,
And gazing on the stars you told
    The trembling story of your love.

I gave to you – one year ago,
    The only jewel that was mine;
My heart took off her lonely crown,
    And all her riches gave to thine.

You loved me, too, when first we met,
    Your tender kisses told me so.
How changed you are from what you were
    In life and love – one year ago.

With mocking words and cold neglect,
    My truth and passion are repaid,
And of a soul, once fresh with love,
    A dreary desert you have made.

Why did you fill my youthful life
    With such wild dreams of hope and bliss?
Why did you say you loved me then,
    If it were all to end in this?

You robbed me of my faith and trust
    In all Life's beauty – Love and Truth,
You left me nothing – nothing save
    A hopeless, blighted, dreamless youth.

Strike if you will, and let the stroke
    Be heavy as my weight of woe;
I shall not shrink, my heart is cold,
    'Tis broken since one year ago.

Drifts That Bar My Door

I.

O ANGELS! will ye never sweep the drifts from my door?
Will ye never wipe the gathering rust from the hinges?
How long must I plead and cry in vain?
Lift back the iron bars, and lead me hence.

Is there not a land of peace beyond my door?
Oh, lead me to it – give me rest – release me from this unequal strife.
> Heaven can attest that I fought bravely when the heavy blows fell fast.
> Was it my sin that my strength failed?
> Was it my sin that the battle was in vain?
> Was it my sin that I lost the prize? I do not sorrow for all the bitter pain and blood it cost me.
> Why do ye stand sobbing in the sunshine?
> I cannot weep.
> There is no sunlight in this dark cell. I am starving for light.
> O angels! sweep the drifts away – unbar my door!

II.

> Oh, is this all?
> Is there nothing more of life?
> See how dark and cold my cell.
> The pictures on the walls are covered with mould.
> The earth-floor is slimy with my wasting blood.
> The embers are smouldering in the ashes.
> The lamp is dimly flickering, and will soon starve for oil in this horrid gloom.
> My wild eyes paint shadows on the walls.
> And I hear the poor ghost of my lost love moaning and sobbing without.
> Shrieks of my unhappiness are borne to me on the wings of the wind.
> I sit cowering in fear, with my tattered garments close around my choking throat.
> I move my pale lips to pray; but my soul has lost her wonted power.
> Faith is weak.
> Hope has laid her whitened corse upon my bosom.
> The lamp sinks lower and lower. O angels! sweep the drifts away – unbar my door!

III.

> Angels, is this my reward?
> Is this the crown ye promised to set down on the foreheads of the loving – the suffering – the deserted?
> Where are the sheaves I toiled for?
> Where the golden grain ye promised?
> These are but withered leaves.
> Oh, is this all?
> Meekly I have toiled and spun the fleece.
> All the work ye assigned, my willing hands have accomplished.
> See how thin they are, and how they bleed.
> Ah me! what meagre pay, e'en when the task is over!

My fainting child, whose golden head graces e'en this dungeon, looks up to me and pleads for life.

O God! my heart is breaking!

Despair and Death have forced their skeleton forms through the grated window of my cell, and stand clamoring for their prey.

The lamp is almost burnt out.

Angels, sweep the drifts away – unbar my door!

IV.

Life is a lie, and Love a cheat.

There is a graveyard in my poor heart – dark, heaped-up graves, from which no flowers spring.

The walls are so high, that the trembling wings of birds do break ere they reach the summit, and they fall, wounded, and die in my bosom.

I wander 'mid the gray old tombs, and talk with the ghosts of my buried hopes.

They tell me of my Eros, and how they fluttered around him, bearing sweet messages of my love, until one day, with his strong arm, he struck them dead at his feet.

Since then, these poor lonely ghosts have haunted me night and day, for it was I who decked them in my crimson heart-tides, and sent them forth in chariots of fire.

Every breath of wind bears me their shrieks and groans.

I hasten to their graves, and tear back folds and folds of their shrouds, and try to pour into their cold, nerveless veins the quickening tide of life once more.

Too late – too late!

Despair hath driven back Death, and clasps me in his black arms.

And the lamp! See, the lamp is dying out!

O angels! sweep the drifts from my door! – lift up the bars!

V.

Oh, let me sleep.

I close my weary eyes to think – to dream.

Is this what dreams are woven of?

I stand on the brink of a precipice, with my shivering child strained to my bare bosom.

A yawning chasm lies below. My trembling feet are on the brink.

I hear again his voice; but he reacheth not out his hand to save me.

Why can I not move my lips to pray?

They are cold.

My soul is dumb, too.

Death hath conquered!

I feel his icy fingers moving slowly along my heartstrings.

How cold and stiff!

The ghosts of my dead hopes are closing around me.
They stifle me.
They whisper that Eros has come back to me.
But I only see a skeleton wrapped in blood-stained cerements.
There are no lips to kiss me back to life.
O ghosts of Love, move back – give me air!
Ye smell of the dusty grave.
Ye have pressed your cold hands upon my eyes until they are eclipsed.
The lamp has burnt out.
O angels! be quick! Sweep the drifts away! – unbar my door!
Oh, light! light!

Aspiration

Poor, impious Soul! that fixes its high hopes
    In the dim distance, on a throne of clouds,
And from the morning's mist would make the ropes
    To draw it up amid acclaim of crowds –
Beware! That soaring path is lined with shrouds;
    And he who braves it, though of sturdy breath,
May meet, half way, the avalanche and death!

O poor young Soul! – whose year-devouring glance
    Fixes in ecstasy upon a star,
Whose feverish brilliance looks a part of earth,
    Yet quivers where the feet of angels are,
And seems the future crown in realms afar –
    Beware! A spark *thou* art, and dost but see
Thine own reflection in Eternity!

Hear, O Israel!

(*From the Hebrew.*)

"And they shall be my people, and I will be their God." – Jeremiah xxxlii. 38.

I.

Hear, O Israel! and plead my cause against the
    ungodly nation!
'Midst the terrible conflict of Love and Peace, I departed from thee, my people, and spread my tent of many colors in the land of Egypt.
In their crimson and fine linen I girded my white form.

Sapphires gleamed their purple light from out the darkness of my hair.
The silver folds of their temple foot-cloth was spread beneath my sandaled feet.
Thus I slumbered through the daylight.
> Slumbered 'midst the vapor of sin,
> Slumbered 'midst the battle and din,
> Wakened 'midst the strangle of breath,
> Wakened 'midst the struggle of death!

II.

Hear, O Israel! my people – to thy goodly tents do I return with unstained hands.
Like as the harts for the water-brooks, in thirst, do pant and bray, so pants and cries my longing soul for the house of Jacob.
My tears have unto me been meat, both in night and day:
And the crimson and fine linen moulders in the dark tents of the enemy.
With bare feet and covered head do I return to thee, O Israel!
With sackcloth have I bound the hem of my garments.
With olive leaves have I trimmed the border of my bosom.
The breaking waves did pass o'er me; yea, were mighty in their strength –
> Strength of the foe's oppression.
My soul was cast out upon the waters of Sin: but it has come back to me.
My transgressions have vanished like a cloud.
The curse of Balaam hath turned to a blessing;
And the doors of Jacob turn not on their hinges against me.
Rise up, O Israel! for it is I who passed through the fiery furnace seven times, and come forth unscathed, to redeem thee from slavery, O my nation! and lead thee back to God.

III.

Brothers mine, fling out your white banners over this Red Sea of wrath!
Hear ye not the Death-cry of a thousand burning, bleeding wrongs?
Against the enemy lift thy sword of fire, even thou, O Israel! whose prophet I am.
For I, of all thy race, with these tear-blinded eyes, still see the watch-fire leaping up its blood-red flame from the ramparts of our Jerusalem!
And my heart alone beats and palpitates, rises and falls with the glimmering and the gleaming of the golden beacon flame, by whose light I shall lead thee, O my people! back to freedom!
Give me time – oh give me time to strike from your brows the shadow-crowns of Wrong!
On the anvil of my heart will I rend the chains that bind ye.
Look upon me – oh look upon me, as I turn from the world – from love, and passion, to lead thee, thou Chosen of God, back to the pastures of Right and Life!

Fear me not; for the best blood that heaves his heart now runs for thee, thou lonely Nation!

Why wear ye not the crown of eternal royalty, that God set down upon your heads?

Back, tyrants of the red hands!

Slouch back to your ungodly tents, and hide the Cainbrand on your foreheads!

Life for life, blood for blood, is the lesson ye teach us.

We, the Children of Israel, will not creep to the kennel graves ye are scooping out with iron hands, like scourged hounds!

Israel! rouse ye from the slumber of ages, and, though Hell welters at your feet, carve a road through these tyrants!

The promised dawn-light is here; and God – O the God of our nation is calling!

Press on – press on!

IV.

Ye, who are kings, princes, priests, and prophets. Ye men of Judah and bards of Jerusalem, hearken unto my voice, and I will speak thy name, O Israel!

Fear not; for God hath at last let loose His thinkers, and their voices now tremble in the mighty depths of this old world!

Rise up from thy blood-stained pillows!

Cast down to dust the hideous, galling chains that bind thy strong hearts down to silence!

Wear ye the badge of slaves?

See ye not the watch-fire?

Look aloft, from thy wilderness of thought!

Come forth with the signs and wonders, and thy strong hands, and stretched-out arms, even as thou didst from Egypt!

Courage, courage! trampled hearts!

Look at these pale hands and frail arms, that have rent asunder the welded chains that an army of the Philistines bound about me!

But the God of all Israel set His seal of fire on my breast, and lighted up, with inspiration, the soul that pants for the Freedom of a nation!

With eager wings she fluttered above the blood-stained bayonet-points of the millions, who are trampling upon the strong throats of God's people.

Rise up, brave hearts!

The sentry cries: "All's well!" from Hope's tower!

Fling out your banners of Right!

The watch fire grows brighter!

All's well; All's well!

Courage! Courage!

The Lord of Hosts is in the field,

The God of Jacob is our shield!

Answer Me

I.

In from the night.

The storm is lifting his black arms up to the sky.

Friend of my heart, who so gently marks out the life-track for me, draw near to-night;

Forget the wailing of the low-voiced wind:

Shut out the moanings of the freezing, and the starving, and the dying, and bend your head low to me:

Clasp my cold, cold hands in yours;

Think of me tenderly and lovingly:

Look down into my eyes the while I question you, and if you love me, answer me –

Oh, answer me!

II.

Is there not a gleam of Peace on all this tiresome earth?

Does not one oasis cheer all this desert-world?

When will all this toil and pain bring me the blessing?

Must I ever plead for help to do the work before me set?

Must I ever stumble and faint by the dark wayside?

Oh the dark, lonely wayside, with its dim-sheeted ghosts peering up through their shallow graves!

Must I ever tremble and pale at the great Beyond?

Must I find Rest only in your bosom, as now I do?

Answer me –

Oh, answer me!

III.

Speak to me tenderly.

Think of me lovingly.

Let your soft hands smooth back my hair.

Take my cold, tear-stained face up to yours.

Let my lonely life creep into your warm bosom, knowing no other rest but this.

Let me question you, while sweet Faith and Trust are folded their white robes around me.

Thus am I purified, even to your love, that came like John the Baptist in the Wilderness of Sin.

You read the starry heavens, and lead me forth.

But tell me if, in this world's Judea, there comes never quiet when once the heart awakes?

Why must it ever hush Love back?

Must it only labor, strive, and ache?

Has it no reward but this?

Has it no inheritance but to bear – and break?

   Answer me –

   Oh, answer me!

IV.

The Storm struggles with the Darkness.

Folded away in your arms, how little do I heed their battle!

The trees clash in vain their naked swords against the door.

I go not forth while the low murmur of your voice is drifting all else back to silence.

The darkness presses his black forehead close to the window pane, and beckons me without.

Love holds a lamp in this little room that hath power to blot back Fear.

But will the lamp ever starve for oil?

Will its blood-red flame ever grow faint and blue?

Will it uprear itself to a slender line of light?

Will it grow pallid and motionless?

Will it sink rayless to everlasting death?

   Answer me –

   Oh, answer me!

V.

Look at these tear-drops.

See how they quiver and die on your open hands.

Fold these white garments close to my breast, while I question you.

Would you have me think that from the warm shelter of your heart I must go to the grave?

And when I am lying in my silent shroud, will you love me?

When I am buried down in the cold, wet earth, will you grieve that you did not save me?

Will your tears reach my pale face through all the withered leaves that will heap themselves upon my grave?

Will you repent that you loosened your arms to let me fall so deep, and so far out of sight?

Will you come and tell me so, when the coffin has shut out the storm?

   Answer me –

   Oh, answer me!

Bibliography

Barclay, George L., editor. *The Life and Remarkable Career of Adah Isaacs Menken, the Celebrated Actress.* An account of her career as a danseuse, an actress, an authoress, a poetess, a sculptress, etc. Philadelphia, 1868.
Brooks, Elizabeth. *Prominent Women of Texas.* Akron, 1896.
Brown, T. Allston. *History of the American Stage*, 2 vols, containing biographical sketches of nearly every member of the profession that has appeared on the American stage, from 1733 to 1970. New York (1870?) and *A History of the New York Stage.* New York, 1903.
Coleman, John. *Charles Reade as I Knew Him.* London, 1903.
Davis, Sam. *The History of Nevada.* Vol 2. Reno, 1913 and Dramatic Recollections, *Nevada Monthly*, July 1880 (pp. 227-230).
Ellis, S. M., editor. *The Hardman Papers (1865-1868).* London, 1930.
Eytinge, Rose. *The Memories of Rose Eytinge.* New York, 1905.
Falk, Bernard. *The Naked Lady.* London, 1934.
Fuller, Jean Overton. *Swinburne - A Critical Biography.* London, 1968.
Freund, John. *Adah Isaacs Menken, Music and the Drama*, New York, June 24, 1882.
Gerson, Noel Bertram. *Queen of the Plaza: A Biography of Adah Isaacs Menken* by Paul Lewis (pseud.). New York, 1964.
Gormon, Herbert. *The Incredible Marquis: Alexandre Dumas.* New York, 1929.
Gosse, Edmund. *The Life of Algernon Charles Swinburne.* New York, 1917, and "Swinburne", *Dictionary of National Biography*, Supplement, 1901-1911.
Gosse, Edmund and Wise, Thomas J., editors. *The Letters of Algernon Charles Swinburne.* London, 1919.
Gottschalk, Louis M. *Notes of a Pianist.* Edited by Clara Gottschalk and translated by Robert E. Peterson. Philadelphia, 1881.
Hamilton, Dr. Allan McLane. *Recollections of an Alienist: Personal and Professional.* New York, 1916.
Hare, Humphrey. *Swinburne - A Biographical Approach.* Witherby, 1949.
Hawkins, Richmond Laurin, editor. *Newly Discovered French Letters of the 17th, 18th and 19th Centuries.* Cambridge, Mass. 1933.
Hibbert, Henry G. *A Playgoer's Memories.* London, 1920.

Hornblower, Arthur. *A History of the Theatre in America.* Philadelphia, 1919.
Howell, John, editor. *Sketches of the Sixties by Bret Harte and Mark Twain (Being Forgotten Material Now Collected for the First Time from "The Californian", 1864-67).* San Francisco, 1926.
Ireland, Joseph N. *Records of the New York Stage (1750-1860).* New York, 1867.
James, Edwin. *Biography of Adah Isaacs Menken.* New York (1881?).
King, Grace. *New Orleans: The Place and The People.* New York, 1904.
Lafourcade, Georges. *Swinburne, a Literary Biography.* London, 1932.
Leavitt, M. B. *Fifty Years in Theatrical Management.* New York, 1912.
Ledger, Edward, editor. *Era Almanac.* London, 1868.
Leith, Lisney (Mrs.). *The Boyhood of Algernon Charles Swinburne.* London, 1917.
Leman, Walter. *Memories of an Old Actor.* San Francisco, 1886.
Le Moyne, William J., editor. *A Scrapbook of Newspaper Clippings Pertaining to the Theatre and the Stage.* Philadelphia, 1856-1889.
Lesser, Allen F. *Adah Isaacs Menken, a daughter of Israel.* Baltimore, 1937. "Reprinted from Publications of the American Jewish Historical Society, 1937". *Enchanting Rebel: The Secret of Adah Isaacs Menken.* New York, 1947. *Weave a Wreath of Laurel: the Lives of Four Jewish Contributors to American Civilization.* New York, 1938. Articles include "La Belle Menken".
Lucas-Dubreton, J. *The Fourth Musketeer: The Life of Alexandre Dumas.* Translated by Maida C. Darnton. New York, 1928.
Lyman, George D. *The Saga of the Comstock Lode.* New York, 1934.
Markens, Isaacs. *The Hebrews in America.* New York, 1888.
McCarthy, Justin. *Portraits of the Sixties.* New York, 1903.
Miller, Joaquin. *Adah Isaacs Menken.* Texas, 1934.
Morais, Henry S. *Jews of Philadelphia.* Philadelphia, 1894.
Moyne, Ethel C. *Enchanters of Men.* London, 1912.
Murdoch, James E. *The Stage.* Philadelphia, 1880.
Muusmann, Carl. *Verdens Henrykkelse.* Copenhagen, 1929.
Newell, Robert H. *Orpheus C. Kerr Papers,* 3 vols, 1862. *Smoked Glass,* 1868. *Walking Doll: Or, the Asters and Disasters of Society,* 1872.
Nicoll, W. Robertson and Wise, Thomas J., editors. *Literary Anecdotes of the Nineteenth Century: Contributions Towards a Literary History of the Period.* London, 1896.
Northcott, Richard. *Adah Isaacs Menken.* London, 1921.
Odell, George C. D. *Annals of the New York Stage.* Vols 6 and 7. New York, 1931.
Paine, Albert B. *Mark Twain, A Biography: The Personal and Literary Life of Samuel Langhorne Clemens.* New York, 1912.
Phelps, H. P. *Players of a Century (The Albany Stage).* Albany, 1880.
Rossetti, William M., editor. *Dante Gabriel Rossetti: His Family-Letters.* With a memoir by William M. Rossetti. Vol. 2. London, 1895.
Rourke, Constance. *Troupers of the Old Gold Coast.* New York, 1928.
Shorter, Clement, editor. *A Fragment of Autobiography.* (Swinburne, Algernon Charles.) London, 1917.
Sims, George Robert. *Glances Back.* London, 1917 and *My Life: Sixty Year Recollections of Bohemian London.* London, 1917.
Stoddard, Charles Warren. "La Belle Menken", *National Magazine,* Boston, February, 1905 (pp. 477-88).
Théâtre de la Gaité. Les Pirates de la Savane: Notice biographique sur Miss Adah Isaacs Menken, artiste Americaine. Paris, 1867.

Welby, Thomas Earle. *Swinburne, a Critical Study*. London, 1914 and *A Study of Swinburne*. New York, 1926.
Wemyss' Chronology of the American Stage from 1752 to 1852. New York, nd.
Willard, George O. *History of the Providence Stage, 1762-1891*. Providence, 1891.
Wise, Thomas J. *A Bibliography of Algernon Charles Swinburne*. Vol 1. London, 1919 and *A Swinburne Library*. London, 1925.
Wood, Clement Scott. *Poets of America*. New York, 1925.
Wyndham, Horace. *Victorian Sensations*. London, 1933.
Yates, Edmund. *His Recollections and Experiences*, 2 vols, London, 1884.

I have been much aided also by having been given access to the original research and thesis on Menken compiled and writtten by Mr. Allen F. Lesser and presently in the American Jewish Archives in Cincinnati. I am profoundly grateful to Mr. Lesser for both his scholarship and his generosity.

Acknowledgements

My thanks are due to the many friends who have responded so helpfully to my persistent enquiries after Menken: J. Richard Abell, Head, History and Literature Department, The Public Library of Cincinnati and Hamilton County; Phillip N. Allen, Head of History and Geography Department, City of Birmingham Public Libraries Department; E. C. Barker Library, University of Texas; Rabbi Murray Blackman, Ph.D., D.D., Temple Sinai, New Orleans; Anthony Blond, New York; Ernest J. Brin, Researcher, City of New Orleans, New Orleans Public Library; Victoria Burgess, Frederick Muller Ltd., London; Joyce Calhoon, Director, Texas State Library; Cyril Clemens, Editor, Mark Twain Journal, Missouri; W. H. Crain, Curator, Harvard Theatre Arts Library, The University of Texas, Humanities Research Center, Austin; Rosemary L. Cullen, Brown University Library, Rhode Island; Ruth Devons, Irvington, New York; Phillip I. Earl, Curator of Exhibits, Nevada Historical Society; Roxanne Etmekjian, Waltham, Massachusetts; Julie K. Fischer, Cincinnati, Ohio; Wendy Fisher, Victoria and Albert Museum, London; Noel B. Gerson, Clinton, Connecticut; Peter E. Hanff, Coordinator Technical Services, The Bancroft Library, Berkeley, California; Noel C. Holobeck, Saint Louis Public Library, Missouri; Susan Krivin, Kennikat Press Corp., Port Washington, New York; Allen Lesser, Washington, D.C.; Mrs. Mabel Leyda, Librarian, Tyrrell Historical Library, Beaumont, Texas; Mr. Jacob A. Marcus, American Jewish Archives, Hebrew Union College, Cincinnati, Ohio; Paul Myers, Curator, Theatre Collection, Library and Museum of the Performing Arts, The New York Public Library; Eric Norris, Bolton-le-Sands, Lancashire; Pamela L. Palmer, Special Collections, Steen Library, Stephen F. Austin University, Texas; Dr. Oskar Pausch, Olterreichilche Nationalbibliothek, Theatersammlung, Vienna; John Philbrook, Reference Librarian, Humanities, Boston Public Library; Mrs. Barbara Rawlings, Research Assistant, San Jacinto Museum of History Association, Deer Park, Texas; Dorothy Sloane, The Jenkins Co., Austin, Texas; Robert Stevens, Assistant Archivist, Rosenberg Library, Galveston, Texas; Dorothy L. Swerdlove, Acting Curator, The Billy Rose Theatre Collection, The New York Public Library.

Also my secretarial assistant, Lori Fischer of Austin, Texas and Hester Slater of Ahakista, Co. Cork.

Photographs and illustrations are reproduced by kind permission of the following: Bettmann Archive. Inc.: 25, 94, 115; BBC Hulton Picture Library: 194; Bibliotèque Rondel, Paris: 167; Courtesy of the Trustees of the Boston Public Library: 4, 242; Harvard Theatrical Collection: 7, 12, 18, 19, 26, 35, 38, 40, 74, 78, 92, 100, 124, 160, 164, 173, 230, 233; Hoblitzelle Theatre Arts Library, Humanities Research Center, The University of Texas at Austin: 65, 85; Mander and Mitchenson Theatre Collection Ltd: 150; Mansell Collection: 21, 107, 117, 122; Museo Teatrale Alla Scala: 48, 162, 180; National Portrait Gallery: 109, 211; New York Library: 10, 88, 105, 176; Osterreichische Nationalbibliothek: 22, 28, 46, 57, 63, 187; Theatre Museum, London: 130, 208.

The author and publisher have taken every care to locate and acknowledge the sources of the illustrations used in this book. If, however, an incorrect attribution has been made we will gladly amend this in future reprints, provided that we are notified.

Index

Albion, The, 149
Aldrich, Louis, 101
Answer Me, poem by M, quoted, 257-8; ref: 82, 197
Anti-semitism, in Europe, 233-4; in Vienna, 190
Appeal to Fallen Women by Charles Dickens, 202
Archduke Charles Hotel, Vienna, 190
Artemus Ward, pseud. of Charles Farrar Browne; his sketch *Women's Rights* quoted 110; ref: 107, 110, 195
Ashbee, Henry Spencer, 212
Ashburnham Place, 212
Aspasia, poem by Newell, quoted, 110-12; ref: 114
Aspiration, sonnet by M, quoted, 108, 254; ref: 197
Astley's Theatre, London, M's contract with, 128-9; illus. 122, 150; ref: 93, 124, 128, 142-3, 214, 215, 232
Athens, 110
Austin, Texas, 44
Austria, 170

Baltimore, 89, 90, 93, 103, 125, 126
Bankhead, Tallulah, 176
Barclay, George Lippard, 41, 182
Barkley, Captain James Paul, his marriage to M, 151-61; death of his son, 193; ref: 127, 146, 165, 166, 170
   Louis Menken, 164-6; his death, 193
Beatty, L. F., 116
Beaudelaire, 223-4
Beecher, Dr. Henry Ward, 85
Bendyshe, Thomas, 210
Benicia, 61
"Bencia Boy, The", *see* Heenan, John Carmel

Bernard, Dr Simon, 14
Black Crook, play, 181
Black-Eyed Susan, play, 84, 89, 103, 149
Blanchard, E. L., review quoted, 135
Bleak House, M's house in New York, 157
Bohemian, The, *see* Harte, Frances Bret
Booth, Edwin, 23, 58
   Junius Brutus, 101-2
Boston University, 188
Boucicault, Dion, 9, 128
Bourgeois, Anicet, 167
Boxing, illegality of, 61-2
Bradleigh, Charles, 211
Brazil, 211
Breckinridge, General, 206
Brice, Joe, 123, 127
Bright and Beautiful, The, poem by M, 37
Broadway, 21
Broadway Theatre, 157-8
Brougham, John, 146
Brown, Thomas Allston, 83, 93
Brown University Library, Provincetown, 241n
Browne, Charles Farrar, *see* Artemus Ward
Bulwer-Lytton, 50
Bunyard's Private Hotel, London, 128
Burton, Isabel, 210, 212
   Sir Richard, 209, 210, 211, 212, 215; illus. 211

Camille, 104
California, 93, 96, 106, 123, 232, and *see* San Francisco
Carline or The Female Brigand, 71
"Casanova" poses, 175
Chatto, Andrew, 195
Celeste, Madame, 6, 18
Charles XII of Sweden, 166
Charles, James S., 49

Charleston Mercury, 72
Charteris, Leslie, 72
Cheyne Walk, Chelsea, 209
Chicago, 83
Children of the Sun, play, 146, 148-9
Cincinnati Commercial, 66
Cincinnati Herald, 11
Cincinnati Independent, 30
Civil War, The, battles of: Fredericksburg, 90; Gettysburg, 95; Vicksburg, 95
 generals of: Stonewall Jackson, 90; Lee, 95; Grant, 95
 Draft Law protests against: 95
Clapp, Henry, 80
Clare, Ada, 23, 81-2, 86, 109, 114, 157
Clemens, Sam, *see* Mark Twain
Cleveland, Ohio, 107
Clipper, The, literary magazine, M reviewed, 71-2; ref: 11, 14, 21, 63, 238, 243
Colleen Bawn, play, 9
Colletti, Mrs., 213
Collins, Mr., 20
Concannon, Alfred, A. C., 196
Conrad, 188
Coolbrith, Ina, 107-8
Crabtree, Lotta, 109, 181
Crescent Dramatic Association, 49, 50
Crisp, William, 52, 53
Cusick, Jim, 61, 64

Daily Picayune, 51, 52
Daily Post, 149
Daily Telegraph, review quoted, 135
Daly, Gus, 157-9
Dan De Quille, pseud. of W. J. Wright, 117-18
Dark Hour, The, poem by M, 79
Dayton, Ohio, 55, 58
Dayton Empire, 55
Dayton Enquirer, 67
Delacroix, 166
Densmore, Gilbert, 107
Detroit, 83
"Diary" of M, hoax, 182-8
 exposed as a hoax, 189
Dickens, Charles, illus. 194; interest in fallen women, 202; his *Appeal to Fallen Women*, 202; ref: 14, 88, 148, 164, 193, 200, 202, 203
Dickensian, The, by B. W. Matz, 203
Didaschelle, by R. H. Newell, 86
Dobie, Frank J., 44
Dolores, poem by Swinburne, quoted, 217-19; ref: 198, 212, 216
Dolorida, poem by Swinburne, 219
Draft Law, protests against, 95
Dreams of Beauty, poem by M, quoted, 40

Drifts That Bar My Door, poem by M, quoted, 251-4
Drury Lane Theatre, 127
Dugue, Ferdinand, 166
Dum Spiro Spero, poem by M, 54
Dumaine, Louis, 235, 237

Eliot, T. S., 176
Ellington, Susette, 165-6, 168, 171, 172, 234, 236, 237, 240
England, 93, 127; and *see* London
English, William, 72
Eton, flagellation at, 212-14

Falk, biographer of M, 53n
Farnie, H. B., review quoted, 136; his version of M's death quoted, 238-9; ref: 141, 238, 241
Fazio or The Italian Wife's Revenge, play, 50; plot of, 51; 104
Fechter, Charles, 146, 148, 206
Fernandez, James, 143
Field, Julian, 233
Figaro, Le, 177
Fish, Provost-Marshal, his conflicts with M's Confederate sympathies, 92-3; 125
Flagellation, 212, 213, 214, 225, 226
Flaherty, Rev. Jonathan, 85
Flogging Block, The, pseudonymous work of Swinburne, 225
Fort Sumpter, surrender of, 83
Fragment of a Heart, poem by M, 79
Free Press of Detroit, review quoted, 83
French Spy, The, play, 84, 101, 103-4, 116, 149, 163, 232
Fredericksburg, Battle of, 90
Front Street Theatre, Baltimore, 89, 90
Fuller, Jean Overton, 212, 213n

Gaiety Theatre, 52
Gautier, Théophile, 146-7, 166
Géante, La, sonnet by Beaudelaire, 223-4
Gerson, Noel Bartram: his account of M's leaving Vienna, 182-5; his biography of M, *Queen of the Plaza*, 182-93; correspondence with Wolf Mankowitz, 188-9; ref: 97, 119, 205, 259
Gettysburg, Battle of, 95
Gilbert's Melodian, theatre, 109
Glasgow Herald, The, 148
Goethe, 13
Gold Hill Evening News, review quoted, 115-16; 169-70
Golden Era, literary journal, aims and characteristics of, 106; contributors to, 107-8; ref: 98, 109, 110, 113-14, 192

Goldsmith, 12
Gonzalez, Captain, 41
Gosse, Edmund, 213, 216, 223, 227
Gottschalk, Louis Moreau, 82, 106
Grant, General, 95, 125
Great Expectations, playbill of, 88
Greeley, Horace, 11
Green Street Theatre, Albany, 6, 9, 18
Griffith Gaunt, by Charles Reade, 159

Hardinge, Emma, 114
Harney, General, 44
Harte, Frances Bret, 107, 151; illus. 107
Harvard Theatre Collection, 174, 189
Harvard University Library, 188
Havana, 184
Hear, O Israel! poem by M, quoted, 254-6
Heenan Has Come, a farce, 72
Heenan, John Carmel ("The Benicia Boy"), his background, 61; world title fights, 61-2; meeting with M, 62; marriage to M, 64; denials of marriage, 72-3; victory over Sayers, 72; ref: 12, illus. 60, 63-4, 67, 71, 84, 112, 140, 155-7, 160, 218n
Herald, 23
Hibbard, Henry Ewing, 182, 188
Hitchcock, Mrs., 107-8
Hotton, John Camden, his publications of *Infelicia*, 195-8; his meeting with M, 203; his publications, 196; his letter to M quoted, 204-5; ref: 216, 241
Houghton, Lord, 212, 213, 214, 222
Howell, Charles Augustus, 209, 210, 211, 212, 215
Hugo, Victor, 191
Humbolt Register, 117
Hunchback, The, play, 55

Illustrated London News, article on M quoted, 137-41
Illustrated Times, The, review quoted, 137
Index Librorum Prohibitorum (of *Pisanus Fraxi*), 212-13
Infelicia, poems by M, publication of, 196-8; reviews of, 198-200; Lesser's opinion of, 198-9; influences on, 199-200; influences of, 200-1; the dedication to Dickens, 203-5; ref: 195-205, 236, 240
Ingomar, or The Barbarian, play, 52
Israelite, newspaper, 54, 57
Ivanhoe, 59

Jackson, Stonewall, 90, 109
James, Ed, his life, 14-16; letter quoted, 24; letters from M, 112-13; dislike of Barkley, 154; account of M's burial quoted 243-4; ref: 11, 13, 21, 24, 29, 64, 83, 90, 91, 93, 94, 104, 119, 123-5, 153-7, 161, 241-3
Jane Eyre, 112, 183
Java, Cunard liner, 161
Jefferson, Colonel Benjamin H., his letter quoted, 96
Jersey (Channel Island), 191
Jersey City, U.S.A., 75, 86
Jew in Parliament, essay by M, 57
Jewess, The, play, 55, 160
Josephine, M's sister, 49
Josephs, Annie, M's sister, 65
Judith, poem by M, quoted, 248-50
  its influence on Oscar Wilde, 200

Karazah to Karl, poem by M, 67, 197
Keate, Dr., of Eton, 212
Kendal, Dame Madge, 146
Kendall, John S., 29-31, 36
Kendall, W. S., 107
King Charles of Württemberg, 170
King, Starr, 98

Lady of Lyons, or Love and Pride, 50
Lafourcade, 223
Lamartine, 191
Laulerack, 42-3
Lawrence, Joe, 98, 106-7
Le Havre, 235
Leaves of Grass, poems by Whitman, 80
Ledger, magazine, 112
Lee, General, 95, 125
Leeds, 149
Lemon, Mark, 136
Lesbia Braudon, by Swinburne, 220
Lesser, Allen, reviews of *Infelicia*, quoted, 198-9; ref: 30, 66, 79, 81, 91n, 151-2, 200, 201
Lesson for Husbands, A, play, 52
Liberty Gazette, quoted, 36-7
Liebert, 177
Lincoln, Abraham, 9, 23, 91
Little Jack Horner, 232
Liverpool, 149, 163
Livingston, Texas, 38, 40, 41, 67
London, 124, 127-8, 147-9, 168, 195, 231-2
London Review, quoted, 137
Longfellow, Henry Wadsworth, 240-1; his verses to M, 241
Louisiana, 49; and see New Orleans
Louisiana, *Historical Quarterly*, quoted, 29-31
Louisville, 58, 160
Lousville Courier, 167
Lovell, Mrs., 52

Lowell, Amy, 201
Ludlow, Fitzhugh, 107

Macbeth, 5, 6, 53
McKenna, John, 148-9
Maguire, Tom, 97, 101, 108, 114, 116
Maguire's Theatre, illus. 94; reception for M, 101; the corps dramatique, 101; ref: 93, 98
Mahabharata, 211
Martin, Dr., 227-8
Martin, Harriet, 71
Marx, Adrian, 237, 240
Masset, Stephen, 74, 114
Matz, B. W., 203
Mayer, Dr. Nathan, 55
Mayo, Frank, 101
Mazeppa, plot of, 16; review by Newell, 24; publicity for in San Francisco, 101-2; in Sacramento, 104; in London, 129-33; at the Broadway Theatre, 157-8; in Paris, 168-9; accidents during performance, 170-1 and 227-8; ref: 7, 12, 49, 79, 85, 90-3, illus. 100, 101, 103, 104, 106, 116, 123-9, 140, 145-7, 166, 186, 214, 215, 234
Mazeppa Waltz, The, 143
Mazzini, 215, 224
Meade, General, 95
Melbourne, 181
Memories, fictive poems by M, 195
Memory, A, poem by M, quoted, 45
Memphis, 52
Menken, The, mining territory, 117
Menken, Adah Isaacs
    I PSEUDONYMS OF: Adele, Adelaide, 36; Dolores de Ricardo Fiertes (*or* Fuentes), 13, 30, 53, 212; Indigena, 195; Infelicissimus, 79, 199; Infelix, 113, 192; Marie Rachel Adelaide de Vere Spencer, 13
    II LIFE OF: birth & parentage, 29-46; capture by Indians, 41-4; study of Hebrew, 54-7; Confederate sympathies, 91; her mother, 182-3; her will, 234; death and burial, 236-44
    III MARRIAGES: to Isaac Menken, 31-3, 66-7; divorce, 69; to J. C. Heenan (*see*), 64; his denials, 72-3; continuing friendship, 156-7; to R. H. Newell (*see*) 86; separation, 86-7; second try, 94-5; their trip to San Francisco, 95-7; their questionable divorce, 123; to J. P. Barkley, 160-1; separation, 161
    IV THEATRICAL WORK: see as follows: *Black-Eyed Susan*, *Children of the Sun*, *Fazio*, *The French Spy*, *The Jewess*, *Lesson for Husbands*, *Macbeth*, *Mazeppa*, *Pirates de la Savane*, *Rookwood*, *Satan in Paris*, *School for Scandal*, *Three Fast Women*; reviews, 50-2, 55, 71-2, 103, 116, 118, 120-1, 135-7, 148-9
    V LITERARY WORK: see under "*Infelicia*; poems by M", and Appendix; ref: 54, 57, 79, 199-200
    VI PORTRAITS OF: in *Mazeppa*, 7, 17, 100, 130, 134; in *Children of the Sun*, 28; in *The French Spy*, 35; in *Pirates de la Savane*, 167; in *Black-Eyed Susan*, 85; semi-nude, 19; with J. C. Heenan, 65; with Alexandre Dumas, 173, 176; with A. C. Swinburne, 208; also 4, 12, 18, 22, 26, 38, 57, 63, 78, 124, 147, 160, 187, 226, 230, 233
Menken, Alexander Isaacs, background of, 50; his letter disavowing divorce, 66-7; ref: 53-6, 73, 84, 159, 182
Menken, Jacob, 54
Menken, Louis Barkley, 165-6, 193
Menken, Shaft and Tunnel Co., 117
Menken, Solomon, 53
Metropolitan Theatre, Sacramento, 104
Miles, R. E. J., 7, 8
Miller, Henry, 176
Miller, Joaquin (*or* Cincinatus), 102, 106, 108, 109, 113-14, 201
Millenburg Joys, 29
Milligan, Rev. J. C. K., 86
Milner, Henry M., 16
Milman, Henry Hart, 50
Milwaukee, 83
Minerva "Minnie", servant to M, 127
Mississippi River, 54
Mr. & Mrs. Barney Williams, comedy act, 91
Moore, George, 221
Moniteur Universal, Le, review quoted, 169
Monroe, Marilyn, 176
Montez, Lola, 8, 12, 55, 83-4, 103, 151, 171, 182
"Morganatic" marriage, rumour of, 171-2
Morrissey, John, 61-2, 66
Mortara, Edgar, 57
Moxon, 196
Mugar Collection of Boston University, 188
Mulford, Prentice, 107
Murdoch, James E., 5-6, 53
My Heritage, poem by M, quoted, 247-8

Nacogdoches, Texas, 40, 49
Naked Lady, The, by Falk, 53n
Napoleon III, 14, 163
Nashville, 160
National Magazine, 190

National Theatre, Cincinatti, 59
Nelaton, Docteur, 171
Nevada, 114, 118; miners' claims in, 115
New Advertisement, poem by M, quoted, 37
New Bowery Theatre, 86
Newell, Robert Henry (pseud. Orpheus C. Kerr), review of *Mazeppa*, 23; meeting with M, 79; views of Whitman, 81-2; his novel about M, 86; marriage to M, 86; separation, 86-7; reunion, trip to San Francisco, 94-5; attempt to end M's acting career, 103-4; his poem *Aspasia* quoted, 110-12; his views on female masochism quoted, 112; questionable nature of divorce, 123, 127; ref: 79-81, 84-6, 110, 114, 119, 155-6
Newlin, Dr. Jean, 189
New Orleans, 13, 29, 30-5, 49, 50, 55, 86, 98, 182-3
New York, 9, 13, 14, 23, 24, 30-1, 62-3, 86, 93, 95, 104, 123, 127, 157, 160, 195
New York Illustrated News, 72
New York Leader, 66

Oakland, California, 107
O'Brien, 89
Ochiltree, Colonel, 40, 171
Offenbach, 172
Oh Calcutta!, 20
Old Bowery Theatre, 13, 71-2
One Year Ago, poem by M, quoted, 250-1
Opelousas, Louisiana, 49
Orchestra, The, review quoted, 136; 142, 238
Orpheus C. Kerr, *see* Newell, Robert Henry
Orpheus C. Kerr Papers, 195
Orpheus in Hades, by Offenbach, 172
Overall, John W., 51-2, 81
Oxenford, John, review quoted, 135

Palace Queen, steamship, 96, 97
Pall Mall Gazette, review of *Infelicia* quoted, 199
Panama, 95-6
Paris, 146-7, 157, 161, 163-78, 181, 191-2, 195
Peasley, Tom, 117
Pearl, Cora, 146, 172
Pére La Chaise, cemetery, Paris, 239, 242
Peter the Great, 166
Pfaff, Charley, 80, 82; his tavern, 80, 82, 89, 106, 123
Philadelphia, 41
Philadelphia Mercury, review quoted, 72
Pirates de la Savane, play, 167-70, 181, 190, 236; its poor reception in Vienna, 190
Plain Dealer, newspaper, 107
Poe, Edgar Allen, 58, 80-1, 89, 93

Poems and Ballads, by A. C. Swinburne, 195-6
Poltava, Battle of, 166
Porcupine, The, 149
Portland, Maine, 83
Portobello, 95
Potter, Mrs., 213
Powell, George, 222
Pre-Raphaelites, 209-12
Private Case of the British Museum, 213, 225
Professor, The, 183
Pro Patria, poem by M, 84, 125, 127
Providence, Rhode Island, 72
Punch, review in verse, quoted, 135; ref: 142, 222
Purity League, The, 107
Pusey Memorial Library, 189

Queen, The, review quoted, 137
Queen, Frank, 63, 74, 83, 93-4, 124, 157, 166, 171
Queen of the Plaza, biography of M by N. B. Gerson, quoted, 182-93; authorship of, 188

Rachel, 55, 128
Raven, The, by Poe, 58
Read, Thomas Buchanan, 240
Reade, Charles, 37, 159
Reitlinger, 174
Resurgam, poem by M, 109, 192
Reynolds, 89
Richmond, Virginia, 38
Robson, Stuart, 58
Rochester (the fictional character), 112
Rochester, New York, 71
Rochfort, Henri, 235-6
Rookwood, play by M, 104
Rosenberg, Dr., 195
Rossetti, Dante Gabriel, 107, illus. 109; his letter quoted, 200; 209, 215, 216
  William, 200
Rothschild, Baron Lionel de, 57, 165
Russ House, M's suite in, 108

Sadowa, Battle of, 190
Salome, by Oscar Wilde, 200
Sand, Georges, 45-6, 163-5, 191, 193, 164
San Francisco, 93, 97-8, 101, 104, 109-10, 114, 119, 181
Satan in Paris, play, 72
Saturday Evening Gazette, 72
Sayers, Tom, 64, 67-8, 72
St. John's Wood, London, 142, 212-13
School for Scandal, 11
Schneider, Hortense, 206
Seal Rocks, 113

Sentinel, review quoted, 83
Seven Weeks War of 1866, 170
Shelley, 209
Sheridan, 12
Shreveport, 49, 50
Shylock, M's essay on, 54, 165
Singer's Restaurant, Baltimore, 125
Sixteen-String Jack, play by M, 55
Smith, Captain John B., 6, 7, 8, 14, 19, 20, 61, 85, 124
Smith, Edward, 124, 128, 141-2, 145
Socrates, 110
Soldier's Daughter, The, play, 52, 55, 63, 83
Solomon, Simeon, 212
Song of the Shirt, by Hood, influence on M, 200
Spirit of the Times, 64; review quoted, 71
Stadt Theatre, New York, 74
Stephenson, W. S., 101
Sterling, George, 201
Stevens, Sarah, 156
Stirling, Edward, 128
Stoddard, Charles Warren, his description of M's portrait, 97; M's letter to, quoted, 191-3; ref: 97, 102, 107, 178, 190, 201, 231-2
Sun, 20
Sunday Delta, 51, 54
Sunday Mercury, 13, 58, 66, 79, 158
Swimming Against the Current, M's essay on Whitman, 80
Swinburne, Algernon Charles; his associates, 210-11; his obsession with flagellation, 213-14, 225-6; his meeting with M, 214-16; his letters to Powell and others, 222-5; ref: 209-28, 232, 241, illus. 208
Swinburne: A Critical Biography, by J. O. Fuller, Chatto & Windus, 1968, 213n; quoted, 213-14

Tennessee, 9
Ternan, Ellen, 202, 203, 206
Territorial Enterprise, 117-18; Twain's review quoted in, 118
Terry, Ellen, 146
Texas, 44, 49, 109
Thaxter, Wallace A., 72
Theatre am der Wien, Vienna, 182, 190, illus. 180
Théâtre de la Gaité, 163, 166, 168; illus. 162
Theodore Sisters, The, 183
Theodorus, Roi d'Abyssinie, play, 235-6
Thomson, John, 195, 214

Thorne, Charles R. Jr., 101
Three Fast Women, play by M: playbill for, illus. 105; characters of (all played by M), 106; ref: 104
Tom Platt's Music Hall, 98
Tribune, 63-4; office of sacked, 95; 158
Twain, Mark (Sam Clemens), his article on *Mazeppa* quoted, 120-1; illus. 117; ref: 117-18

Union, newspaper, 116, 118
Unprotected Female, An, play by M, 103
"Urania Cottage", 202

Varieties Theatre, Liverpool, 116, 118
Varney, Gus, 41, 42
Verlaine, Paul, his satire on Dumas, 174
Vicksburg, 52; Battle of, 95
Vienna, 182-93, 231, 233-6
Voltaire, 166

Ward, Artemus, *see* Artemus Ward
War Department, 127
Watts-Dutton, Theodore, 221, 225
Waverley Magazine, 112
Webb, Charles Henry, 107
Weekly Dispatch, 195
Westchester House, New York, 72-3
Westminster Palace Hotel, London, 143, 232
"Whipping ladies", 212
Whippingham Papers, The, by Swinburne, 225
Whistler, 210
Whitman, Walt, illus. 21; ref: 21-4, 76, 80, 81, 188, 198, 199, 201
Wife's Prayer, by M, quoted, 58
Wilde, Oscar, 200
Wilke's, George, M's letter to, quoted, 65-6; his review in *Spirit of the Times*, 71; ref: 64-5, 67, 69
Winter, William, review quoted, 158-9
Wood, George, 20, 22, 23, 157; his theatre in Cincinnati, 53-4, 159-60
Women's Rights, a sketch by Artemus Ward, quoted, 110
Working and Waiting, poem by M, 200
Wright, William, "Joggle", *see* Dan De Quille
Wuthering Heights, 183

Yellow fever, epidemic of in New Orleans, 182-3

Zanea, Juan Clemente, 31

DATE DUE